D1878904

HUMAN RIGHTS CONCERN OF THE FUTURE

HUMAN RIGHTS
CONCERN OF THE FUTURE

Editor
GOPAL BHARGAVA

KALPAZ PUBLICATIONS
DELHI-110052

Human Rights: Concern of the Future

© Gopal Bhargava

ISBN: 81-7835-060-2

All rights reserved. No part of this book may be reproduced in any manner without written permission.

Reprinted in 2012 in India by
Kalpaz Publications,
C-30, Satyawati Nagar,
Delhi-110 052
E-mail: kalpaz@hotmail.com

Printed at: G. Print Process, Delhi

human rights of their inhabitants. International instruments require states to enact legislation and otherwise ensure that the rights are respected. In some legal systems international human rights obligations may be self-executing and will be given effect by officials and courts without domestic legislation. The denial of human rights and fundamental freedoms not only is an individual and personal tragedy but also creates conditions of social and political unrest sowing the seeds of violence and conflict within and between societies and nations.

The human rights movement has progressed to a point where in its fundamental conception it treats of members of the human race as members of a global community and, therefore, broadly entitled to a common pattern of human rights. The pervasive presence of human rights in almost all the dimensions of daily life in most societies provides a cementing influence in the realisation of the world recognising the need in the current political climate for examining issues on a global basis, the internationalisation of human rights values can be excepted to proceed apace.

This work will prove ideal and dependable reference book for academics, policy-makers, human rights activists alike.

Editor

Preface

Human rights and fundamental freedoms allow us to develop fully and use our human qualities, our intelligence, our talents and our conscience and to satisfy our spiritual and other needs. They are based on mankind's increasing demand for a life in which the inherent dignity and worth of each human being will receive respect and protection. In the language of United Nations Centre for human rights 'human rights could be generally defined and those rights which are inherent in our nature and without which we cannot live as human beings'.

This book views the human rights as an on going attempt to define human dignity and worth and to create human rights' culture in future for society. The basic principles of a human rights' culture will survive only if people continue to see a point in it doing so. It needs to be constantly defended. We have a right to this. It is not just what we want or need. It is your right. There is a responsibility to be met. The concept of human rights tells a detailed story of the attempts made to define basic dignity and worth of the human beings and his or her most fundamental entitlement.

Human rights are rights to be enjoyed by individuals in their own societies and implemented and enforced under their laws and institutions. International undertakings are designed to help assure that national societies in fact respect the

Contents

Preface v

1. Introduction 1
2. Human Rights and Human Duties 36
3. Human Rights in India: Some Issues 51
4. Constitutional Protection of Human Rights 78
5. The Implementation System: International Measures 105
6. Enforcement of Fundamental Rights Under Indian Constitution 159
7. Human Rights: Global Responsibilities 221
8. Human Rights Development 243
9. Changing Perspectives 267

Index 325

1

Introduction

If we look at the contemporary world in a wide perspective, we find that the most challenging problem of our time is how to utilize the vast knowledge and resources available to day for the welfare and development of all mankind. It is gratifying to note that there is growing and recognition of this basic objective. The international community, as organized and represented at the United Nations has not only taken the initial steps in its long journey towards the goal but also set the meaning and direction of that journey. It has spelt out that the welfare and development of mankind includes universal respect for and observance of human rights and fundamental freedom for all without distinction as to race, colour, sex, language, religion, political and other beliefs, descent, birth or other status.

Following the establishment of the United Nations, whose Charter proclaims the protection of human rights as one of its principal purpose, scores of international instruments have been adopted, spelling out norms and standards to promote universal respect for, and observance of, human rights and fundamental freedoms for all. Most instruments contain a set of rights and freedoms which they seek to protect. Some are general, such as the Universal Declaration of Human Rights, and the International Covenants on Human Rights, while other deals with specific rights, for instance, the rights of association and collective bargaining, or for specific groups like women and children and other vulnerable sections of the society.

Other instruments are directed to eliminate such evil practices as racial discrimination, discrimination against women, torture, slavery and slave-like practices. Most instruments establish some machinery for their supervision and implementation and impose an obligation on the member-states to report periodically to an international body on the measures they have adopted to implement the provisions of the instruments, while some also provide procedures for individual petitions or inter-state complaints against violation of rights, However, overall experience of international supervision and enforcement has been rather poor.

It was, in part, to augment the international system of supervision and enforcement, that initiative for regional arrangements were made—such as contained in European Convention on Human Rights, the American Declaration and Convention and the African Charter on Human and Peoples Rights. Notwithstanding, the vast array of international and regional measures gross violation of human rights are widely rampant. In many parts of the world observance of, and respect for, civil and political rights are conspicuous by their absence. Arbitrary arrests, long term detention without trial, political disappearances, torture, summary executions, enforced disappearances and abuse of psychiatry for political ends are widely rampant.

The prerequisites for enjoyment of civil and political rights i.e., rule of law and democratic system of government have been ignored with impunity. One-man one-party, military dictatorship and other kind of dictatorial regimes characterise a larger part of the world.

Thus, most of the Governments lacks what the Universal Declaration of Human Rights refers to as the foundation of human right system—the principle that the will of the people shall be the basis of authority of government, expressed through periodic and genuinely free elections. It is not surprising therefore that various parts of the world have been experiencing turbulance and turmoil of one kind or the other. The continuing armed conflicts/civil wars have resulted not only in flagrant violations of human rights but also killing of innocent people including women and children and also surging increase of refugees, estimated to be 17 million, with another 25 million displaced within their own homeland. There is more to the disturbing situation in the context of denial of basic human rights. Some 1.5 billion people in different parts of the world, mostly in developing countries, live in absolute poverty, with another one billion on the margin of poverty -enduring unemployment, hunger, disease and shelterlessness. Against this background one may well visualize the situation In the context of the right to life—a primordial right which constitutes the raison d'etre of all other rights. In Asia alone, some 900 million people i.e. 40 per cent of the total population, live below poverty line; 29 per cent of the people living in urban areas and 80 per cent of the people in rural areas do not have access to even safe (drinking) water. There are no sanitary facilities for 47 per cent of the people in urban areas and for 87 per cent in rural areas. This is partly why diarrhoeal diseases, which are transmitted by human faecal contamination of soil, food and water are so widespread. What aggravates their plight is lack of medical facilities and the necessary resources needed to provide for health care. Thus, millions of people are trapped in a vicious circle of poverty, malnutrition and disease.

What has been-referred to above are instances illustrative of oppression and denial of basic human needs that characterize the lives of millions of people; a more sordid reality is that among the victims, women and children are the worst sufferers.

There is more to the situation. When people are denied freedom of expression, political and religious rights or are oppressed and discriminated against because of their race, religion, colour or class, descent etc., those who are sufferers include both men and women. However, women suffer another kind of discrimination. Often referred to as 'better halves of mankind' and constituting the majority of the world population, they are denied equality of status in their own, societies simply because they are "women" and not "men". This is true even in the case of so called advanced countries for instance, Australia, Canada, United Kingdom U.S.A., Switzerland. Indeed, judged by virtually every index of gender comparison, women's enjoyment of human rights is much inferior to that of men. This is not just a matter of economic inequity, important as that is. A continuing inequality persist notwithstanding the fact that some countries have recently had women as heads of Governments.

The socio-legal situation apart, the other hard reality is that some 75 per cent of the world's 17 million refugees and some 80 per cent of 1.5 billion people in various parts of the world enduring poverty, hunger, disease and shelterness, are women and children. Indeed among the most vulnerable of all groups are the children. Of course, concern of the international community for the well-being of a child or his/her family, without any distinction and discrimination whatsoever has been repeatedly expressed in various instruments. The two specific ones, the Declaration and the Convention on the Rights of the Child, respectively, set forth some basic principles which include enjoyment of special protection and provision for special opportunities and facilities, by law and other means, to enable a child develop physically, mentally, morally, socially, in a healthy and normal manner. Every child is entitled to adequate nutrition, medical .care, education, housing and recreation. He is to be protected from all forms of neglect, cruelty and exploitation. "Mankind owes the child the best it has to give" proclaims the UN Declaration.

Fine words and pious hopes, indeed. Countless Children—50 million at a conservative estimate—are surviving in the streets through menial work, begging, theft and prostitution, with no proper home or family care. In Asia, Africa and Latin America, 14 per cent of the children die within a year of their birth because of lack of medical facilities and necessary nutrition. Among those who survive, nearly 40 per cent do not ever get a chance to go to primary school, 68 per cent do not move up to secondary school and more than 90 per cent do not make to higher studies level. There is no question of parks, playground or other recreational facilities for them. Open rough fields, if available nearby, or narrow dingy streets, serve as their only playgrounds. They donot know the better and perhaps life could he still enjoyable for them. But this is not to be. A very high percentage of children (no reliable statistics arc available in that regard) are subjected to forced labour and exploitation. Child labour is a common phenomenon in almost all countries of the Third World.

What is still worse is 50 per cent do not get the basic needs of life; for 30 per cent, there is no shelter from the sun, or the wind, rain or cold. They suffer from hidden hunger—what is referred to, in the UN jargon, as "invisible malnutrition". UNICEF reports indicate that invisible malnutrition touches the life of approximately 25 per cent children of the developing count countries' and three-fourth of them are in Asia. It quietly steals away their energy; it gently restrains their growth; it gradually lowers their resistance and in both cause and consequence it is inextricably interlocked with illness and infections which both sharpen, and are sharpened by, malnutrition.

UNICEF reports present a pathetic picture, which statistics cannot express, of how a child quietly passess away—to see a mother sitting, hour after anxious hour leaning her child's body against her own; to see the child turn on limbs which are unnaturally still, stiller than is sleep. The child yawns and one sees the living pink at the roof of the child's mouth in shocking contrast to the already dead-looking greyness of the skin—the colours of its life and death; to see the uncomprehending panic in eyes which are still clear and lucid eyes of a child and then to know in one endless moment that life has gone. Some 40,000 children die like this in a world where even cats and dogs can afford fillet of beef.

Malnutrition, it is estimated, can be overcome specifically in terms of 'calorie intake', if only one per cent of the grain production of the world, or 15 per cent of what is kept in cold storage, at an approximate cost of $ 16 billion for maintaining stability in market prices, or less than 20 per cent of what is fed to cattle (to obtain juicy beef) in the industrially advanced and affluent countries in the North, is used to meet the needs of hungry children in the developing countries of the South. What is analysed above covers only a part of the grim human rights situation prevalent to day. It does not present the whole picture. Indeed, given the complex dimensions of the existing state of human rights, the whole scenario cannot be encapsuled into a single study, whatever its size. One aspect of the situation however is very clear that the promises and aspirations set out in the Universal Declaration of

Human Rights and elaborated in several international instruments, remains largely unfulfilled. The right to life - to an adequate standard of living, to freedom of expression, to protection from torture, inhuman treatment or arbitrary arrest and many of the "common standards of achievement for all peoples and nations" are as far from realization now as ever. If this is a depressing evaluation, it is nonetheless a reality for the majority of human-kind, particularly those living in poor countries. Among the people of the affluent Western nations also, there is either indifference, or a deeply felt sense of dissatisfaction and frustration about the lack of progress towards universal respect for and observance of human rights.

Human Rights problems cannot be tackled in isolation with other pressing problems. For instance, arms control; a world that spends more than 3 billion dollars a day on armed forces and armament; but cannot afford a tiny fraction of that amount towards eradication of poverty, shelterlessness, disease etc., is .it world with very topsy turvy priorities. Who is responsible for the poor developing countries spending a major part or their meagre resources on acquisition of arms'? Who supply the arms to them and why and for whose benefit? Another problem relates to North-South issues. While local national efforts are essential to meet the socio-economic needs of the people, there is urgency for equitable management of the world economy.

Human rights are essentially the rights of people both as individuals and in groups. It is therefore obvious that the activity on behalf of human rights cannot yield much practical results if it remains confined to actions by Governments or to discussions and recommendations at the intergovernmental level and acceptance of their recommendations (which In practice are disregarded with impunity) by the

Governments. Over the decades and most especially since the 1970s, there has been an explosive emergence of local, national and international organizations formed by people themselves on every continent and in almost every country of the world working for the promotion and protection of human rights. These nongovernmental organizations (NGOs) vary enormously in their membership, In the scope of their activities and programmes, and the influence or impact they have in domestic, regional and international arena. This is so because NGOs have emerged in response to specific conditions and crises and are the product of social action, history and culture. Nonethless these NGOs in all their diversity comprise a human rights movement, the dynamo that had driven the struggle against arbitrary rule, for self determination for social and economic justice. However, there is still need for evolving an all pervasive peoples' forum, at global level.

While inter-governmental conferences have become a 'routine', there is still no forum where people in their individual capacity or in organized groups (NGOs) could meet periodically (with the active participation of experts from inter-governmental organizations concerned with human rights) for exchange of views and information and to plan concerted actions to promote the common objectives. Further, NGOs especially in the developing countries, have little opportunity for exchange of experiences, information sharing and solidarity-building among themselves. Thus, there is a clear need for greater interaction leading to the development of more enduring linkages between human rights activists, educationists and jurists as individuals or in organized groups. Furthermore, a forum providing periodical meetings among them could perform its role as a catalyst: to review the progress or lack of it, in the implementation of international norms of human rights and to draw attention of inter-governmental organizations, especially the United Nations and its specialized agencies concerned with human rights problems, to situations which have been neglected and/or have not attracted adequate attention. And thereby prompting inter-governmental bodies, as also Governments, to take necessary action against violation of human rights.

Furthermore, most of the non-governmental organizations generally focus attention only on some specific facets of human rights problems. As for example, most of the NGOs, operating at international level, focus attention on denial of civil and political rights - arbitrary arrests, extra-judicial executions, political killings, detention without trial etc. 'Mere are some who focus attention on elimination of' discrimination against women, Others concentrate on such social-economic problems like liberation of bonded labour, rights and welfare of the child etc., rights of refugees and stateless persons is another problem claiming specific attention. Then there are groups focusing attention on the need for safe-environments.

Indeed, the problems emanating from denial of human rights in various forms are so massive and complex that no single group could adequately provide vigilance and launch movements for redressal of grievances relating to various aspects of human rights. Again, while denial of civil and political rights, arbitrary arrests, extra-judicial executions have attracted world-wide attention of the media as also inter-governmental organizations, hunger, poverty, shelterlessness, illiteracy, diseases, widely prevalent in developing countries have not attracted the attention they deserve; nor have adequate steps, at national and much less at into national level, been taken for removal of these social and economic menace which amount to negation of basic human rights.

There is more to the need for a global forum. Concerted views expressed by NGOs, through such a forum, would carry more weight in terms of consideration and action by intergovernmental organizations (IGO) as also Governments, than views expressed by individual NGOs having 'consultative status' with the United Nations and its specialized agencies. Indeed, a global forum (at non-governmental level) has the potential to become a new force in the world-wide movement for effective implementation of international norms of human rights.

The idea of holding periodical congregation of human rights activists, educationists, jurists and representatives of various non-governmental organizations drawn from different parts of the world as well as the official representatives of intergovernmental agencies concerned with human rights was mooted, in various international conferences, both inter-governmental and non-governmental.

In formulating the agenda for the third World Congress the approach was naturally global, rather than sectoral or regional, it was designed to cover all important issues relating to promotion and protection of Human Rights which are of vital concern to the international community in the 1990s and beyond. Hence, ten major themes were chosen: (I) Civil and Political Rights: Protection of Personal Integrity; (ii) Role of NGOs In Human Rights; (III) Economic, Social and Cultural Rights: Protection of Human Dignity; (iv) Natural Resource Conflicts and the Right to Safe Environment; (v) Effective Realization of the Rights of Women; (vi) Ethnic, Social and Religious Conflicts; (vii) Rights of Refugees and Stateless Persons; (viii) Protection of the Rights of Vulnerable Sections of the Society; (ix) Human Rights Information, Teaching and Research; (x) Mechanisms for Implementation of Human Rights. Withing the ten broad themes, sub themes covering related aspects were also included. Efforts were made to request such human rights educationists, activists and jurists, in different parts of the world, who were having expertise in the respective fields. It is gratifying that these experts could find time to contribute papers which formed the basis of detailed discussion and deliberations of the Congress.

The universalization of human rights is a political fact. The Universal Declaration of Human Rights adopted by the General Assembly in 1948 has been accepted by virtually all of today's 150 states; even those, notably the European Communist states, which had abstained when the Declaration was approved, have now accepted it formally in the Final Act of the Conference on Security and Cooperation. Every state has adhered to at least one human rights agreement; and more than a third of the world's states have accepted the comprehensive agreements, the International Covenant on Civil and Political Rights, and the International Covenant on Economic, Social, and Cultural Rights, with more states joining every year. The universal acceptance of the idea of human rights and its general content may be only formal and superficial, in some cases even hypocritical, but no government dissents from the ideology of human rights today or offers an alternative to it.

The steady internationalization of human rights is equally impressive. Before the Second World War, how a state treated its own inhabitants was its own business, a matter of "domestic jurisdiction," not of "international concern." Today it is the stuff of daily diplomacy among states. Numerous international organizations deal with it regularly, and it is never absent from the agenda of every organ and agency of the United Nations and of major regional organizations. There are dozens of international human rights agreements, and some of them have been adhered to by more than one hundred states. New international bodies-commissions, committees, and courts-occupy themselves with human rights daily.

The contemporary philosophical respectability of human rights is itself remarkable. The idea of limitations on government, on majorities-even on the "public good"-in favor of individual autonomy, dignity, and need, has taken root and no present political system, no contemporary political theory, rejects it. Earlier philosophical objections have subsided or have become irrelevant. Eighteenth century notions of natural rights suffered the onslaughts of legal positivism in the nineteenth and early twentieth centuries, but human rights now are attended by resurgent "neo-natural-rights" theories, and are finding a prominent place in contemporary political, ethical, and moral philosophy, now again preoccupied with "justice," "liberty," "equality," and "rights." Today, it is human rights that claims the mantle of natural law, not-as in the past-slavery or the divine right of kings, not the inferiority of women, of particular races or of the poor. The establishment of human rights in national law and in international law has disarmed legal positivists as well. It is human rights that are positive national and international law, not the antihuman laws of Hitler or some other jurisprudence of terror. And it is individual civil-political rights as well as economic-social and cultural rights that are the law, not unmitigated collectivism or laissez-faire.

The idea of human rights is not an abstraction; it has specific content. What the world has accepted are the civil, political, economic, social, and cultural rights set forth in the Universal Declaration and the international covenants. They include rights of freedom from mistreatment and undue governmental intrusion, as well as rights to governmental support for the economic and social welfare of every human being. Although specific, the rights are flexible enough to rise above differences among political systems; they are consistent with different degrees and forms of free enterprise as well as with socialism. Debates about conflicts or priorities between rights only confirm rather than depreciate any of the rights declared in the Declaration or protected by the covenants.

Concern by some governments with the condition of individuals in other countries is not new. Centuries ago, princes and popes interceded for coreligionists and others in various countries. The nineteenth century saw a number of "humanitarian interventions" by big powers, through diplomacy and sometimes through force, to protest, end, or prevent massacres, pogroms, and other atrocities. These, however, were personal expressions of "noblesse oblige," or extraordinary reactions to egregious events; they were sharp deviations from the international political system's assumption that, in principle, how a state treated its own citizens was its own business. Surely there was no serious disposition to render the treatment of the individual human being in his own country a subject of international diplomacy and law.

Human rights did not become the concern of international politics or law until after the Second World War, but individual welfare was not wholly beyond the ken of the international system even before then. International law and human rights were linked in the history of ideas, both having antecedents in natural law and in Roman law, and common progenitors in Grotius, Vattel, and Locke. In fact, international law early included some of what we would today as human rights obligations; for example, treaty provisions in which parties undertook to tolerate heterodox religious worship and not to impose civil disabilities on religious dissenters. Customary international law, too, has long imposed on states a responsibility not to deny justice to aliens. In the last century, nations sought to mitigate the horrors of war by developing law to forbid particularly cruel weapons, and to protect prisoners of war and civilian populations during war. Following the First World War, the dominant powers required several states to adhere to "Minority treaties," in which they assumed obligations to respect the rights of ethnic, national, linguistic, religious, or other minorities among their inhabitants. The League of Nations Covenant provided that the mandate system established for dependent areas should be governed by the principle that "the well being and development of such peoples form a sacred trust of civilization," and imposed "conditions which will guarantee freedom of conscience and religion" and other rights. Members of the League undertook "to secure just treatment of the native inhabitants of territories under their control"; mandatory powers were required to promote the welfare and rights of the inhabitants of mandated territories.

The Preamble of the UN Charter reaffirms "faith in fundamental human rights, in the dignity and worth of the human person, in the equal rights of men and women," and declares the determination of peoples "to promote social progress and better standards of life in larger freedom." The purposes of the UN include international cooperation "in promoting and encouraging respect for human rights and for fundamental freedoms for all without distinction as to race, sex, language, or religion" (Articles 1, 55(c)). Human rights are among the responsibilities for study and recommendation of the General Assembly (Article 13) and the Economic and Social Council (Article 62(2)), and a commission on human rights is expressly required (Article 68). Human rights provisions are prominent in Chapters XI and XII dealing with non-self-governing territories and international trusteeship. Members pledged themselves to cooperate with the UN organization for the achievement of its human rights purposes (Article 56). The various UN bodies have devoted years of arduous effort to promoting human rights. Human rights have been on every agenda of every body and have become a staple of UN activity. A universal declaration of human rights was prepared and adopted. Even particular human rights violations have received attention, early as in the case of Russian wives of non-Russians and the treatment of Indians in South Africa, more recently in Chile and elsewhere .6 Some violations-e.g., apartheid in South Africa-are perennially on the UN agenda. Other violations in other places-the treatment of Soviet Jews, allegations of torture in Chile-were the subject of extended international debate over many years. Despite resistance, it was established that within the meaning of Article 2(7) of the Charter, UN preoccupation with human rights was not forbidden intervention. The prevailing view was that UN consideration was not intervention, and, more importantly, that human rights are an international, not a domestic concern.

The UN Charter ushered in a new international law of human rights. The new law buried the old dogma that the individual is not a "subject" of international politics and law and that a government's behaviour toward its own nationals is a matter of domestic, not international, concern. It penetrated national frontiers and the veil of sovereignty. It removed the exclusive identification of an individual with his government. It gave the individual a part in international politics and rights in international law, independently of his government. It also gave the individual protectors other than his government, indeed protectors and remedies against his government. The international law of human rights differs from other international law in its motivations and impulses as well. Generally, international law is made, international obligations are undertaken, to serve common or reciprocal national interests; early human rights laws, too, we have seen, largely served states' political or economic purposes. The move to a comprehensive human rights law also sought to appeal to national and transnational interests, perhaps in an effort to de-emphasize its radical nature. Human rights, it was urged, are related to international peace, for states that violate human rights at home are not trustworthy in international relations, and violations of those rights afford occasions, temptations, and pretexts for interventions or war. The international human rights law also had a different kind of political motivation: states that had minority treaties or human rights provisions in peace treaties imposed on them resented being singled out and sought to universalize their undertakings. But whatever reasons (or rationalizations) were provided to mask it, the fact is that the new comprehensive international human rights law generally serves no patent, particular national interest.

The international law of human rights parallels and supplements national law, superseding and supplying the deficiencies of national constitutions and laws; but it does not replace, and indeed depends on, national institutions. The constituency in every society that supports human rights law is different from the constituency that supports, say, international trade agreements, or military alliances, or peaceful settlements, or even international organization and cooperation. The pressures on a government to adhere to international human rights law are also different from those to adhere to other law, and indeed, a state's adherence to human rights conventions is far less important if in fact it behaves at home, toward its own, consistently with their terms. In other respects, too, international law and politics see human rights in the context of the international political system. Although human rights are universal, they are the claims of an individual upon his society, not on other societies. Although the society in which one lives may be crucial to life and dignity, although a right to change one's society might well be deemed fundamental, the individual does not have an absolute right to join another society and seek his rights there. Even those who are oppressed at home do not yet have an international human right to asylum elsewhere; those who are starving at home do not have an internationally recognized human right to be taken in by the more affluent societies or to be fed by them.

Like other international law, human rights law is made by treaty or convention; there is also customary human rights law made by national practice with a developing sense of legal obligation. The declarations and resolutions of UN organs and other international bodies on human rights may have greater weight in achieving international law here than on other matters, since they purport to express the conscience of mankind on a matter of conscience. And though all law-making is a political process, humanitarian law has its own politics in both making and enforcing law.

The normative human rights provisions of the UN Charter are general and preliminary: essentially, by Articles 55 and 56, member states pledge themselves to take joint and separate action in cooperation with the United Nations to achieve respect for human rights. Human rights are not defined or specified in the Charter, and there is no clear undertaking by every state not to commit one or another violation. The institutions, procedures, and programs for inducing national respect for rights, for monitoring the condition of human rights in different countries, and for preventing, deterring, or ending violation, are not provided. But the words of the Charter are words of legal obligation and surely the pledge of Article 56 is violated if a member state itself persists in committing gross violations of rights universally recognized as fundamental.

No doubt, however, the members of the UN themselves recognized that the Charter law was insufficient. Immediately they proceeded to prepare and promulgate the Universal Declaration of Human Rights, making specific the general Charter references to human rights and freedoms for all.

The Declaration is a remarkable juncture of political-civil and economic-social rights, with equality and freedom from discrimination a principal and recurrent theme. It declares the rights to life, liberty, and security of person, to fair criminal process, to freedom of conscience, thought, expression, association, and privacy; the right to seek and enjoy asylum, to leave one's country and return to it; rights to marriage and family, and rights of property. It declares the will of the people to be the basis of the authority of government, and provides for universal suffrage and bona fide elections. It speaks of the right to work and leisure, health care, and education. The Universal Declaration was not generally conceived as law but as "a common standard of achievement" for all to aspire to; hence its approval without dissent.

The international law of human rights developed by the two covenants parallels the Universal Declaration. It provides protections like those in the constitutions and laws of enlightened democratic-liberal countries as well as the promises of socialist and "welfare" constitutions. Before, during, and since the negotiation of these two major covenants, the UN system also promoted specialized declarations and conventions—on genocide, on the status of refugees and stateless persons, on the rights of women, and on the elimination of all forms of racial discrimination." These emphasize, extend, and supplement the protections afforded by the principal covenants. They have also made it possible to "extract" legal obligations on these particular subjects from governments not prepared to adhere to all the obligations of the general covenants.

International human rights instruments do not legislate human rights; they "recognize" them and build upon that recognition." Human rights was an eighteenth century idea, rooted in notions of natural law and natural rights, and woven of several strands: original autonomy of the individual, converted in society to popular sovereignty; government by social compact of the people and subject to the continued consent of the governed; government for limited purposes only; the rights reserved for the individual even against the people's representatives in government. The international human rights movement took these eighteenth-century ideas of individual autonomy and freedom and combined them with nineteenth- and twentieth-century ideas of socialism and the welfare state. International human rights, however, reflect no single, comprehensive theory of the relation of the individual to society.

That there are "fundamental human rights" was a declared article of faith, "reaffirmed" by "the peoples of the United Nations" in the UN Charter. The Universal Declaration of Human Rights, striving for a pronouncement that would appeal to diverse political systems governing diverse peoples, built on that faith and shunned philosophical exploration. Because of that faith-and of political and ideological forces-governments accepted the concept of human rights, agreed that they were appropriate for international concern, cooperated to define them, assumed international obligations to respect them, and submitted to some international scrutiny as to their compliance with these obligations.

Those who built international human rights perhaps also saw these rights as "natural," but in a contemporary sense: human rights correspond to the nature of man and of human society, to his psychology and its sociology:

— rights "derive from the inherent dignity of the human person";

— "recognition . . . of the equal and inalienable rights of all members of the human family, is the foundation of freedom, justice and peace in the world";[14]

— respect for, and observance of, human rights will help create "conditions of stability and well-being which are necessary for peaceful and friendly relations among nations."

We are not told what theory justifies "human dignity" as the source of rights, or how the needs of human dignity are determined. We are not told what conception of justice is reflected in human rights, or how preserving human rights will promote peace in the world. International human rights are recognized as inherent, but it is not necessarily assumed that man is in principle autonomous, or that rights antecede government. The international instruments nod to popular sovereignty, but there is no other hint of social compact or of continuing consent of the governed. Respect for retained rights is not a condition of government, or a basis of its legitimacy; violation of rights does not warrant undoing government by revolution.

International human rights imply rights for the individual against society, but they are not seen as against the interests of society. Rather, it is believed, a good society is one in which individual rights flourish, and the promotion and protection of individual rights is a public good. Any apparent conflict between the individual and society, between individual rights and a more general public good, is only temporary and superficial; in the longer, deeper view the society is better if the individual's rights are respected.

Like the eighteenth century idea of rights, international human rights also, inevitably, implicate the purposes for which governments are created. Rights against government imply limitations on government, but there is no a priori assumption that in general government is for limited purposes only. To the contrary, born after various socialisms were established and spreading, and after commitment to welfare economics and the welfare state was nearly universal, international human rights imply a conception of government as designed for many purposes and seasons. The rights deemed to be fundamental include not only civil and political rights which government must not invade, but also rights to economic and social well-being which government must actively provide or promote. The rights declared and enumerated imply a government that is activist, intervening, that is committed to economic-social planning for the society which would redound as economic-social rights to the individual.

Human Rights as International Law

Human rights are rights which the individual has, or should have, in his society. If societies respected these rights adequately, there would be no need for international law and institutions to help protect them. International human rights law and institutions are designed to induce states to remedy the inadequacies of their national laws and institutions so that human rights will be respected and vindicated. The individual must pursue his rights through his own laws and institutions. Even when these fail him, international law and institutions cannot provide those rights; they can only press the state to provide them. International human rights obligations are met when, and only when, national laws and institutions meet the minimum international standards and give effect to the minimum of human rights. International human rights agreements are international agreements like all others. They create rights and duties between states parties to the agreement; they may create also rights in third parties, whether states or individuals. Failure to honour these undertakings brings the same consequences as for other international agreements: other parties can demand compliance and seek reparations, and may resort to any tribunal which has jurisdiction over such claims between these parties. 16 Some agreements also provide for special remedies before particular bodies.

The United Nations Charter made human rights a legitimate subject for discussion and recommendation by the Assembly and its sub-organs. Human rights may also properly come into the ken of the Security Council when it implicates peace and security, e.g., in South Africa. By discussing human rights the General Assembly does not intervene in matters "which are essentially within the domestic jurisdiction of any state" (Article 2(a)). Intervention, strictly, means dictatorial interference by force, and there have been no UN military interventions in support of human rights; discussion and recommendation are not intervention. Human rights, moreover, are a matter of international concern, not essentially within any state's domestic jurisdiction. Enforcement measures by the Security Council are in any event exempted from Article 2(7).

Article 2(7) speaks only to intervention by the UN, not by member states, but most challenges to activities by states on behalf of human rights as "intervention" are equally unfounded. Peaceful objections by states to human rights violations by other states are not interventions. Generally, human rights are no longer within a state's domestic jurisdiction. That which is governed by international law or agreement is ipso facto and by definition a matter of international concern, not a matter of any state's domestic jurisdiction. Certainly, any state that adheres to an international human rights agreement has made the subject of that agreement a matter of international concern. It has submitted its performance to scrutiny and to appropriate, peaceful reaction by other parties, and to any special procedures or machinery provided by the agreement for its implementation.

The international instruments speak of human rights, but they do not purport to create them; they recognize"' their preexistence in some other moral or legal order. They confirm the concept of human rights and give it status and value in the international system. Like other international agreements, the international human rights agreements create rights and obligations among the states parties to the agreement: every party is obligated to every other state to carry out its undertakings; every other state has the right to have the obligation carried out. But these are the legal rights of states, not the human rights of the individual. If states are the promisors and promisees, however, the authentic beneficiaries are the individual inhabitants whose "human rights" the state promises to respect. Whether the international agreements also create international legal rights for the individual is debated. Some have strongly denied it. Others argue that as third-party beneficiaries, and the true beneficiaries, individuals have rights under international law, even when they have no direct remedy but must rely on states and international bodies to vindicate their rights. And some instruments for example the Optional Protocol to the International Covenant on Civil and Political Rights, the Convention on the Elimination of All Forms of Racial Discrimination, and the European and the American Conventions on Human Rights-also provide some remedy for the individual to pursue his international legal rights by international legal remedies.

Human rights are rights to be enjoyed by individuals in their own societies and implemented and enforced under their laws and institutions. International undertakings are designed to help assure that national societies in fact respect the human rights of their inhabitants. International instruments require states to enact legislation and otherwise ensure that the rights are respected. In some legal systems international human rights obligations may be "self-executing" and will be given effect by officials and courts without domestic legislation. The international system also provides "enforcement machinery." Such international instrumentalities, however, do not operate directly to grant the individual his rights; they work on the state and are designed to induce the state to carry out its obligations. Even when the individual is given some kind of an international remedy, for example, the right to "communicate" to the Human Rights Committee pursuant to the Optional Protocol to the Covenant, the communication does not produce an international mandate conferring the right; it serves only to trigger an international process to induce the state to desist from violation or to provide a remedy for past violations.

The principal international human rights agreements are the two covenants deriving from the Universal Declaration. Both covenants have been in force since 1976. The Covenant on Economic, Social, and Cultural Rights, which requires a state to take steps "to the maximum of its available resources" with a view to achieving "progressively" rights that may depend on the society's economic-social development, has, understandably, not been a subject of international controversy or of individual complaints of violations. Compliance with that Covenant is not the charge of a special monitoring body but of political bodies, the Economic and Social Council and the General Assembly, that have not built up any substantial jurisprudence of interpretation of that Covenant. The Covenant on Civil and Political Rights, on the other hand, is acquiring an ever-growing jurisprudence. Reports by states on their compliance have been scrutinized and discussed by the Human Rights Committee created pursuant to the Covenant. Governments and especially nongovernmental organizations have invoked the Covenant. Disputes about compliance by particular parties are daily fare, reflecting differences of interpretation that cry to be discussed.

The Covenant is binding international law, like any other international agreement. That the agreement is for the benefit of individuals, and that the beneficiaries are each state party's own citizens and inhabitants, in no way detracts from its binding legal quality. Like any international agreement it creates rights and obligations among the states parties to it and affords each party the usual remedies for inducing compliance or obtaining reparation if a violation occurs. Again, that the true beneficiaries are the state's own inhabitants does not detract from the rights, obligations, or remedies available to the parties. Neither does the fact that special machinery is provided to scrutinize and induce compliance vitiate the usual remedies between states parties to the agreement.

The Content of the Covenant

The Covenant tracks closely the provisions of the Declaration. At the beginning of this Covenant (as well as the Covenant on Economic, Social, and Cultural Rights), however, are provisions dealing with the right of peoples to self-determination and to sovereignty over their resources, which have no counterpart in the Declaration.

Self-determination has been a major slogan and a political principle in international life in the twentieth century; that it is also a norm of international law was long disputed. Whether as political principle or legal norm, important controversies revolved about its meaning and scope. What (or who) is a people entitled to self-determination? How shall a people make and indicate its determination? Are all options available to a people, or are some precluded as inconsistent with the principle of self-determination? Does self-determination mean only freedom from classical forms of colonialism, or also from various forms of "neo-colonialism?" Does it imply the right of any part of a state to secede? Is self-determination "external" only, or does it imply also the right of people freely to determine the form and substance of their government?

Article 1 of the Covenant provides: "All peoples have the right of self-determination. By virtue of that right they freely determine their political status and freely pursue their economic, social and cultural development." That provision does not readily resolve any of the disputes about the jurisprudential character of the principle of self-determination. Clearly, the Covenant does not create the right; it recognizes it. (It does not indicate whether it is a moral or a legal right, or in which moral or legal order.) Parties to the Covenant assume the legal obligations implied in recognizing that right. Such legal obligations presumably run towards other states parties, although any "people" entitled to such self-determination may be a third-party beneficiary of such obligations.

There were political-ideological differences as to the appropriateness of including provisions on self-determination since they asserted rights of "peoples," not of individuals. Most governments, however, supported inclusion, arguing that these rights inured to individuals and were the foundation of all other rights. Since all now accept both political and economic self-determination in principle (although with important differences as to what they imply), it may not matter much whether these "rights of peoples" are included in the lexicon of individual human rights or in other instruments. Including them in the Covenant, however, links self-determination to the rights of individuals, as Cassese demonstrates. The other, individual rights follow the general order of the Declaration. In the Covenant, the substantive rights appear in Part III and are not formally grouped, but in fact reflect a grouping which we have sharpened in the scheme of this volume. The order of rights suggests no hierarchy of importance but follows some rationale of organization. The right to life, physical liberty, and integrity of the person form a -natural" package and a natural place to begin. Understandably, indeed inevitably, these rights come first in the elaboration of individual rights in the Covenant. They are the matrix, the indispensable condition of all human rights, giving meaning to all others. Other rights, while they also have important, intrinsic, independent validity, can be seen as developments and elaborations of these rights. Every society, every ideology proclaims the sanctity and primacy of these rights and none would admit to violating them. But there are important issues as to the scope of these rights and of the limitations upon them. These rights include the right to life itself, to physical integrity, to treatment with dignity; freedom from coercion, slavery, and forced labour; and freedom from arbitrary detention and arrest (see essay 5 by Yoram Dinstein).

The rights to life, liberty, and physical integrity are particularly implicated in a society's criminal law. The law, the procedures, the institutions, and the sanctions of the criminal law weigh heavily on the individual and sometimes take his life.; international human rights seek to assure that their reach is carefully circumscribed so that individual rights are invaded only to the extent essential to achieve the law's legitimate purposes. The substantive provisions of the Covenant forbid making criminal what should not be. Other provisions are designed to prevent abuse of criminal law and process, as by unlawful or arbitrary arrest and detention. In a civilized system-and under international human rights—the legitimate purposes of the criminal law are not served by the conviction and punishment of the innocent. Moreover, as the most threatening form of action by the state against an individual, the criminal process in particular requires fairness, decency, and respect for individual integrity and dignity. The rights of even the guilty ought not be invaded more than need be; hence, limitations on being convicted twice for the same offense, on cruel and excessive punishment, and a general requirement that "all persons deprived of their liberty" including those convicted of crime-"shall be treated with humanity and with respect for the inherent dignity of the human person" (Article 10(l)).

Limitations on Rights

As in even the most enlightened and libertarian national rights systems, most of the rights in the Covenant are not absolute. The freedom of expression, in the classic reference, does not permit one falsely to cry "fire" in a crowded theatre; the most libertarian societies do not permit slander; all countries impose some limits on freedom of movement in some circumstances to protect national security or public order. In the rights jurisprudence of the United States these permissible limitations are not expressed in the Constitution, although sometimes read into general phrases: search and seizure is forbidden only if "unreasonable," punishment only if "cruel and unusual," infringements on liberty only if they deny "due process of law."

The Framers of the Covenant sought to define the permissible scope of limitations as strictly as possible, although inevitably in general phrases. For example, the freedom of movement within a country or the right to leave it "shall not be subject to any restrictions except those which are provided by law, are necessary to protect national security, public order (order public), public health or morals, or the rights and freedoms of others, and are consistent with the other rights recognized" in the Covenant (Article 12(3)). Or, "the Press and the public may be excluded from all or part of a trial for reasons of morals, public order (order public) or national security in a democratic society, or when the interest of the private lives of the parties so requires, or to the extent strictly necessary in the opinion of the court in special circumstances where publicity would prejudice the interests of justice" (Article 14(l)). One can debate the merits of these and other limitations or their particular formulations, but few would question that in principle some such limitations are inevitable and probably desirable. The limitations themselves, however, are governed by law, not by the whim of the state. Whether a particular limitation on a right is permissible under the Covenant is a question of international law, and the state's action can be scrutinized and challenged as a violation of the Covenant.

Like all international human rights agreements the Covenant does not eliminate the essential dependence of individual human rights on national laws and institutions. The Covenant requires states to respect the individual's rights and to "ensure" them, and the state can do that only through its own laws and institutions. Indeed, the Covenant expressly requires states to "adopt such legislative or other measures" as are necessary to give effect to rights recognized by the Covenant.

Permissible Reservations

Unlike some other international agreements, the Covenant does not expressly bar reservations generally or to particular clauses. In view of the character of the Covenant, one may assume that there was no intention to bar reservations; it is desirable to have states adhere to as much of the Covenant as possible, even if they insist on excluding some particular provision. But any state may object to a reservation by another state and may even reject a treaty relation with the reserving state as regards the Covenant as a whole. Also, there can be no reservation "incompatible with the object and purpose" of the Covenant.

Major reservations that contradict the basic spirit of the Covenant would be out of order even if other parties were prepared to acquiesce in them. Surely, for a hypothetical example, South Africa could not purport to ratify the Covenant but reserve the right to maintain apartheid. Even as regards particular provisions, it would seem improper for a state to reserve a major exception permitting it to violate an important right in an important way against ail important segment of its population. Even if most states acquiesced, a single objecting state might challenge the propriety of a reservation under the Vienna Convention and impugn the claim of the reserving state to be a party to the Convention.

It has been suggested that those articles of the Covenant which are not subject to derogation in time of emergency ought not to be-perhaps a fortiori-subject to reservation generally. That argument is plausible, with some limitations. First, a state may wish to make a reservation to the nonderogation clause itself, and if the reservation is not "total," it might not be a reservation that defeats the object and purpose of the Covenant. Second, some clauses are not subject to derogation not because of their fundamental importance but because they are of a character to which public emergency is irrelevant and surely not 11 strictly required," for example imprisonment for contract debt (Article 11). That such a clause is nonderogable, then, is no sign that it should also be not subject to reservation. Even articles that are not subject to derogation for reasons of their importance, moreover, might be treated differently for reservation purposes. The exemption from derogation is stated in terms of whole articles of the Covenant and might be deemed to exempt the entire article. But while a reservation to any of those articles as a whole may w ll be unacceptable as inconsistent with the object and purpose of the Covenant, a reservation to some single aspect of it might pass. Thus, for example, the right to life (Article 6) is not subject to derogation and should not be subject to reservation as a whole, But it might not be inconsistent with the object and purpose of the Covenant for a state to reserve, say, a right to impose capital punishment on persons over 17 (rather than 18) years of age. In principle, "nonderogability" should be strong but not conclusive evidence that a reservation is inconsistent with the object and purpose of the Covenant.

As for any international agreement, the rights and duties created by the Covenant, and whether they are observed or violated, are determined by reference to its provisions as properly construed. The Covenant is not an exercise in rhetoric but an instrument for practical application in every society. Like any instrument, it must be read with good sense in the light of its character and purpose. In the case of the Covenant the character and purpose are a paramount guide. The Covenant is part of the International Bill of Rights, a historic milestone in the struggle for human freedom and dignity. It is designed to help protect and ensure individual rights everywhere, and to establish a legal, political, and economic climate in which individual freedom and dignity can flourish. The Covenant, then, is not to be read like a technical commercial instrument, but "as an instrument of constitutional dimension which elevates the protection of the individual to a fundamental principle of international public policy." Rights are to be read broadly, and limitations on rights should be read narrowly, to accord with that design.

Interpretation is hardly an exact science, in international or in national law, and international interpretation must take account also of differences of doctrine or style in interpretation between different legal systems, different states, courts, lawyers, or scholars. Nevertheless, international instruments are not "wide open"; words are not wholly uncertain: communication, surely agreement, would be impossible if words and sentences did not have essentially clear and indisputable meaning, whatever ambiguities or uncertainties may arise at the periphery and in unanticipated circumstances. Despite some impressions to the contrary, the provisions of the Covenant are no more ambiguous than other international or national instruments, probably no more ambiguous than instruments serving such purposes had to be. Provisions permitting derogation and limitation are in general terms and have twilight zones, but they, too, are not more ambiguous than they had to be. In any event, that lines may have to be drawn in the interpretation or application of a clause or phrase, say "public order," does not mean that they may be drawn anywhere. Every clause has a broad clear zone of unambiguous meaning with twilight only at the margin. Uncertainties and ambiguities may loom larger, however, because the application of human rights provisions, and the facts of any human rights issue, are largely in the control of the state. Other states or international bodies often do not have the interest or the ability to challenge interpretations of Covenant provisions and their applications in particular circumstances.

Interpretation is the pursuit of meaning; and international law has developed rules, canons, and attitudes of interpretation, codified recently in the Vienna Convention on the Law of Treaties. "A treaty shall be interpreted in good faith in accordance with the ordinary meaning to be given to the terms of the treaty in their context and in the light of its object and purpose" (Article 31). "Recourse may be had to supplementary means of interpretation, including the preparatory work of the treaty and the circumstances of its conclusion, in order to confirm the meaning," or to determine the meaning when the text "leaves the meaning ambiguous or obscure," or "leads to a result which is manifestly absurd or unreasonable" (Article 32).

For interpreting the Covenant this means of course that we begin with the text, but we don't necessarily stop there. The travaux préparatoires, including all the various stages of the preparation, are relevant to resolve ambiguities and uncertainties, though obviously not against the textual grain. Since the drafting process took many years and the subjects received different degrees of attention, at different hands, the travaux have to be used cautiously and intelligently, but they are often indispensable to understanding the text and giving it the designed effect. Borrowed terms bring with them a freight of meaning they had in the context from which they were borrowed. Early interpretation shapes meaning and determines later interpretation. What governments applying an agreement say or act as though it means, and how other governments react; interpretation by international bodies whose job it is to monitor the implementation of the agreement, by the International Court of justice and other international adjudicatory or arbitral bodies; by national courts or by scholars; or authoritative interpretations of similar language in other instruments-all fairly enter the process of pursuit of meaning. Interpretation, moreover, cannot be static; inevitably, it contributes to the development of various provisions, applying them to new, often unforeseen contexts and cases in the light of the purposes of a provision and the overall aims of the agreement.

A cardinal principal of interpretation is that an instrument shall be construed in consonance with its dominant purpose. In the case of the Covenant, it must never be forgotten that it is a human rights instrument, dedicated to the protection of the individual against governmental excesses. That general principle of construction is expressly developed in Article 5(l): "Nothing in the present Covenant may be interpreted as implying for any State, group or person any right to engage in any activity or perform any act aimed at the destruction of any of the rights and freedoms recognized herein or at their limitation to a greater extent than is provided for in the present Covenant." Another general principle, particularly relevant to the Covenant, is that "limitations clauses"-provisions permitting derogations from rights and limitations on rights-shall be strictly and narrowly construed. That principle is recognized in Article 5(1) and underscored elsewhere in the Covenant. Derogation where permitted is only allowed to the extent "strictly required" (Article 4(l)); limitations on rights are permitted only as "necessary," or "strictly necessary" (Articles 12(3), 14(l)).

Historically, spiritually, and conceptually the Covenant-like its sibling the Covenant on Economic, Social, and Cultural Rights-is a child of the Declaration and that ancestry is not irrelevant to the Covenant's meaning. Since the Declaration has been universally accepted, it is plausible to argue that it be seen as a guide to what is in the Covenant, rather than as having been rejected and replaced by it. Thus, for one example, the presence in the Declaration of Article 17 recognizing a right to own property and not to be arbitrarily deprived of it lends support to the view that such a right is intended to be protected also by the Covenant, if only by implication from Article 5(2).23 The transformation of the Declaration into two covenants has significance for the meaning of both of them. While each Covenant rests on its own bottom, the existence of an obligation in one Covenant may suggest that it was not intended to be implied also in the other. That a provision is designated a civil-political right and included in that Covenant may also be relevant to its interpretation.

It is not possible to anticipate all the issues that may arise under the Covenant. But good faith in applying the Covenant in the spirit in which it was conceived, and for the purpose for which it was created, should resolve most issues. The important and controlling considerations are: that the Covenant is a bill of rights for the individual even against his own society, even when it acts in what it sees as the public good; that derogations from and limitations upon rights are exceptional and to be sparingly and strictly invoked. Especially because the individual is at the mercy of his government and it is the government that decides in the first instance what his rights are, it is of supreme importance that all recognize that a government's interpretation or application is not final but is subject to scrutiny by other states parties, by the Human Rights Committee and other international bodies, and by organizations and individual men and women of good will who represent what the Covenant reflects, the conscience of mankind.

2

Human Rights and Human Duties

At the United Nations Conference on Human Rights in Vienna, Western nations are pushing for a more general acceptance of their human rights standards in the rest of the world. A special international court as well as a High Commissioner for Human Rights are supposed to guard against violations of fundamental human rights. Minimum human rights standards are also made conditions for development cooperation by Northern donor countries. No visit by a high-ranking official from a Western democratic state in a developing country will pass without the human rights situation being discussed and mentioned in the final press conference as an important point on the agenda. In spite of this, it is hard to say whether the human rights situation in the world has actually improved. While in some countries, freedom, democracy and the rule of law have certainly gained ground, there are other countries where the situation is worse than ever. The most basic of all human rights is the right to life and security, butthis right seems to be increasingly in danger. Statistics show that the number of wars in the world has been rising steadily since the end of World War Two. At the moment almost 50 wars of different types are being waged around the world, most of them in Asia and Africa. Millions of people are affected by these wars and are either killed and wounded or drift around as refugees. Many are expelled from their homes as part of "ethnic cleansing"—a common phenomenon not only in former Yugoslavia but also in many other civil-war type conflicts.

All these are serious human rights violations. But how can they be redressed? Can the international community be held responsible and asked to intervene in all these cases to help the victims of wars, oppression and persecution to assert their human rights? Can the United Nations possibly be expected to be mounting peace-making and peace-keeping operations in 50 war-type conflicts around the globe? Who is supposed to provide the troops, the logistics, and the money for such a gigantic undertaking?

When we speak of human rights, we should also speak of human duties and responsibilities. Take the case of Somalia. The 8 million people in that war-ridden country have the right to live in peace and personal freedom and security But they also have the duty to compromise and to bring their own house in order. It is intolerable that a handful of tribal clans can hold a whole nation to ransom and cause a chaos which costs the international community billions of dollars to correct The same can be said of Cambodia or the former Yugoslavia. Enormous relief funds are needed to mitigate the effects of relentless civil wars. Much more money will still be needed for peacekeeping operations once the wars there come to an end. The interventions by the United Nations in these areas are motivated by humanitarian concerns and intended to safeguard human rights. But we should not forget that it is the foremost duty and responsibility of the people in the area to find a modus vivendi and not to stick to maximalist positions. The right to self-determination, for instance, cannot mean that every village becomes a sovereign state.

The definition of human rights, in the eyes of the Third World, not only includes political, but also social and economic rights. They rightly argue that a person cannot enjoy and use his civil liberties unless he can meet his basic needs of food, shelter, and health care. Hence the demand to the rich industrial North not only to preach democracy and the rule of law, but also to assist the South in eradicating widespread poverty But when we speak of a "right to development" we must also talk about the duty of the more prosperous groups in a society to share their wealth with the less fortunate ones. As long as the upper classes in a given developing country show no inclination to bring their flight capital home to invest in their own countries, as long as they are not prepared to pay their taxes to enable the state to help the poor, the international community cannot be held responsible for taking on this job. And as long as governments do little or nothing to control the population growth which does so much to aggravate the problems of poverty, they are ill placed to claim international aid as a human right.

Our world of terror and horror, of hunger and handicaps, of hopes of a human order where people everywhere will be sovereign and, as groups and as individuals, will be free, where society will guarantee full person hood in its holistic richness to every member of the world community, presents many problems of social dynamics and jural pragmatism. Here we have challenges, ideological and other, to creative law-persons, humanist jurists and sensitive statesmen. The task is to strive for a social order concretizing, by positive law, the aspirations of mankind for the full and free development of every individual which is one of the basic principles of socialist society. The International Human Rights

Conference in Tehran called by the General Assembly of the United Nations to mark the International Year of Human Rights came out with a pregnant proclamation.

> Since human rights and fundamental freedoms are indivisible, the full realisation of civil and political rights without the enjoyment of economic, social and cultural rights, is impossible.

This process of realisation calls for legal positivisation, not political polemics nor diplomatic clap-trap but normative formulation, by lawyers who know the art of effective expression with no compromise on the spirit and substance of the project. We may assert that 'it is the essence of law that it becomes positive'.

The creative commitment of democratic jurists must catalyse the living values enshrined in human rights jurisprudence, especially in the current politicised context of distorted perspectives and cold war objectives. While it is a welcome phenomenon of our times that universal faith in fundamental human rights and global awareness of the dignity and worth of the human, person as part of the larger freedoms is rising, it is a poignant paradox that this very humanist appeal is being used by cannibal powers as a sanctimonious strategy, wearing a moral mask painted with human rights to hide the designs of those who hold the neutron bomb in one hand and a politicised packet of "human rights" in the other.

Democratic lawyers must expose the 'human rights' hoax and restore 'human rights' truth. But what are human rights? Going to its spiritual roots, we discover that the Religion of Man-be it located in the Vedas, Buddhist texts, the Bible, the Quoran or the holy literature of other authentic teachers - upholds human divinity. Every human being is a divine being and has title to dignity, liberty, equality and other basic rights. This natural or idealistic view, however, was to be read down according to the laws of social dynamics.

We cannot understand or evaluate human rights divorced from the historical and social context. Idle ideals and empty assertions cut no ice. The status of human rights takes us to the life-style of a society. That is why the Indian constitutional approach is soaked in the social milieu and human condition and is not a trans-Atlantic transplant.

Even the Afagna Carta' the Bill of Rights or the Rights of Man, are products of their society. After all, King John responded to his barons only, Jefferson himself was a slave owner and the French Declaration of the Rights of Man did not apply to women or end slavery, although these several muniments of human rights were achievements in their own way and time. Lenin's Declaration of the Rights of the Working and Exploited People had a burning relevance to the Russian Revolution even as the Objectives Resolution moved by Nehru in the Constituent Assembly was history in the making, not hortative rhetoric.

This dialectical angle reveals that the compulsions of the global holocaust and Nazi savagery accounted for the integrated agenda of Peace, Human Survival and the Dignity and Worth of the Human Person and the glorious developments, at the international, level, of the rainbow of human rights. A flashback of history will be light now the U.N. Charter is the off-spring of the peoples' struggle for civilised life. It is the living product of the blood, toil, tears and sweat of mankind everywhere, not a legal parchment drafted by clever diplomats. The Universal Declaration of Human Rights, again an imperative of the forces at work, took the programme to a higher level of concreteness. Although many counterforces side-tracked and procrastinated the formulation, in its fullness, of a, codified covenant of human rights, the universal pressure of the peoples or our planet resulted in be ultimate acceptance by the U.N. of the two great instruments—the Covenants on Civil and Political Rights an , equally important and integral, the Economic, Social and Cultural Rights. These thirty years of international life have been a witness to a fasciculus of declarations, Covenants, conventions and what not, such as

— the Declaration on the Granting of Independence to Colonial Countries and Peoples, dated 14 December 1960;

— the Declaration on the Elimination of All Forms or Racial Discrimination, dated 20 November 1963;

— the Declaration on the Promotion among Youth of the ideals of Peace, Mutual Respect and Understanding between Peoples, dated 7 December 1965;

— the Declaration on Social Progress and Development, dated 11 December 1969;

— the Declaration on the Elimination of Discrimination against Women, dated 7 November 1967;

— the Declaration on Principles of International Law concerning friendly Relations and Co-operation among States in accordance with the Charter of the United Nations, dated 24 October 1970;

— the Charter of Economic Rights and Duties of States, dated 12 December 1974; and

— the Declaration on the Use of Scientific and Technological Progress in the Interests of Peace and for the Benefit of Mankind, dated 10 November 1975,

The higher consciousness of the human family, in the setting of political, economic and cultural developments among nations, is reflected in the enrichment of human rights and their codification. Viewed from the Indian standpoint, human rights have been synthesised, as it were, into an integrated fabric by the Preambular promises and constitutional clauses of the National Charter of 1950, surely influenced inter alia by the U.N. Charter and the Universal Declaration of Human Rights. We may briefly consider the current status of human rights in India vis a vis international developments in this field. Not being a research paper but a tribute to a great humanist jurist, no attempt is made here to be exhaustive, save to convey a feel of the humanization of the basic rights which belong to the Indian people.

India is a sovereign, socialist, secular, democratic Republic. Every attribute of the Republic is bed-rocked an human rights - the sovereignty of the people over the entire resources of the nation, the secular liberation which interdicts discrimination against individuals and groups on religious grounds, the socialist harvest of economic, cultural and other rights and the democratic participation through political and civil rights. These are meaningfully implicit in the system of the Republic and made more explicit in the Preamble and Parts III and IV which have been called the conscience of the Constitution. A word about the Indian constitutional position on the polemics of political versus economic rights.

The Indian constitutional perspective is, that all human rights hang together, that, in the backdrop of the people's appalling and pervasive poverty, the 'founding fathers' viewed the economic and cultural rights as basic, not merely the traditional political' rights which too were regarded as fundamental. Mahatma Gandhi, the inspirer of the Anal freedom struggle, used to say:

> There is on the face of the earth no other country that has the problem that India has of chronic starvation and slow death - a process of dehumanization. The solution must, therefore, be original. In trying to find it, we must discover the causes of the tremendous tragedy.

The State shall, in particular, direct its policy towards securing

(a) that the citizen, men and women equally, have the right to an adequate means of livelihood;

(b) that the ownership and control of the material resources of the community are so distributed as best to subserve the common good;

(c) that the operation of the economic system does not result in the concentration of wealth and means of production to the common detriment;

Article 41 runs :
The State shall, within the limits of its economic capacity and development, make effective provision for securing the right to work to education and to public assistance in cases of unemployment, old age, sickness and disablement, and in other cases of undeserved want.

The holistic approach to both categories of human rights in the constitutional law of India is instructive. While the political and civil rights are made fundamental and judicially enforceable, they are subject to 'reasonable restrictions' for social good. The economic and social rights are also made fundamental, though not justiciable. The State is mandated to enforce them administratively and legislatively. Moreover, the two sets of rights have been, by deliberate design, orchestrated as it were by judicial interpretation. The Supreme Court has held that both parts must be harmonised and

Parliament has gone further in Arts. 31 A, B, C to give primacy to the Directive Principles of State Policy (Part M relating to socio-economic rights in the community setting. The net effect is that constitutional immunity has been conferred on legislation to promote and protect economic and social rights, which cannot be rendered void even if fundamental (political and civil) rights are transgressed. Maybe, this is an over-simplified statement of the legal status of the two classes of human rights but, in substance, it is sound although vested interests are challenging this position through litigation.

Two constitutional developments deserve passing mention before moving on to another aspect of the subject. Although Part IV of the Constitution of India has been described as setting out basic socialist principles, it was only in 1976, by the 42nd Amendment Act, that the Republic was specifically described as socialist. Inevitably, economic rights came to command great moment. Article 43A which too was brought in by the same Amendment, reads:

> 43A. The State shall take steps, by suitable legislation or in any other way, to secure the participation of workers in the management of undertakings, establishments or other organisations engaged in any industry.

The other circumstance demanding attention is that by the 44th amendment Act of 1979, Parliament deleted the right to property, often relied upon by the powerful vested interests in the country, from the category of fundamental rights. Thus, in India today property rights are not sacrosanct and it is no longer tenable for the Proprietariat to demand, as before, the rich man's right to property and compensation on its taking by the State whenever economic legislation is enacted affecting the capitalist order. The extra-ordinary significance of economic, educational and cultural rights in India cannot be grasped unless the sub-human and omnipresent 'absolute poverty' degrading the vast majority of the people is realised. It is beyond Western imagination, perhaps world comprehension.

On top of this dreadful agrestic and urban indigence and massive illiteracy, is the problem of 'backward classes' and that other agonising bracket constitutionally described as Scheduled Castes and Scheduled Tribes. This latter human segment, around 22½% of the total of 680 million people suffer globally unique social suppression and economic exploitation. The Freedom Struggle against imperial Britain was not just a political battle but a human liberation struggle. The harijans and girijans - over a fifth of Indian humanity—had to be freed from serfdom, untouchability, unapproachability, degrading forms of feudal life and labour. Women had to be released from domestic subjugation and, beyond breaking their chains, allowed to unfold their personhood. Indian children, under stark privative situations and physical, mental and educational disabilities are the largest segment of the handicapped innocents in the world. The declaration of the rights of the child in Arts. 4, 5 and 6 provides for State remedial action in favour of children, their nutrition, education and material advancement. The Indian Constitution has, provision in this behalf. On a moderate estimate, the World Bank figure of 290 million 'absolute poor', sans nutrition, even clean drinking water, clothing and shelter, is the dimension of Indian destitution. We have five-star hotels and ill-starred humans. In such a sombre social scenario, to talk of human rights as only political and civil is to shock social conscience, shame human justice and outrage sanity. Rightly, therefore, freedom, in the India of Gandhi, Nehru and Ambedkar became a broad concept. And this is reflected in the spectrum of provisions in the Constitution, with flesh and blood given to them by scores of legislation for the protection of backward sections of people, women and children, workers, handicapped groups and the like. Constitutional realism and humanism converge here.

The courts too have adventured on the same lines in interpretation and application of the laws. Illustratively, a few passages from a couple of judgments may be excerpted later. Before that, a panoramic over-view of human rights jurisprudence on the international plane may be proper.

Article 51 of the Indian Constitution bits the nail on the head when it directs the State to (a) promote international peace and security; (b) maintain just and honourable relations between nations; and (c) foster respect for international law and treaty to obligations in the dealings of organised peoples with one another. India views human rights in the perspective of world peace and international co-operation. The commitment to peace is cardinal to human rights and the intensification to cold war is fatal to human survival. No peace, no life; no life, no rights. Karl Marx has said that the 'full and free development of every individual' is one of basic principles of socialist society.

The International Human Rights Conference in Terhan, called by the General Assembly of the United Nations to mark the International Year of Human Rights, came out with a pregnant Proclamation: 'Since human rights and fundamental freedom are indivisible to full realisation of civil and political rights without the enjoyment of economic, social and cultural rights is impossible'. This conceptual integrality is quint-essential to humanrights reality. A dischotomy and down-grading of economic rights spells doom on political rights as well, for, devoid of economic and social stamina, political rights become decorative paper rights, the husk without the grain. A rapid survey would reveal the genesis in the United Nations

Declaration of January 1942, then the U.N. Charter with its stress upon respect for observance of human rights.

The drafters of the charters of the major regional organisations have also displayed the same sensitivity to the unity of human rights. Article 3 of the Statute of the Council of Europe, the numerous references to human rights in the Charter of the Organisations of American States are instances. The basic documents, however, are the universal declaration of human rights in 1948, the numerous covenants and conventions, some of which have specific concern, especially those adopted in 1966 on civil and political rights and on economic, social and cultural rights. The Council of Europe adopted the European conventions for the protection of human rights and fundamental freedoms;, likewise the European social charter has also entered into force and affirmed economic, social and cultural rights. In 1948 the American States affirmed through the American declaration of rights and duties of action and in 1969 the American convention oil human rights, the fundamental freedoms referred to above. Many international human rights agencies have been responsible for reinforcing human rights. What is significant to notice is the growing emphasis on both classes of human rights on the basis that they are inseparable. The problem of priority, as between the two classes of human rights is a false chase and, in one sense, depends on the circumstances of each case. Strictly speaking, ail these rights are of equal importance because exercise of one right is associated in action with the exercise of another. The traditional western view of confining human rights to civil and political rights is no longer current coin among international jurists. Even the Inter-American Juridical Committee supported the stand that economic, social and cultural rights are vital human rights. The committee noted way back in 1945;

> A generation or more ago States had but a limited understanding of the obligation of the community to promote the welfare of its individual citizens. The rights of the individual were rights against the interference of the State, not rights to the active assistance of the State. But within more recent years, it has come to be understood that the individual cannot always by his own efforts attain standards of living 'adequate to the development of his given personality, (and the) relation between spiritual development and standards of material welfare has come to be more generally recognised .... Thus the fundamental rights of the individual may be regarded as growing with the growth of civilization, taking on new forms with newer ideals of social justice.

Even Pope John XXIII in his Encyclical Pacem In Terris stated'

> Man has the right to life. He has the right to bodily integrity and to the means necessary for the proper development of life, particularly food, clothing, shelter, medical care, rest and finally, the necessary social services. In consequence, he has the right to be looked after in the event of ill-health; disability stemming from his work; widow-hood; old age; enforced unemployment; or whenever through no fault of his own he is deprived of the means of livelihood

The Inter-American Juridical Committee had no doubt about the importance of economic, social and cultural rights, and, in its report, states:

> In more recent years the existence of cyclical unemployment upon a vast scale has led to the assertion of a fundamental right of man to work as the basis of a duty on the part of the

> state to regulate private industry so as to avoid as far as possible the recurrent business cycles with mass unemployment in times of depression, and at the same time the duty on the part the state itself to provide opportunities of labour which enable persons to earn a livelihood by their own efforts. It is beneath the dignity of the human person to be continuously the object of charity and state aid; and at the same time it is demoralizing for him to remain in idleness.

In the socialist countries it has always been regarded that economic rights are as important as, if not more than, political rights. The Constitutions of the socialist countries bear testimony to this equal emphasis. The Indian Constitution acts up to this synthesis and philosophy and describes, in Parts III and IV, both classes of human rights as fundamental. Indeed, the recent amendments to the Indian Constitution of 1976, 1979 and 1980 leave no doubt that the conspectus of human rights, so far as the Indian people are concerned, makes no distinction between political, civil, economic and cultural rights. The founding fathers of Indian Freedom, right from the beginning of the battle to overthrow the British Empire, envisioned a comprehensive conceptualisation and articulated the demand for freedom in its political, economic and social dimensions. Today, these are not mere agitational demands but rights with constitutional status. The Indian Supreme Court has, in several rulings, adopted a harmonious approach and has read political, economic and social justice into the living law of the land. The constitutional clauses, played upon interpretatively by a sensitized court, has activated the national rule of law to rise to the international level of human rights, especially in the field of prison justice, right to be defended by a lawyer and according to the rules of natural justice, immunity from imprisonment for civil debts, death penalty, worker's rights and equal status of women. Legislation has also given effect to international covenants and resolutions and rules so that the Indian legal status of human rights is conscionable. In this sense, most of the articles of the Universal Declaration of Human Rights and the two International Covenants are building blocks of any Indian's constitutional right.

One may conclude that the Indian and international human rights movement has for its focus:

> Everyone has the right in all circumstances to be treated with humanity and with respect for the inherent dignity of the human person. Thus, international law, in the field of human rights, is no longer the vanishing point of jurisprudence but is a catalyst for the free and full development of every individual in the fertile milieu of a just society.

If we want to act on the improvement of human rights, we must therefore, first shoulder our human duties: The duty to keep the peace at home and to work for compromise between the various groups in society; the duty to balance out the economic interests and remove the staggering discrepancies in incomes and standards of living; the duty, also, to remove unfair barriers to international trade so that all nations have a chance to compete on equal terms. It is no use clamouring for human rights if we are not prepared to accept our human duties.

3

Human Rights in India: Some Issues

The concept of human rights has assumed importance globally during the past few decades. Ever since the proclamation of the Universal Declaration of Human Rights, the term human right has gained currency. Human rights have been the crucial element of philosophical, social and political debates in the second portion of the twentieth century. They will probably also constitute a major discourse of the twenty first century. While there is increasingly widespread concern for universal respect and observance of human rights, gross violation of internationally recognised norms continue unabated in almost all parts of the world. Countless people around the world suffer hunger, disease and lack of opportunity, there being denied the enjoyment of the most basic economic, social and cultural rights as well as civil and political rights, which is of paramount importance for full realization of human dignity and for the attainment of legitimate aspiration of every individual. The challenge of violation of human rights faces the mankind in its stark nakedness. The challenge is global, concern universal and the issue is basic.

In a developing society such as ours where around 50 per cent of the people are living below poverty line and around 70 per cent of the people are illiterate and large number of men and women are living a life of want and destitution, misery and suffering, this subject assumes much greater importance. Despite much type and holloa a vast number of Indian masses continue to live indignified and uncongenial life. Most of the fundamental human rights and fundamental freedoms enshrined in the Indian Constitution have remained paper aspirations, which compel many to rethink about India's commitment and seriousness to these issues. There is wide gap between rhetoric and reality and sometimes human rights appear more or less a myth in India.

Though in large parts of the world we boast of a democratic set-up with a comprehensive charter of rights written into its constitution protected by an independent Judiciary, and we pride ourselves on observance of the rule of law, large scale violation of individuals' rights has almost become a permanent feature. Hardly any day passes when we do not witness one or other types of human rights violations of women and children, of lower caste and otherwise disadvantaged communities, of religious and ethnic minorities, and of workers. These violations range over whole conspectus of human rights, civil and political rights, as well as social and economic.

There are mass killings and widespread disappearances, torture, wide displacement of communities from traditional abode; arbitrary detentions and extensive censorship of thought and expression. Cases of human rights violation in India are innumerable, repetitive, enduring and have almost become a permanent feature of the state system. The state is a major culprit, brutalising whole population, but massive violations also take place in and through civil society sometimes with connivance of the state and frequently reflecting feudalistic and patriarchal dimension of culture. Justice V.R. Krishna Iyer writes that "India with all its thousands of years of cultural heritage and Vedic vintage, has not been able to assure to its people even a pretence of the preamble's grand undertaking of justice, liberty, equality and fraternity to every citizens."

However, the notion of human rights is not new for India which can claim to be one of the oldest civilizations of the world, where the modem democratic ideals had been their way of life under their enlightened emperors. India can boast of having rulers like Ashoka and Akbar whose concern for the people and their welfare can hardly be over emphasized. Later when India was colonized resistance to foreign rule manifested in the form of demand for fundamental freedoms and civil and political rights for the people. The freedom struggle in India when viewed in its historical perspective is also found to be a struggle for human rights. As early as in 1895 the-Swaraj Bili inspired by B.G. Tilak emphasised the importance of human rights. In the Delhi session of December 19M, Indian National Congress included the principles of self-determination as one of the basic rights of human beings. Madras Congress of the INC in 1927 demanded incorporation of Declaration of fundamental rights in any future constitutional frame work. Lahore Congress of 1930 declared freedom from foreign rule as a fundamental right.

The famous resolution on "Fundamental Rights and Social Change" was adopted by the Indian National Congress at the Karachi session on March 29, 1931. The Karachi Resolution envisaged the future constitution of free India providing for classical freedoms and equality, non-discrimination, religious neutrality of the state, adult suffrage, as well as right to free primary education, living wages for workers under healthy conditions of work, freedom from serfdom, prohibition of child labour and social security system for old age, sickness and unemployment. There was wide public acceptance with such thinking concerning fundamental human rights and freedom. These were perhaps the powerful factors in ensuring that the Constitution of India when it came into being, based itself on an emphatic articulation of essential human rights.

Promulgation of the constitution by the people of India in January 1950 was the culmination of India's long struggle for fundamental freedom and human rights. The Preamble, Fundamental Rights and the Directive Principles together provide the basic human rights for people of India. Democratic socialism spelt out in the Preamble and the Directive Principles is meant to provide the context in which the fulfilment of Fundamental Rights has to be achieved. Fundamental Rights contained in Part III are essentially civil and political rights which are declared supreme under Article 13 of the constitution and as such are judicially enforceable. While Directive Principles of State Policy contained in Part IV are by and large social and economic rights which as per Article 37 of the constitution, are not enforceable in courts of law but, nevertheless, fundamental in the governance of the country.

After independence and adoption of a constitution which contained in it a long list of people's rights including civil and political and economic and social right, it was hoped by millions of poor people in India that now they would get the chance to improve their lot under the guidance and protection of democratic government. Pandit Nehru voiced the hopes of people : "I trust that the constitution itself will lead us to real freedom that we have clamoured for and real freedom in turn will bring food to our starving people, clothing for them, housing for them and all manners of opportunities of progress."

Now the question arises how far the dream of the founding fathers has been realised in India in its 50 years of journey after independence? It is pertinent to discuss whether the concept of human rights enshrined in the Indian constitution is really being honoured or not. This needs thorough examination of working of political process, institutional structure, development process and the condition of the man who is the base component of the entire system. Though this examination is beyond the scope of this paper but a cursory look at the whole situation would certainly lead to disappointment. Constitutional goal of socio-economic justice has become mirage. Directive Principles have been transformed into 'Decorative Principles of State Policy'. Inspite of claimed rapid economic development half of the population in India still live in miserable and pathetic condition. People are still dying due to starvation in some part of the country. Half of the people are illiterate and equal number of them are living below poverty line. Managing two times meal is still dream for many and difficult task for others. In absence of basic necessities of life, talking of human rights appears to be cruel joke for them. We must be mindful of the fact that inspite of constitutional, safeguards an statutory provisions evils like untouchability and other social discriminations are still prevalent in many part of the country. In many areas S.C. & S.Ts and down trodden are not allowed to go to the place of worship. What is more shameful that even today these people in some part of the country are not allowed to pass nearby the houses of land lords wearing shoes or Chappals. We cannot ignore the fact that there can neither be human freedom nor respect for human dignity till socio-economic rights are not protected.

The situation is not better on civil liberties front. This also represents a very gloomy picture. Civil liberties and fundamental freedoms of the people are often violated by the state machinery and by those who hold money and power in the society. The use of force and coercive method is normally used by police and bureaucracy in their dealing with the people. While the criminals and anti-social elements are left scot-free, innocent people are often harassed and some time killed in the name of law and order. Secret trials, incognito witness, presumption of guilt, hearing in unknown places and far away states, draconian refusal of bail and restriction on appeals and shoot-at-sight with no habeas corpus remedy and other Star Chamber processes, preventive detentions, sound-proof - sight-proof system of law with a hands-off mandate to human rights and total blackout of the rule of law - this subjects not only the terrorists but all citizens indiscriminately to a regime where decencies of justice are outlawed. Despite the non-derogable rights available to the people, state has used the device of national emergency to rob humans of their right to life and like core rights.

Moreover the condition of Minorities, Dalits, Women and Children are even worse in India. Women represents the most vulnerable section of the society inspite of their celebrated and privileged position as referred to by the ancient Indian scriptures. Women are treated as unequal by society for genetic sin of her discriminated sex. She suffers gender devaluation at home, at work, in literacy, in matrimony, in inheritance and allied rights, in economic opportunity, public life and power process. The gender violence is common and takes many forms across culture, race and class. According to a recent data given by the Ministry of Women and Child Development, there is one rape every 54 minutes, one molestation every 26 minutes, one kidnapping or abduction every 43 minutes, one dowry death every one hour 42 minutes, one act of cruelty every 33 minutes, and one criminal offence against women every 7 minutes. These statistics do not take into account domestic violence which is believed to be the most common yet least reported crime, With more than 500 cases of rape reported every year sexual crimes against women have assumed dangerous proportions. Men are reluctant to report such incidents for fear of serious reprisals from offenders, societal ostracism, damaging marriage prospects$ bringing shame to the family and being victimised.

The woman's dignity is most vulnerable in caste and communal wars, women become the soft targets and are made to face physical and psychological violence. There are numerous example when the caste animities are avenged at the cost of women. They are raped, humiliated, harassed and tortured. A decade ago Chief Justice of Guwahati High Court in his Judgment in "A Police Gang-Rape Case" observed : "It is really unfortunate that in this year of 1988 when we have crossed four decades of our independence and Constitutional guarantees, our woman folk and amongst them also the poor down-trodden are still treated as vegetables to provide tastes to the sex lust for resourceful males." The primary reason why women are subjected to intimidation and violence is their subordinate status in a male dominated patriarchal society. It is, considered a male privilege to legitimise gender hierarchy within the family and the use of violence against women. Thus there Is need for better protection through stringent legislation and policy and reform in criminal justice system. Education and legal awareness widens a woman's perspective, lends confidence to stand up to the oppressor, and if need be take recourse to the courts for redressal. There is need to make an all opt attempt to reorient the society and transform social ethos, educate people about concept of women's dignity and the need to treat women as a human being and individual and a person demanding and needing respect and dignity.

There are other rightless groups such as the suppressed, oppressed Dalits. Inspite of the untouchability being abolished, provision for reservation in jobs and legislation and special protection in criminal justice system neither their is any spectacular change in their condition nor violation of human rights against them has disappeared. Instead atrocities against them have increased including their women.

Widespread atrocities and all-around discrimination against Dalits and the ruthless attempts to suppress them whenever they try to assert their rights pose the problem of denial of human rights to a substantial section of our population. The violence against Dalits takes many form, Most common are murder, rape, grievous hurt, arson and other types of offences. Atrocities on Dalits are not new but what is new in the situation today is that now atrocities and violence against them are carried out in an organised and concerted manner and almost with impunity. More pervasively, there is denial of civil rights provided under law and the Constitution. Reality today is that Dalits are not allowed to enjoy these rights rather they are prevented from exercising these rights. During the elections, they are prevented from voting in marry villages, or if they exercise their franchise at their free will against the dictates of the landlords, they are physically assaulted, their properties destroyed and they are even murdered in some places. What is more important that the state which is supposed to create the necessary conditions to enable the weaker sections to exercise their rights and protect them when they are attacked often behave in a manner which helps only the oppressors and exploiters. They also suffer from a number of social disabilities. For centuries, they have been segregated from the mainstream of society. Evil practice of untouchability is still prevalent in many parts of the country and especially in the rural areas. In many village they cannot still draw water from the common village tank. Going on a bicycle in front of a Brahmin's house nutritive food and deprived of elementary education. The sad is still a crime in rural areas. In many tea-shops in the villages Dalits have no entry. Even if they are served they have to sit in a separate place and to wash the glasses after drinking. In some villages they are not allowed to take out marriage processions without permission from the caste Hindu landlords.

There are a large number of places where they are not allowed to use certain public thorough fares. In short they are discriminated against in every sphere of life. In these circumstances there is no other way left for the suffering people except to rally unitedly and fight and defend their rights. A sense of resistance to injustice and oppression should grow among the Dalits. Ultimately it is their united will and determination to fight and defend their rights which will help them in achieving their goal or social equality. Besides all progressive forces, right thinking people and nil those who believe in social justice and social equality should conic to the aid of the Dallis In their struggle against atrocities and social oppression. Abuse of Child Rights is another am which requires our special attention. We should not forget that the children also have rights like other human beings, to be respected with regard to their integrity, dignity, interest and opinion. But significantly enough children in India are deprived of even the basic human rights due to them, as they ought to be in any civilized society. Human rights violations of children are numerous and of various types. It is shocking to learn that about a million babies, out of 21 million born every year in India are abandoned soon after their birth due to various socio-economic pressures. We are guilty of many crimes and errors but our worst crime is abandoning our children. The problem of child labour in India is an alarming one and constitutes egregious violation of children's rights. India continues to be in the stranglehold of child labour even after five decades of planned development.

The fact remains that these are around 20 million child labourers In India working in various hazardous and non-hazardous industries. Driven by the poverty of their parents, they are working for long hours in miserable conditions and most unhealthy environment, denied plight of there innocent children remain an untold story and offshoot of unequitable socio-economic ambience. Child rape and child prostitution is another dimension of violation of child rights and dignity. There are various reported Incidents when girls have been raped by their fathers. This is a kind of custodial rape that has not so far received adequate attention from the social activists. Because of silence born of fear and shame this kind of child abuse continues for years without any punishment and without any relief to child. There are violations in various ways of' the basic rights of the children, but nothing is more than exploiting them sexually and engaging them in prostitution. Using children to satisfy an adult's sexual needs is something so cruel and mean that it does not exist even in the animal kingdom. Besides govt's concerted efforts general people should be sensitised to children's merciless exploitation and child abuse to put an end to the violation of child rights. Much more attention requires to be given to children's needs for health care, games and recreation and much harsher punishment needs to be given to those who sexually abuse the child.

Minorities in India are another disadvantaged group whose human rights are frequently violated in one or other ways. Minorities who are numerically weak and enjoy Inadequate share in power are subjected to discrimination exclusion by the dominant majority especially when they assert their right to distinct identify and are not prepared to get assimilated. Inspite of the fact that India is party to several international covenants and declarations which particularly deal with minorities rights and Constitutional safeguard, practical experience of minorities has been quite narrowing. Their general educational backwardness, poverty low representation in political institutions and government services and recurrent riots testify to it.

Communal violence has been the most serious problem faced by the minorities from very beginning which causes large scale violations of their many rights. Regardless of which side starts the riot, the minorities are generally the relative losers in terms of lives lost and property destroyed.

Communal violence resulting in extensive destruction of lives and property of the Muslim minority continues unabated. Problem of violence against Christian is a recent .phenomena. What is even more perturbing that in many cases police and other law enforcing agencies have been guilty of active or passive connivance, complicity or participation in rioting against the vulnerable minorities. This fact was recently highlighted by the Srikrishna Commission on the Mumbai Communal Riots of 1992-93 : 'the built in bias of Police forces against Muslims became pronounced." A Tamil Nadu PUCL report spoke of the nexus between a section of the local police and the Hindu fundamentalist forces in the Coimbatore riots of November 1997. "The manner in which the Police indulged in senseless killing would shame even hardened criminals" it said. Thus there is urgent need to protect the rights of minorities which can be done by ensuring their adequate representation in all walks of life and police and law enforcing agencies. State should take special care for their education, employment and overall upliftment in cooperation with NGOs and members of minority groups. This is not merely a humanitarian task, but the very interests of the country's development and national advance require such cooperation and help from all progressive and democratic sections. As long as a considerable section of our people is forced to live a life of utter misery and is denied even the basic rights granted to them in constitution, there cannot be any national progress in the real sense. Such a situation will act as a drag on the country's forward march. Although much has been written and pronounced about human rights through the centuries, yet one would still be hard put to define the term. But again as one author has aptly remarked- "Human rights may be difficult to define but impossible to ignore."

Human rights is a dynamic concept and endeavours to adopt itself to the needs of the day. For this reason, the definition and understanding of tile term depend much on tile condition and opinions prevailing in the given society at a given time and it attains new dimension with the march of history. Since the socio-economic environment with which the question of human rights is intrinsically bound up, keep changing, so do the form and content of human rights. Hence, what constitute human rights cannot be spelt out, in absolute terms for all times and all situations. Inspite of the complications involve in defining human rights attempts are made to comprehend it. To put it simply, human rights constitute those very rights which one has precisely because of being a human. To have a human rights one need not to do anything special than be born a human being. In their basic meanings, human rights are claims of the individual for such conditions as are essential for the fullest realization of the innate characteristic which nature has bestowed him/her with as a human being. They are inherent in our nature and without which we cannot live as human beings. Human rights pertain to all persons and are possessed by everybody in the world because they are human beings. They are not earned, bought or inherited nor are they created by any contractual authority. Differences of sex, race, language and colour do not change these rights. Nor do the differences of property, social origins, political ideals or religious beliefs. Every one regardless of who they are and what they do or think, is born with human rights. The colour of the skin may be white or black, the level of mental make-up may be high or low, the way of life of a people may be modern or primitive, to the core the essential reality of all belonging to the species of human race cannot be dismissed by any stretch of imagination.

Human Rights are essential for full development of human personality and for human happiness. They are indispensable for physical and mental upliftment of the human race. These rights are inalienable because the enlightened conscience of the community would not perm the surrender of these rights by any person even of his own volition. These rights are inviolable because they are not only vital for the development of human personality but also because without them men would be reduced to the level of animals. These rights are expression of what is a life minimally worth living and are based upon primary material and immaterial necessities of life. Of course there cannot be single opinion about quality of life minimally worth living, about primary necessities of life and thus about human rights. But still some rights must be regarded as fundamental like right to life with dignity, right to freedom of conscience and of course right to minimal means of subsistence. Human rights are based on mankind's increasingly demand for a decent and civilized life in which the inherent dignity of each human being will receive respect and protection.

There is no doubt that the term "Human right" is a twentieth century phraseological invention. However, the idea of the inalienable rights of man is much older and infact was often articulated by poets, philosophers and politicians since antiquity. The genesis of human rights is the utopian concept of natural rights traceable from the days of the Greeks or even earlier. The doctrine of natural rights rests on a belief in "Nature", as the original creating force which gave to every man the power of finding by reason the right principles on which to organise his life. Natural right refers to some conditions, situation or conduct that is right, as opposed to being, neutral or wrong for human beings. For example, if we have the natural right to be free, then being free is right, not wrong for us by nature.

The Charter of the United Nations, however, did not define or specify the contents of human rights and this task was left to organisation itself. For this purpose in December 1948, after three years of preparatory work, the UN General Assembly proclaimed the Universal Declaration of Human Rights. The UNDHR was primarily an enunciation of common standard to be adopted by all people and all nations in the promotion and Protection of human rights across the globe. It was a yardstick of international standards and a path-finding Instrument, It defines specific rights-civil and political as well as economic, social and cultural-with equality and freedom from discrimination as a principal and recurrent theme. It spells out the rights to life, liberty and security of person, to fair trial by due process of law, to freedom of conscience, thought, expression, association and privacy, freedom of movement. It also enumerates such economic, social and cultural rights as the right to equal pay for equal work, right to form and join trade unions, right to rest and leisure, and the right to health care and education and so on.

The UNDHR is not, of course, a perfect or even complete compilation. It must be seen as the beginning of a process, not its end. The Declaration does not include many rights which have become enormously significant since then, such as right to self-determination, and the right to development. These rights have been subsequently embodied in declaration of their own, the formular and format modelled on their precursor, the Universal Declaration. The Declaration though devoid of legal authority and enforceability it has exercised a profound influence upon the minds of men and practice of states throughout the world. It stirred the moral consciousness as well as the political assertiveness of people in various countries.

Various parts of the Declaration have been cited in national constitutions and other international instruments as well as regional treaties and conventions. It has also been invoked and invoked by a broad range of decision makers, national and international, judicial and others. Adoption of Declaration was really an event of great significance which launched a new era of hopes and aspirations for human civilization in the protection and promotion of human rights across the globe. Mrs. Eleanor Rosevelt rightly called it the "Magna Carta" of all mankind, as it constitutes a landmark in the history of human rights. It should, however, be noted that the UNDHR was devoid of legal sanction to compel states to meet the obligation of ensuring observance and implementation of human right,, enshrined in it. So to transform the 'principles' into provisions Lasting binding legal obligation on the part of ratifying states, the General Assembly promulgated in December 1966 International Covenants comprising three instruments : International Covenants on Economic, Social, and Cultural rights. International Covenants on Civil and Political Rights; and Optional Protocol to the Covenants on Civil and Political Rights. Besides over the decades, scores of other instruments dealing with specific rights-rights of stateless person, of the refugees, of women, elimination of all forms of, discrimination, and so on have also been proclaimed. All these embody political commitments by signatory states and also provide for the conduct of international relations in the field of human rights and bring the domestic policies in line with international code of ethics. International covenants and instruments are beacon lights showing the path of justice and humanity to the nations. However, what has been traversed so far could be regarded its the initial steps towards a long and arduous journey, Progressive steps forward on this journey call for ceaseless struggle by people in different parts of the world, to ensure that human rights are respected and upheld universally. Though the human rights issue is basically universal in nature, it has been politically manipulated by the Western powers as a means of exercising domination over the, Third World countries. Political use of the issue of human rights has made the intention of the most western countries sceptic in the eye of the majority of the people of the Third World countries.

Most importantly the USA and other countries, which have not been slow to condemn violation of human rights in the third world countries have not only been the worst violators of human rights of these countries but also among the most laggard in respect of signature and ratification of the covenants and conventions on human rights drafted and adopted in or outside the UN. Interestingly, the country which is readily agree to serve the interests of the West, inspite of the large scale violations of human rights therein, is given clean chit. But if a country questions the policies of West and refuse to be a tool in their hand and rejects their model of development, suddenly the issue of human rights is invoked. Does it not lead to think that should the non-western countries need certificate of human rights record from western world? This is a perennial question to deal with.

Frequent recourse to the sanction of human rights in the untenably narrow sense of civil and political ones, accentuates the irony of the situation. The powerful countries of west (particularly the USA) are trying to use their clout in ways palpably harmful to the economic -interests of the poor countries. The tendency in the west to link unrelated issues such on labour standards, social conditions and environment to the new trading regimes work to the disadvantage of the developing countries. Ironically, the sanction of human rights Is further Invoked by the self-appointed policeman of the world—the US to pressurise threshold nuclear power countries to sign the NPT and CTBT, while it and Its allies remain free to use nuclear blackmail to secure their strategic objectives. If the history of Imperialism is any guide, it is these powerful countries which need to be disciplined first.

It is also worthy to note that the western scholars use academic Jargon rationalising the limited definition of human rights which fits in with the emerging post-cold war US policy of establishing political hegemony over third world countries, justifying control over their economy and polity. Not only that the US is funding to scholars and politicians of third world who offers their service in rationalising American ideology and political and economic interests. India is going to be target of this kind of programme because India is a potential market with its over 200 million middle class population, not only for consumer goods, but also for mass media products. If these facts are any guide one can speculate on a latent political objective behind the current fashion of the frequent use of the terms human rights, democracy etc.

However, our enthusiasm in speculating, American hidden agenda must not blind us with the fact that violation of human rights has become every day's affairs in many of the third world countries. Politics of convenience, authoriarianism and repressive state practices, politically motivated ethnic and communal earnages, massive corruption and virtual collapse of any system of accountability have become some of the striking features of the modern state system in the third world. The strategy for third world countries, therefore, should be two fold. At one level they must unitedly chalkout their plan to shield themselves against any design of the western intrusion into their sovereign domain and at the other level they should also strive to do away from there evils which have crept into their society and show great respect for the human rights of their own citizens. They must set their own house in order alongwith their crusade against western imperialism.

Promoting human rights is a historic process and no country can be exception. If one country or several countries act as a permanent guard of human rights, supervise and attack other countries which can only be watched and have no right to speech, this in itself violates the principle and spirit of human rights. Despite the many achievements of the international community.

In the field of human rights, the question of the universality of human rights versus relativism again revisited against the background of the 50th anniversary of the Universal Declaration of Human Rights. Many scholars and states have contended the view that the Universal Declaration serves as the universally valid standard of human rights and morality to which one country could appeal in making judgements about another country or countries with altogether a different culture and tradition. They are of the view that while human rights are universal in nature they must be considered in the context of a dynamic and evolving process of international norm setting, bearing in mind the significance of national and regional particularities and various historical, cultural and religious background. But unfortunately not only do human rights as set forth in the Universal Declaration reveal a strong western bias, but there has been a tendency to view human rights and morality and In isolation from their social, political and economic milieu. In its White Paper "Human Rights in China," the Chinese government stated that "despite its international aspect, the issue of human rights falls by and large within the sovereignty of each state." The Chinese White Paper further states that the evolution of the situation in regard to human rights is circumscribed by the historical, social, economic and cultural conditions of various nations, and involves a process of historical development. Owing to tremendous differences in historical background, social system, cultural tradition and economic development, countries differ in their understanding and practice of human rights.

The concept of universality of human rights caused sharp differences of opinion among the states during Vienna Conference (June, 1993). Lien Huapiu, the head of the Chinese delegation stated that "one should not and cannot think the human rights standards and models of certain countries as the only proper ones and demand that all countries comply with them. It is neither realistic nor workable to make international economic assistance or even international cooperation conditional on them." Similar view was expressed by the Iranian Deputy Foreign Minister at the Bangkok Regional Conference—"The political predominance of the group of countries which is temporary by nature cannot provide a license for the imposition of a set of guidelines and norms for the behaviour of the entire international community, especially since these states do not present an ideal, feasible or practical model in theory or practice.

Respect and observance of human rights are always conditional upon economic conditions of respective states. Unfortunately, this fact is often ignored by the Western scholars and states. Any discourse on human rights situation in the Third World countries would be incomplete unless it takes into account prevailing economic condition. According to UN statistics, the world's total population is about 5.7 billion, with 4.9 billion living in developing countries and about 1.3 billion living in hunger. Poverty has been one of the most potent cause of the violation of human rights in third world countries. Poverty undermines human dignity and without human dignity there is no human right. If unprejudiced, one can easily understand a simple argument: one can enjoy human right only after one manages to live on. The Civil and Political rights are neither meaningful nor feasible in conditions of want and destitute. When there is a grim struggle for, existence, many of the principles of human rights appear to be impractical and devoid of merit. When employment itself is scarce, insistence on payment of minimum wages, abolition of child labour, abolition of bonded labour etc. appear to be constraints in getting employment. For a poor man, if his child could earn any amount, it is an addition to his income and will keep the pot boiling. He is unable to see any merit in the virtues of universal education and prevention of child labour.

If human rights are really universal, it implies entitlement of world's resources to satisfy, to start with, the most basic want of hunger. Normatively, suffering on this account anywhere in the world should be the concern of the world community everywhere. But irony of the situation is that if millions of people are dying in many states of third world due to hunger, many rich countries of the west are dumping huge quantities of food grains in the sea as a price stabilisation measure and huge amount in these countries are spent on nutritional needs of dogs and cats. Are the lives of poor masses of the third world are more worthless than cats and dogs of the west? Similarly, the current emphasis on environmental problem is shared world wide. But there appear to be some subtle attempts to compel the already poor third world countries to invest in environmental protection measures so that the affluent countries do not suffer in terms of competition on account of such investment in their countries.

One of the most strident objections made by Third World countries against Universal Declaration is that it lays greater emphasis on civil and political rights than on economic, social and cultural rights. The balance of Declaration, according to critics is somewhat upset "because it does not properly examine social, economic and cultural rights." Similarly in the developed Western countries the emphasis has always been on civil and political rights and human rights are sought to be equated only with civil and political rights. It is believed In many third world countries that it was on the insistence of the United States that originally proposed as one document, the International Covenant of Human Rights had to be split into two because the US did not want to see the same force given to implementing economic and social rights. Hence, more stringent monitoring and implementation procedures were agreed for civil and political covenant (ICCPR), including an Optional Protocol which provides international machinery for individuals to use in making a complaint about the violation of any of the rights covered in ICCPR. But unfortunately no such mechanism was tried for to ensure the implementation of social and economic rights which needed more for Third World countries.

Thus we see that the protection of economic and social rights compared to the civil and political rights at both national and international level has been weak and irregular. Very often social and economic rights are considered as aspirational and non-justiciable. There is also fallacious thinking that negative rights which gather around our liberties are more important than positive rights that evolve from basic needs. The reason for Western emphasis (undue) on civil and political rights seems to be that having attained a fairly high stage of development in material and economic resources, the social and economic rights did not find much preoccupation in their minds and their concerns were largely confined to civil and political rights. The socio-economic condition being totally reverse in the Third World countries their priority must be different from the West. Majority of the developing countries are reeling in extreme poverty, ignorance, illiteracy, mal-nutrition, disease and suffering and in the prevailing situation civil and political rights loose much of its relevance.

However, the West's unwillingness to recognise and give proper weight to economic and social rights is itself a distortion of universal human rights. What is now needed is a renewed and wonder recognition of the interdependence and indivisibility of all human rights —civil and political as well as social, economic and cultural. It is a matter of satisfaction that there are in fact optimistic signs that the inter-relationships between political freedoms and economic and social development are being increasingly recognised.

The Vienna World Conference on Human, Rights realised this need and stated in no unclear/less certain terms that all human rights are "universal, indivisible and interrelated." The Vienna Declaration stressed that economic and social rights are as important as civil and political rights. The Vienna Declaration tried to set at rest the debate between the primacy of civil and political rights on one hand and economic and social rights on the other. The divide between the two sets of rights was in fact a product of the cold war with the West pushing for civil and political rights and East insisting on economic, social and cultural rights. Indeed, acceptance at Vienna by the developed countries the importance and validity of-economic and social rights and interdependence of these rights with civil and political freedoms represents a positive sign.

In simple terms the indivisibility concept is based on the belief that freedom and food both are essential for ensuring the dignity of person. This fact was very much appreciated in the Universal Declaration which declares that human beings to safeguard their dignity should enjoy freedom of speech and belief and freedom from fear and want. There is indeed a close relationship between these two sets of rights and their relationship is so obvious that the International human Rights Conference in Tehran called by the General Assembly in 1968 declared in a final proclamation : "Since human rights and fundamental freedoms are indivisible, the full realisation of civil and political rights without the enjoyment of social, economic and cultural rights is impossible." The ideas of the Tehran Conference had a profound impact on the Declaration on Social Progress and Development adopted by the UN General Assembly in 1969 proclaiming that "international peace arid security on the one hand and social progress and economic development on the other are closely interdependent and, influence each other and it is of cardinal importance to accelerate social and economic progress everywhere, thus contributing to international peace and—solidarity."

Another major step in the direction of the recognition of indivisibility concept was the adoption of Resolution 32/130 on "Alternative approaches ... for improving the effective enjoyment of human rights" by General Assembly in 1977. This resolution stressed that the approach to be followed by the UN system with respect to human rights should be based on the concept that all human rights are—indivisible and equal attention should be given to the promotion and protection of both civil and political, and economic, social and cultural rights. One of the outcomes of this Resolution was the recognition of the link between the realisation of a new international economic order and the promotion Of human rights. Another Important outcome was the initiation of debate on the right to development which paved the way for the adoption of the UN Declaration on Right to Development in 1986. However, it took almost a decade to General Assembly to adopt this much cherished demand of developing countries of the Third World but alas developed world showed very little interest In passing of this long &waited resolution.

The Declaration on Right to Development ties the realisation of human rights in developing countries to international economic aid for them and gives the people the right to participate in, contribute to, and enjoy economic, social, cultural and political development, in which all human rights and fundamental freedoms can be fully realised. The Declaration which also recognises the concept of indivisibility of human rights, emphasised that the denial of civil and political rights as well as economic, social and cultural rights would constitute a serious obstacle to development. Further, the Declaration also stressed that promotion of one set of rights cannot justify the denial of other human rights. Most importantly the Declaration recognised that the "human person is the central subject of development and should be an active participant and beneficiary of the right to development."

The right to development is one of the most important basic human rights and it constitutes the culminating point of the evolution of the concept of human rights. This super-right, transcends the differentiation of civil and political rights and socio-economic cultural rights. It includes within its ambit both sets of rights. It correctly links the both because with hunger and ill health freedom can have no meaning. The importance of the indivisibility concept is not restricted to international normative developments, it also provides an effective antidote against efforts to undermine human rights under "trade-off theory." Under this theory many dictators of Third World countries proposed that to achieve development civil and political rights should be atleast temporarily sacrificed. But in reality the ultimate result of this trade-off was denial of civil and political rights as well as impoverishment rather than development. Thus the trade-off theory could only be effectively countered by stressing on the indivisibility concept of human rights.

A question which has become central to the relationship between human rights and development is the issue of politic conditionalities. This means that the continuance of development assistance would be dependent on political conditions such as " good governance" and the observance of civil and political rights. The European Council in its one resolution passed on November 28, 1991 emphasised that respect I for human rights, the rule of law and the existence of political institutions which are effective, accountable and enjoy democratic legitimacy are the basis for equitable development. It also stressed the safeguarding of human rights as an essential condition for its relations with other states. Similarly, the US House of Representative passed the Burton Bill on June 1992 cutting 24 million dollars of development assistance to Third World countries including India on grounds of poor human rights records. The Canadian House of Commons Standing Committee on External Affairs and International Trade recommended as early as in May 1987 that progress on human rights should be central element of development assistance.

However, the developing countries by and large have resented the link between human rights and aid on the ground that such conditions infringe on their national sovereignty. They see these intercessions in political terms as efforts to appropriate human rights as an instrument in the political and ideological hagemony of the North over the South. The policy of donor countries may appear genuine but inconsistency in its application and selective approach is bound to create doubts and suspicions. And it will also invite strong criticism and rebuff from the developing countries. If the developed countries of the West really want to see their policy being effective it should not only be credible, consistent and non-discriminatory but it also appears to be so. Is the decision to suspend or terminate developmental assistance based solely on human rights considerations or is it more probable that factors such as geopolitical importance, the economic model pursued by the recipient country and the domestic politics of the donor country are likely to influence such decisions? Although no one would allow developing states to use "primacy of development" or "cultural relativism" as a pretext for diluting of derogating from universal human rights but the political use of the concept of human rights by thc West could not either be tolerated.

The concept of indivisibility of human rights assumes greater importance in the changed global, situation which is dominated by a single development model based on multinational capital and corporation. By and large the experience of countries that have gone through the process of restructuring and privatising their economies has been a negative one. This economic model has contributed to increased inequalities, dismantling of social services with adverse effect on the poor, restrictions on trade union rights, implementation of development projects with negative impact on the local populations, particularly indigenous people and the tendency to centralise the decision making process. However, it is yet to be seen whether the end of the Cold War and rhetoric of human rights and good governance can prevent some of the fragrant violations that were witnessed in the past centuries that 'embarked on restructuring and privatising their economy, whether on their own or on dictate of the North.

Whatever be the current of attitudes and policies of governments, the reality of popular demands of human rights, including both greater economic justice and greater political freedom, is beyond debate. A deepening and widening concern for the promotion and protection of human rights, has now unmistakably woven into the fabric of contemporary world affairs. We have a great opportunity now to make progress in protecting and fully realising the human rights that the arehitects of the post war settlement so eloquently laid down. The end of the Cold War has been accompanied by a growing recognition that successful sustainable development is impossible where rights are divided and economic and social rights downgraded. Poverty and inequality remain the two great barriers to the realisation of "all human rights for all". Fifty years after signing of the UNCHR, it is more than very necessary to reaffirm, as the Preamble declares, our "faith in fundamental human rights, in the dignity and worth of the human person and in the equal rights of men and women and (determine) to promote social progress and better standard of life in larger freedom."

4

Constitutional Protection of Human Rights

The definition and protection of human rights remains one of the major themes of political, philosophical and legal discourse. Although the idea of human rights has been repeatedly and comprehensively criticised, it retains considerable popularity and support. A substantial body of opinion holds that there are such things as human rights and that they ought to have legal protection. This view has, from time to time, received expression in the form of general declarations of the fundamental rights which persons are supposed to have. Clearly the making of such declarations is not sufficient to ensure the actual protection of human rights, and such general declarations of rights have often been dismissed as mere rhetoric. The advocate of human rights must address the issue of how the move from the rhetorical affirmation of rights to the actual protection of human rights is best made. No disparagement of general declarations of rights is intended by this statement, for they have it role to play in the exchange of ideas and the formulation of opinion. In that sense, to talk of mere rhetoric is to miss the point because rhetoric undoubtedly has its effect.

What that effect might be is not, however, the principal concern to this chapter. Rather, the concern 46 to show what implications the choice of mechanism for the protection of rights has, in moving from rhetorical affirmation to real protection of human rights.

Although the notion of human rights has traditionally been less popular amongst lawyers in the UK than it is in other jurisdictions, a significant number of lawyers prefer to analyse the legal system in terms of human rights. Those lawyers who do analyse the legal system in terms of human rights have tended to consider the legal protection of human rights in isolation from philosophical questions concerning the definition and elaboration of human rights. They seem to assume that the definition of human rights at a philosophical level is unproblematic and that one need only determine the most appropriate legal mechanism for the protection of human rights. To give but one example, since the early 1970s a major debate has been taking place on the desirability of enacting a fundamental guarantee of human rights into the UK constitution, possibly by incorporating into UK law the European Convention on Human Rights. Those in favour of a fundamental guarantee of human rights have pointed to numerous infringements of, and threats to, liberty in the UK, and lamented the inability of the British courts, limited as they are by the doctrine of the Sovereignty of Parliament, to protect the individual from the excesses of the modern state. A Bill of Rights or some similar instrument would, they think, provide much better protection.

The opposition to this movement has pointed to the vaguenes of fundamental guarantees of human rights, the numerous qualifications and exceptions to the absoluteness of such rights which are typically made, the inflexibility of such mechanisms and their supposedly undemocratic nature.

There is good reason to be profoundly dissatisfied with this debate. The opponents of Bills of Rights too readily assume that constitutionally entrenched guarantees of human rights are inimical to democracy and that severe difficulties in translating general declarations of rights into concrete and specific legal rules make the enterprise worthless. The supporters of Bills of rights generally, fail to meet arguments directed against the validity of the concept of human rights. They also fail to explain the significance of couching arguments in terms of human rights rather than some other concept. Last of all, they show no sign of having learned very much from the experience of other jurisdictions, particularly the USA.

What UK advocates of a Bill of Rights fail to realise is that, if attention is focussed entirely on legal mechanisms for the protection of human rights, and theoretical disputes about human rights are left unresolved, these latter disputes will simply re-emerge when interpretation of legal instruments protecting human rights is required. The enterprise of protecting human rights through law can only proceed on the basis of a fully worked out theory of human rights . It is suggested that legal analysis in this field must, therefore, pay close attention to moral and philosophical debates about the meaning and significance of rights, whichever mechanism for' the protection of human rights is chosen.

Thus the purpose of this chapter is not so much to argue directly for or against Bills of Rights as to discuss some important implications of the Bill of Rights model for protecting human rights.

There are several variants of the Bill of Rights model. One which has found favour in a number of jurisdictions is the constitutionally entrenched guarantee of human rights accompanied by judicial review of state action. Under this model the constitutional guarantees of rights have overriding authority over other laws and the judiciary has power to declare unconstitutional state legislation or other actions of the state which conflict with the terms of the constitutional guarantees. The principal alternative approach is the piecemeal one of protecting human rights by the enactment of ordinary legislation dealing with individual rights and the development of judge-made case law. This, of course, is the approach which has been adopted in the UK, although it might be more accurate here to speak of the protection of civil liberties rather than of human rights. Intermediate approaches are possible such as enacting a Bill of Rights which has the same constitutional status as a state's other legislation, but space does not permit consideration of such variants, and subsequent references to Bills of Rights or constitutional guarantees of human rights are references to the model described above.

The issues raised by the use of the Bill of Rights model have received very considerable attention in the USA and, given that the USA possesses a highly developed jurisprudence of constitutional protection of human rights, it deems appropriate to draw on the American experience and see what lessons can be learned from it.

In the American Bill of Rights, the enumeration of protected rights includes both fairly specific rights and rights which are expressed at a very high level of generality. Rights in the criminal process are comparatively specific. Other rights are gar less specific in their terms, for example, 'Congress shall make no law...abridging the freedom of speech, or of the press; and 'No person shall...be deprived of life, liberty or property without due process of law.

The vagueness and generality of the latter sort of definition is, of course, a serious defect, as far as the opponents of Bills of Rights are concerned They consider that such general phrases do not give the individual an adequate account of what his or her rights are, do not give courts sufficient guidance to make decisions in concrete cases, and give the judiciary a degree of power that is inappropriate in a democratic society. The language of such provisions is so open-ended that, in any particular case, radically differing views as to whether or not state action is constitutional are possible. This is apparent from such cases as Buckley v. Valeo in which the US Supreme Court had to consider the constitutionality of limitations on expenditure on political .campaigns. The legislation was held to be an unconstitutional abridgement of freedom of speech because It limited the ability of persons to engage in free communication. Yet supporters of the measure had argued that the legislation encouraged - freedom of speech by 'equalising the relative abilities of individuals and groups to influence the outcome of elections and, therefore, protected and furthered First Amendment values.

This sort of case of inevitably leads to criticism that judges are making important policy choices which ought to be left to the elected representatives of the people; in the guise of exercising a judicial function of protecting settled legal rights.

The American approach to this Predicament has been to look for a method of interpretation of constitutional provisions which can be considered the right method: A method which simultaneously removes the problem of the vagueness of constitutional guarantees and takes proper account of the anti-majoritarian difficulty.

A number of distinct and mutually inconsistent approaches can be discerned in the decided cases and in scholarly writing. This section will attempt briefly to describe and criticize each.

The first approach to be considered is what has been called interpretivism. Interpretivists argue that the answers to constitutional questions can and should be supplied by the actual text of the document or by clear inferences from it. Where simply scrutinising the text would not provide sufficient guidance, reference is to be made to the intentions of the framers of the Constitution which are to be discovered primarily in the legislative history of the Constitution and its Amendments, and also from other sources such as the history of the political circumstances which gave rise to the provision in question.

Certain Supreme Court justices, for example, justice Black, have invoked what appears to be an interpretivist approach but this, more often than not, masks the imposition of value judgements which are neither uncontroversial inferences from the text of the Constitution nor clear applications of the intentions of the framers.

The interpretivist thesis that adjudication should rest on the text and the intentions of the framers solves neither of the twin problems, the vagueness of constitutional provisions and the anti-majoritarian difficulty, which are the principal pre-occupations of American constitutional scholarship. Nor does it, seem satisfactory as a means of protecting human rights. The difficulties posed by the extreme generality of the terms of the Constitution itself cannot be met by reference to the framer's intent. First, perusal of legislative history shows that different groups and individuals held a variety of views as to the possible meaning and effect of the various positions. Second, the views expressed in debates are, in any event, only an imperfect guide to the actual reasons which motivated votes in favour of particular texts at constitutional conventions. Third, it is not clear why the supposed views of, for example, Congressmen should be preferred to the views of those voting in state legislatures to adopt constitutional amendments. Last of all, an interpretivist is unable to deal with situations which were not, nor could have been, foreseen at the time the constitution or any amendment thereto was adopted. The same point can found the more general criticism that no evolution or growth of constitutional protection of human rights is possible if such a thesis is strictly Applied.

The interpretivist thesis solves the problem of legitimacy at one level by apparently restricting the actions of popularly accountable institutions only when such A restriction can be tracted to a document which by agreement forms the basis of the political system. However, if the concern is that limiting the freedom of action of elected institutions is undemocratic, then it is not clear why a consensus, or majority, of the past should be able to override a modern consensus or majority.

A further criticism relevant to both vagueness And legitimacy is that the Interpretivist thesis does not accord with accepted methods of legal interpretation which include reference to precedent, changing historical and social circumstances, logical consistency and background principles such as a sense of justice, as well as to the original understanding of the meaning of any provision.

One must also have grave misgivings about an interpretivist thesis if one is truly concerned with the protection of human rights. Uncritical acceptance of the (apparent) original understanding may tie constitutional interpretation to views which simply are not protective of human rights. Some interpretivists have taken the view that segregation of the races is not unconstitutional discrimination because the framers of the Fourteenth Amendment did not intend to outlaw segregation. Indeed, not all interpretivists would agree that the Constitutions is or should be about the protection of human rights. The second approach to be considered is that controversies about the meaning of the Constitution's provisions should be settled by reference to tradition. If certain rights have traditionally been seen as fundamental in American political culture then they are deserving of protection. By Implication, interpretations of the scope and content of rights which do not have a basis in traditional are to be rejected as undeserving of special constitutional protection.

In *Moore v, City of East Cleveland*, the plurality opinion of justice Powell, in a case invalidating, on due process clause grounds, a city ordinance which limited the class of persons who could live together as a family, stated that 'the Constitution protects the family precisely because the institution of the family is deeply rooted in this Nations's .history and tradition'.

A third approach, closely related to the second; Is the view that interpretation should be based on some identifiable consensus in society or, in other words, on conventional morality. Those moral principles which can claim to have sufficient weight in conventional morality should guide constitutional interpretation.

In *Breithaupt v. Abram*, in which the Court upheld the constitutionality, under the process clause, of taking a blood sample from an unconscious motorist for use as evidence against him In criminal proceedings, the majority referred to 'that 'whole community sense of decency and fairness" that has been woven by common experience into the fabric of acceptable conduct' as being the test of constitutionality in this instance. Justice Douglas, although dissenting, appeared to agree that the test of constitutionality was 'the decencies of a civilised state.

Both these approaches can be dealt with briefly. Appeals to consensus or to tradition are radically indeterminate. Neither the USA nor any other country has a single unambiguous tradition nor shows a consensus of views on such matters as for example, the rights and wrongs of abortion or the appropriate scope of the freedom of speech. Arguments from these sources can be, and have, been, used to support almost any position. Even where it is possible to identify a dominant well-established tradition or widely-inclusive consensus, this may simply amount to the unjustified subordination of the interests and desires of a minority to those of the majority. Neither consensus nor tradition provide plausible answers to the problem of legitimacy. This is so partly because they often do not provide clear guidance, and partly because they involve invoking some alleged will or spirit of the people against the decisions of their elected representatives. References to consensus and tradition also ignore the plausible argument that the enterprise of protecting human rights through constitutional guarantees implies that democracy need not be a purely majoritarian political system. Last of all, it may be said that interpreting constitutional guarantees by reference to consensus or tradition is unlikely to be protective of human rights. There is no necessary connection and, in many political and social circumstances, no actual connection between what tradition or consensus dictates and the human rights persons have.

The fourth approach considers that, whatever may be desirable in the abstract, judges cannot avoid simply substituting their own value judgements for those of the legislature or other branches of the state apparatus, because there is no objective method of adjudication. Judges and commentator should, therefore, admit that this is what is going on. On this view, the only limits that there are on constitutional decision-making are those of prudence and plausibility. The view that judges impose their own values faces the difficulty that there seems little reason to permit unelected judges to replace the choices of accountable political institutions with their own choices. Of course, if one accepts the supposition of this approach that there is no objective judicial method then it inevitably follows that adjudication involves the infusion of the judges' personal beliefs into the process of adjudication. If, however, it can be shown that the 'subjectivist' account of the judicial process is not descriptively correct, then there is little to commend thio approach to constitutional interpretation. If there is reason to suppose that an objective judicial method is possible, a matter which will be dealt with shortly, then that supposition should be the basis of any theory of constitutional interpretation.

The fifth approach, usually referred to as process-based theory, is that judicial review should he based on the presuppositions of the democratic system. The decision as to whether or not to invalidate state action depends on whether or not the political process has mal-functioned, in the sense of illegitimately interfering with participation or representation in the political process. This view places particular emphasis on rights of from speech and political participation and the rights of minorities not to be unfairly discriminated against.

The traditional 'double standard' of review in constitutional cases ushered In by the Now Deal and summed up in the Carolene Products footnote has been Interpreted as supporting this view. Under the 'double standard' state action in the economic sphere is presumptively constitutional and will be upheld if it appears to have a rational basis. State action impinging on preferred rights (basically civil and political rights) is subject to more searching constitutional scrutiny.

On this view, the need to make controversial value choices, whether by reference to tradition, consensus or any other source of value, can be obviated by invoking the presuppositions of the democratic system. The judge is concerned not with the rightness or wrongness on substantive grounds of legislative choices, but with the question of whether the democratic system has malfuntioned judicial review is orientated towards participation and representation In the political process. The emphasis, in terms of particular rights, is therefore on freedom of expression, voting rights and the rights of minorities not to be discriminated against. If adequate participation and representation can be assured, then there is no reason to interfere with the outcomes of the political process, and every reason to assume that the outcomes generated by the political process will be reasonably fair and just.

On first inspection, this view may seem to go a long way towards dealing with the problem of vagueness and the anti-majoritarian difficulty in that it provides principles of interpretation which are based on the presuppositions of a democratic system.

However, closer examination reveals that it solves neither of these problems. It is not possible to apply this theory to concrete cases without making the substantive value judgements which it claims to eschew. One cannot decide whether a particular minority or person has been unconstitutionally denied effective representation or participation unless one has a substantive ideal of what that minority is entitled to. One can imagine infringements of the rights of minority groups being passed into law after a, full debate by a legislature in which that majority has the same voting rights as any other group of persons. It would be odd if the constitutional conclusion to be drawn in that situation was that, because the political process had functioned regularly, they had no grievance. Process-based theory, therefore, rests on substantive moral principles, the nature of which it does not itself explain.

A second criticism is that this theory, being based on the presuppositions of a democratic system, can only hope for acceptance if there is a consensus about the essentials of a fair democratic process. Since there is no consensus about what opportunities for participation and what procedures for representation are most appropriate to a democracy, process-based theory must be seen as based on a particular contestable conception of democracy for, which independent justification must be provided. That justification has not yet been forthcoming. Process-based theory, therefore, seems to be neither a clear nor a value-neutral guide to constitutional adjudication.

The third criticism that can be made is that the American Bill of Rights seems to include numerous provisions which are clearly expressions of belief in substantive values, for example, religious liberty and security of property. More generally it can be said that process-based theory does not seem to be a theory of human rights in any meaningful sense. The concentration on the proper functioning of the political process implies that the 'rights: protected by the constitution are simply means towards the end to ensuring that the political process gives opportunities to all to participate, and provides all with some measure of representation. Such 'rights' do not seem to be valued, in themselves, as rights persons possess because they are persons.

The differences between each of these approaches are obvious, yet they do have something in common. With the exception of the fourth option-the 'subjectivist' approach-they seek to provide a neutral method of constitutional interpretation which can evade the charge that judges simply substitute their own view for that of the other branches of government.

The sixth and final approach to be considered is that which bases constitutional adjudication on substantive moral values and, in particular, on a theory of fundamental rights. Using this method of interpretation a judge would reach decisions in, for example, freedom of expression cases by asking whether or not the state action in issue infringed the moral right of freedom of expression. This view is implicit, if not explicit, in many judicial opinions, and has been attacked on the grounds that there is no agreed method of moral philosophy, so that resolving constitutional questions by reference to moral theory really amounts to the imposition of individual beliefs which can claim no superior status over any other beliefs because they are ultimately subjective.

It does, therefore, seem as if attempts to construct value neutral methods of constitutional interpretation have failed. The various allegedly neutral approaches already discussed either do not provide determinate answers to difficult constitutional questions or provide answers based on concealed value judgements of there own or combine both defects. Nor does it seem likely that any new theories which might be put forward will be both determine in their outcomes and value-neutral in their outcomes.

This realisation might lead some to conclude, in desperation, that constitutional adjudication is inevitably confined to the 'subjective pit of will and power' and that the only improvement which could be ' made in constitutional adjudication is that the judges be more honest about this. This would, however, be too hasty a conclusion, Similar problems of interpretive 'method and legitimacy arise in systems without constitutional guarantees of human rights and judicial review, nor are such problems confined to cases involving human rights issues. The American system of government simply raises these issues in a more stark and obvious form, and in a context where they have greater personal significance. These difficulties require attention whatever legal mechanisms are used. It would also be a mistake to assume that these difficulties are incapable of solution. The mistake being made here is this assumption that only a value-neutral method of adjudication can properly be called objective. This is where the sixth view of constitutional interpretation becomes relevant. If it can be shown that the process of moral reasoning can be objective then there seems good reason to allow the process of constitutional interpretation to be guided by substantive moral beliefs. If it is possible for judges, or indeed anyone else concerned with the interpretation of the constitution, to make objective moral judgements, then constitutional interpretation can be rescued from ultimate subjectively. At least one theorist, in advancing the claim that good constitutional arguments are based on good moral arguments, has explicitly stated that the validity of his thesis depends on there being 'right' answers to moral questions.

It is worth nothing that the framers of the American Constitution assumed that there were right answers to moral questions, and this view received expression in the theory of self-evident natural rights which was current at that time. That view of moral objectivity is no longer accepted, nor indeed tenable, but the idea of the transcendent indisputable moral truth does to exhaust the possibility of moral objectivity. Modern moral theories, whilst granting a less exalted status to moral statements, do not deny that they can be objective.

It would not be appropriate in this chapter to embark on a detailed account of contemporary moral theory or to attempt a comprehensive proof of the proposition that moral reasoning can be objective, but it is worth examining briefly some arguments for the objectivity of moral reasoning. The simple statement that moral propositions are ultimately based on value judgements which cannot themselves intelligibly be described as correct or incorrect does not do justice to the complexity of the reasoning processes involved in modern moral theories. One method of moral reasoning which has a substantial number of adherents has been called 'wide reflective equilibrium'. The method of intuitionism is to reason from basic principles or values which are arrived at solely by intuition, to particular results. The only constraint on the reasoning process is that of logical coherence: the resulting judgements must follow from the principles. Intuitionism clearly implies that moral view-points are ultimately subjective. Wide reflective equilibrium goes beyond intuitionism by attempting to achieve coherence amongst three different sets of beliefs a person may hold. These are a set of considered moral judgements, a set of moral principles, and a set of relevant background theories.

One begins by collecting those initial moral judgements of which a person is relatively confident, and which were made under conditions appropriate to avoiding errors of judgement. Next, one proposes various sets of moral principles which might account for those judgements. Having achieved the greatest possible degree of coherence between principles and judgements, one goes on to argue the relative strengths and weaknesses of the alternative sets of principles. This is where some improvement on intuitionism is achieved. Simply settling for the best fit of principles with judgements would not be an essentially different method from intuitionism. The arguments about the strengths of the principles are inferred from a set of relevant background theories for example, a theory of the person, a theory of the role of morality in society and so on-the background theories must show that the moral principles which are eventually preferred are better than others on grounds other than simple coherence 'between principles and particular judgements. If this were not so the method would still closely resemble intuitionism. The outcome of the process is that one set of principles is eventually deemed superior, This may, and often will, 'lead 'persons' to revise particular moral judgements, adopt different principles and possibly also adjust background theories. Once order and coherence amongst particular judgements; principles and background theories have been achieved, a person has arrived at the point of wide reflective equilibrium which gives the theory Its name.

Adopting this method of moral reasoning will not, of course, eliminate disagreements about the correctness of particular moral judgements or the appropriateness of particular moral principles. Individuals may start out with widely differing sets of moral judgements and principles and may employ crucially different background theories. However, it can be argued that it produces fruitful moral debate. By reasoning out fully the implications of shared principles and judgements, and by comparing and evaluating background theories, initial disagreements may be resolved. If disagreements are not resolved it may be possible to identify the precise locus of disagreement such as the terms of a particular background theory, and this may in time lead to resolution of differences. Provided at least some part of the framework is shared, moral debate can advance and can possibly lead to a consensus on moral issues which one might have reason to trust because that consensus is the product of a process of rational inquiry,

Despite the importance Which it attaches to consensus, the method of wide reflective equilibrium clearly remains rather individualistic in nature. The emphasis is very much on how individuals should argue and little attention is paid to the conditions under which interpersonal agreement might arise, including the opportunities available to persons to participate in moral discourse. However, these omissions can be supplied, and a more complete idea of the nature of objectivity in moral reasoning arrived at, by reference to another approach, that adopted by

Habermas. Habermas has been concerned to refute the claim that moral statements cannot be rationally grounded. He does so- by means of an extended critique of the positivist philosophy of science which serves as the starting point of his argument that moral statements can be true. He considers the criteria for the validity of purported statements of fact in science to be based ultimately on conventions and expectations within the scientific community, which cannot themselves be demonstrated to be true. The point is not that scientific statements ire ultimately subjective or irrational but that certain assumptions which "'List be made, for example, that observation statements can be trusted under certain conditions, are the conditions of the possibility of scientific knowledge. A similar approach is taken to the possibility of moral 'knowledge'. The basic question is, what conditions make rational consensus about what is right or In answer to this question Habermas posits a the 'ideal speech situation' which, he considers, provides appropriate criteria for the validation of ethical propositions. Moral truth is found, under this approach, in consensus. However, not all consensus or agreement is considered rational, and it is the function of the ideal speech situation to distinguish between rationally and irrationally grounded moral consensus.

Rational agreement about moral statements is defined as that agreement which has been brought about solely by the force of the arguments used and has not been influenced by any other factors. Moral consensus achieves this ideal of resting only on the force of the arguments used when the two principal requirements of freedom to shift the level of discourse and symmetry are satisfied.

Requiring freedom to shift the level of discourse encourages a completely self-aware, self-critical discourse in which nothing, not even the most basic assumption, is taken for ground. Thus one begins with a particular moral statement or judgement which is disputed. It is in turn supported or refuted by reference to general norms being accepted as binding. The validity of general norms themselves are tested according to their ability to satisfy generally accepted needs and interests. This of course assumes that some human needs or interests can be generalised.

From this point it must be possible to go on to question the total conceptual framework within which moral debate has taken place; for example, participants can question whether the language system used was appropriate, whether different basic assumptions could have been made, and so on. Ultimately it must be possible for participants to reflect on what it is possible for human beings to know and what to do.

Symmetry requires, complete equality of participation in the discourse. Everyone has the right to participate and all participants are entitled to make their views known, They are entitled to hear as well as to be heard, and generally to adopt the different possible roles involved in any discussion. The opportunity to do all these things must be given to all equally. If all the requirements described above are satisfied, and consensus is arrived at, that consensus is considered rationally grounded.

It is admitted, however, that the ideal speech situation is a fiction: that such a state of affairs in moral debate never has occurred and never will. Nonetheless, Habermas sees the ideal speech situation as an unavoidable supposition of moral discourse and an ideal which is anticipated in every actual moral discourse. To put it more simply, it functions as a regulative ideal against which actual situations can be measured, but which itself can never be achieved.

Habermas admits that, at the practical level of the creation of political institutions and the formation of societal policy, restrictions will inevitably operate upon discourse. Considerations of time, space, economy and organisational efficiency dictate that. What is crucial, however, is that in specific historical and social circumstances, political and social institutions and their functioning are such that we can reasonably assume that the political and social decisions taken would have been agreed to by all had they had complete freedom to participate in the formation of decisions. In other words, we could reasonably assume that the decisions arrived at would be essentially similar to those that would have been reached in the hypothetical ideal speech situation.

The foregoing account of two related theories of moral reasoning may serve to indicate a plausible approach to constructing the methodology of objectively valid moral judgements. Such theories could be subjected to extensive criticism, and others could have been considered. Space does not permit consideration of all the many possible theories and the counter-arguments to them, but enough has been said to indicate the sort of theoretical approach which can be arrived at by focussing on the rational, informed consensus as a possible condition of the objectivity of moral reasoning. The moral judgements which are arrived at through these processes of reasoning ire not represented is timeless and eternal truths, but are considered right because they have been arrived at under the best possible conditions for agreeing on moral truth. To pursue the argument that what is proposed is not true objectivity would, perhaps, be to set too high a standard. After all, when comparisons are made with modern theories Of the validity of scientific propositions, it can readily be seen that the concept of objectivity in relation to those propositions has undergone extensive revision. At one stage in intellectual history, it was possible to contrast science as the domain of the indisputably objective with moral discourse as the domain of the irredeemably subjective, Scientific propositions could make sense whereas moral propositions could not. That stages has passed and the status of scientific propositions as reflections of independent reality has increasingly been called into question. Such doubts have not led the questioners to assert that science is not objective or valid; they have simply led to a rethinking of the meaning of objectivity. For propositions to count as scientific they must have been arrived at in a certain way. Objectivity resides in the procedures and the methods adopted and their consensual acceptance by the scientific community rather than in a direct correspondence to independent reality. Given that the objectivity of science is being viewed in a less transcendental or absolute sense, it seems reasonable to apply a similarly qualified standard to moral reasoning. An irrefutable case for the objectivity of moral reasoning has not yet been made but it does seem reasonable to proceed on the basis that objectivity in moral reasoning is possible.

The principal implication of the foregoing discussion of moral theory is that theories of constitutional interpretation based on moral arguments can purport to have some validity and judges can legitimately make decisions which are ultimately based on moral principles. Theories of human rights have, of course, generally been based on moral principles. That does not in itself demonstrate that human rights theories are valid and convincing as moral theories. The theories of moral reasoning already described in this essay do not automatically imply a human rights approach as the answer to the question of what qualities a morally sound society should exhibit. That may seem a serious defect in the argument, but to assume such a thing would be to misunderstand the point which is being made. Such tentative 'proofs' of the objectivity of moral reasoning undermine the principal criticism of the explicitly moral philosophical approach to constitutional ' interpretation. Furthermore, whilst a human rights approach does not automatically follow from these theories of moral reasoning, clearly such methods of moral reasoning could readily produce moral arguments expressed in terms of human rights.

Having established, albeit tentatively, that there is some justification for basing constitutional interpretation on moral principles it would, of course, be necessary to go on to show that a rights-based approach was preferable to other approaches, for example, a utilitarian approach,

All this may seem far removed from what judges do and can reasonably be expected to do. The Judicial process does not closely resemble, for example, Habermas's ideal speech situation (although the use of the amicus brief in the Supreme Court effectively increases the number of participants and the range of views canvassed in particular cases). That is not so grave a criticism as might, At first, appear, for it ignores the way in which moral reasoning becomes relevant to, and can be used by, judges. Judges are part of a wider legal and political culture, including practising lawyers, academics, politicians and citizens, all of whom may have something to say about the meaning of the Constitution and all of whom may cast their view of the Constitution in terms of a moral theory of human rights. The views which judges may acquire about the moral demands of human rights are acquired not apart from, but within, this culture, and they are able if they wish to continue to learn from it.

Clearly, it is something of a pipe dream to expect judicial decisions to proceed from exhaustive accounts of moral epistemology, through fully articulated and complex moral theories, to particular decisions. However, the possibility of judges learning from elaboration of such issues in a wider legal and political culture remains. This may not seem an entirely satisfactory answer but, given the absence of a neutral criterion of constitutional interpretation, it is the only real option.

Clearly we cannot assert that judges will be able to deduce from general guarantees of freedom of expression and of other rights, self-evident answers to the problems posed by specific cases. The methods of moral reasoning which have been described have little to say about concrete problems. They are too open-ended to prescribe particular, unarguably correct decisions. But they offer at least the prospect of resolving particular issues in a rational manner. The human rights doctrine that is evolved, when attention is focussed explicitly on the moral requirements of a human rights approach, has more chance of being coherent and properly protective of rights than doctrine which attempts to avoid difficult philosophical issues. The American experience should serve as a warning. Legal doctrine and theory there have been confused by the unhappy combination of a variety of approaches to the problem, of finding guiding considerations. At one time or another, guidance has been sought from the intentions of the framers, from tradition, from societal consensus and from a supposedly value-neutral model of the properly functioning democratic process. The common element of these approaches is avoidance of difficult moral choices and overt moral reasoning. However, it is only in accepting the need to make such difficult choices and to indulge in moral reasoning that there lies any hope for coherence in doctrine.

The bare injunction to include moral analysis in constitutional interpretation is not, of course, very helpful. At the level of decision-making in concrete cases, analytical techniques must be evolved which can guide judges more fully and still keep faith with the basic moral imperatives of human rights theory.

Once ouch candidate for an analytical technique is the idea of the core. It is not the only possible technique which might be used in adjudicating human rights cases under a constitution but it does illustrate how it more explicit human rights approach might be exemplified in actual doctrine. The idea of the core includes at least two related notions, one of which is the objective or purpose of the right in question. It is useful to focus on the core because asking, in relation to any right, what the, purpose of that rights is makes it more likely that one will be able to make rational decisions about its application in concrete cases. Incoherent doctrine is partly the product of failure to attend to the question of what the purpose of a right is, or of failure to identify the purpose of a right correctly. Some examples drawn from American jurisprudence should show this. In evolving constitutional doctrine on freedom of speech, judges have grappled with such unhelpful distinctions as that between speech and conduct, and that between protected and unprotected speech, for example, obscenity, rather than getting to grips with the real issues.

The lack of sympathy for the 'obscene' ignores the possible role of erotic material as implicit advocacy of an alternative way of life. The speech—conduct distinction unjustifiably favours standard and well-established modes of expressing ideas and emotions over other modes. What the speech-conduct and protected-unprotected speech distinctions have in common is a failure to address the question of what the purpose of a right is.

Each of these strands of doctrine indicates a willingness to make decisions on the basis of assumptions about the proper role of free speech without making a detailed examination of what the point of a human right of freedom of expression is mid without critically examining the assumptions which have determined decisions. Nor can assumptions about freedom of expression employed in different doctoral areas be happily reconciled one with another.

These criticism should not be seen as an attempt to dictate particular arguable moral propositions about freedom of expression under the guise of a neutral analytical technique. Rational doctrine on free speech could take a number of forms. The point being made is that the Supreme Court is unlikely to achieve a happy resolution of these issues until the issue of the underlying propose of freedom of expression is clearly addressed. Until then, different strands of doctrine will point in different directions, because underlying differences of outlook never directly confront one another. Identification of the core of the right of freedom of expression carries more hope for coherent doctrine because doctrine could be elaborated in the light of an explicitly stated and well-argued theoretical base.

Similar problems have arisen with the abortion cases. In Roe v. Wade the Supreme Court held that a women's right to choose whether or no to terminate a pregnancy was fundamental. That simple statement, however, conceals the confusion that is evident injustice Blackmun's majority opinion, which drew on historical beliefs, modern scientific evidence, a principle of freedom of choice in reproductive matters, and the concept of the professional judgement of the physician, without making clear which source of value was more important or how potential conflicts between each rationale for the decision could be resolved. It was not clear whether the fundamental constitutional right to choose to have an abortion was based on a moral principle of reproductive self-determination, or on the view that, since abortion is a health problem, denial of important medical treatment was an infringement of liberty, or on the view that a focus could not reasonably be said to have rights because it is not a person. The decision, in fact, seems to have been based on each of these ideas but the relationship between them was not made chear. The implications of this for the right to choose and abortion are clear. The different possible rationales for the decision each have different implications for the further development of the right in issue. Thus the emphasis on the medical aspects of abortion may have the effect of changing the content of the right over time. The Court held that the state had a compelling interest in protecting potential life from the point when the focus became viable, yet viability clearly depends on the state of medical science at a given point. Advances in medical science would logically permit states to proscribe abortion at ever earlier stages of pregnancy. On the other hand, if the rationale of the rights is firmly based in a moral principle of complete reproductive self-determination, attempts by states to further limit the right to choose an abortion would remain impermissible. By basing doctrine on such a clear and explicit formulation of moral principle, the content and limits of the right could be made clear.

What the immediately foregoing passage demonstrates is that techniques of analysis can be evolved which give judges more guidance than the simple injunction to introduce overtly moral reasoning into the decision-making process, In this way the task of interpreting broad constitution" guarantees of human rights can be made manageable. This may leave some unconvinced about the utility of Bills of Rights. They might admit that this is the course which judges interpreting a Bill of Rights must follow, whilst asserting that a Bill of Rights should not be introduced into the UK, or any other country which does not already have a Bill of Rights, because the task is one which judges need not perform. This, however, would be to misunderstand the task of judges under a system which preferred to piecemeal legislative approach to protection of human rights.

In the UK, Parliament has dealt with a number of human rights issues by particular enactments, such as the Race Relations Act, 1970, and the Sex discrimination Act, 1975. Judges interpreting these statutes are not freed from the need to make controversial judgements of value. Both these Acts provide detailed specification of the various situations in which discrimination is forbidden, for example, in the field of employment, in education, in housing, in the provision of goods, facilities and services and so forth. However, whilst the scope of the Act, in terms of areas of human conduct, is clearly delineated, the definition of discrimination itself is frame at a high level of generality. Section 1 of the Sex Discrimination Act, 1975, has a two-part definition of discrimination. It makes clear that indirect discrimination (where ex facie neutral requirements have discriminatory impact) is unlawful. So too is direct discrimination. However, the basic definition of direct discrimination is 'a person discriminates against a woman in any circumstances relevant for the purposes of any provisions of this act, if-(a) on the ground of her sex lie treats her less favourably than he treats or would treat a man.' The Act does not further define the meaning of less favourable treatment, except in the sense that certain specific declarations are made about differences in treatment which are not to count as discrimination, as where sex is a genuine occupational qualification. Judges are still left with the task of defining the meaning of discrimination in modem society on the basis of an essentially open-ended definition and they will be required- to make difficult decisions in many cases where the terms of the statute do not provide a clearly correct legal answer.

Here, the opponent of Bills of Rights might make the more precise criticism that one could accept the need to indulge in moral reasoning in human rights cases whilst still denying the appropriateness of constitutional guarantees of rights. Although judges would face similar difficulties under a piecemeal legislative approach, they would perhaps arise less often and without the consequence of invalidation of democratically enacted legislation. These are persuasive points, but they do not dispose of the issue. The choice of mechanism ultimately depends not only on such questions as whether moral reasoning can be objective and whether human rights Is an intelligible philosophical concept, but also on other considerations. The historical, political and social contexts must, for reasons of prudence, play a large part in the decision, and there may be circumstances in which real protection of human rights requires us to accept the expanded judicial role and the consequences for democratically elected institutions which a Bill of Rights entails.

What can be said is that the objections to the Bill of Rights model are not as great as is often supposed in the U.K. Insofar as the objections are based on the view that Bills of Rights raise issues which are incapable of objective judicial resolution, they are misconceived. Both in the UK and in the USA there is a widespread failure to appreciate that the existing differences in constitutional structure create not major differences in the problems of interpretation and of judicial method caused by enacting legal guarantees of human rights. In neither situation is it possible or desirable to separate moral concerns from legal reasoning. The shift from rhetoric to reality in human rights matters must follow the path of moral reasoning.

5

The Implementation System: International Measures

International law has been often deprecated because there are no formal executive institutions to enforce it. In fact, however, international obligations are generally observed, without any special "enforcement machinery." The basis of international treaty relationships is good faith; it is assumed that states accept treaty relations in good faith with the intention of respecting their obligations, and that they will respect them. And, in fact, governments generally do respect them. It has long been recognized, however, that in some areas of international agreement and convention, especially those dealing with how a state treats its own inhabitants, reliance on good faith is insufficient. That was reflected in the system established earlier in the twentieth century for implementing the International Labour Conventions. Repeated violations of human rights by states that had pledged themselves to respect such rights in the Charter of the United Nations was a principal reason for moving from the Charter and the Universal Declaration to covenants with legal obligations and machinery to enforce them.

Opponents of enforcement systems have sometimes argued that international systems intervene in the internal affairs of sovereign states. The argument is unfounded, if not disingenuous. Matters as to which states have accepted international obligations are, by hypothesis, of international concern and no longer exclusively a matter of their domestic jurisdiction. A state that has assumed obligations cannot object to measures to implement them. Surely, it is appropriate to seek such measures by agreement of the parties.

The Development of the Covenant System

Though the decision to include "measures of implementation" in the Covenants was taken i the early days of the United Nations, when the in influence of the Western democracies was predominant, there were widely different opinions about the form those measures should take. Early proposals submitted to the Commission on Human Rights included an Australian proposal for the establishment of an International Court on Human Rights.

René Cassin (France) proposed the creation of an International Investigation Commission empowered to consider petitions presented by individuals, coupled with the appointment of an Attorney General. India suggested a conciliation committee which could investigate complaints, attempt conciliation and, if necessary, refer the matter to the General Assembly. Israel proposed the creation of a new specialized agency for the implementation of the Covenants with its own Assembly and elaborate procedures for hearing complaints by states and petitions of nongovernmental organizations though not of individuals. The attitude of the United Kingdom and the United States was more cautious: they proposed the establishment of a panel of independent experts from which a Human Rights Committee of five members would be selected to examine interstate complaints (but not individual petitions) and only with a view to establishing the facts. The USSR was opposed to all measures of implementation, which one Soviet delegate described as "a means of interfering in the internal affairs of a State party to the Convention, and of undermining the sovereignty and independence of particular States." In 1949 the Soviet Government stated, in reply to a questionnaire, that "the implementation of the Declaration of Human Rights and the Covenant is a matter which solely concerns the domestic jurisdiction of the State" and accordingly it saw "no need for any international agreements on the subject." Nevertheless, the General Assembly in 1950 requested the Commission to consider provisions for the receipt and examination of petitions from individuals and organizations.

In 1951 Uruguay tabled a proposal for the establishment of an Office of the United Nations High Commissioner (Attomey-General) for Human Rights, an idea which has been relaunched from time to time independently of the Covenant-notably by Costa Rica in 1965 and by President Carter of the United States in 1977-and has found a considerable measure of support both in the Commission and in the General Assembly, but has met with such strong opposition from certain countries that no final decision has yet been taken.

In 1950 the Commission decided that there should be some implementation measures in the Covenant, that there should be a permanent body to consider, violations, and that this organ should be empowered to consider interstate complaints. But it rejected, by narrow majorities, the possibility of access to it by nongovernmental organizations and individuals.

Much further discussion took place in the Commission, the Economic and Social Council, and the

Third Committee of the General Assembly during the three following years, but there was little change of substance from the Commission's position in 1950, though detailed articles were drafted about periodic reports by states on the implementation of the two covenants. As a result, the draft Covenant on Civil and Political Rights submitted by the Commission to the General Assembly in 1954 called for the establishment of a Human Rights Committee of nine members, with competence to consider interstate complaints but not communications from nongovernmental organizations or individual petitions, and an obligation on states to submit periodic reports.

It is useful to study the system proposed in 1954 in order to understand the changes introduced during the next twelve years. The 1954 draft Covenant would have established a Human Rights Committee, its members to be elected by the International Court of Justice from a list of names proposed by the states parties. The draft envisaged that if one state party considered that another state party was violating a provision of the Covenant, it might address a communication to the latter to that effect; the receiving state would be required to provide an explanation within three months. Only if a satisfactory solution by bilateral negotiations was not reached within six months would either state have the right to refer the matter to the Human Rights Committee. The latter would normally deal with a matter only after the individual victim of the alleged violation had exhausted domestic remedies (Article 41). The Committee would have the right to call upon the states concerned for any relevant information (Article 42). The Committee would have the task of ascertaining the facts and making available its good offices with a view to a friendly solution of the matter on the basis of respect for human rights; within eighteen months of the original reference of the case to it, it would draw up a report, which would be published; if a solution was not reached the report would state the facts and the opinion of the Committee on the question of violation (Article 43). The Committee would have the right to request (through ECOSOC) an advisory opinion of the International Court of Justice on any legal aspect of the matter (Article 44), and the states-parties would also have the right to refer the case to the Court in the absence of a friendly settlement (Article 46). The Committee would submit an annual report on its activities to the General Assembly (Article 45).

Article 49 of the 1954 draft would have required states parties to submit reports on the legislative and other measures, including judicial remedies, adopted for the implementation of the Covenants; these reports would be submitted to the Economic and Social Council, which might transmit them to the Commission on Human Rights "for information, study and, if necessary, general recommendations." This words "general recommendations" were used in conformity with "a widely held view that the reports should not give rise to particular recommendations to individual States." It will be observed that the function of studying the reports and possibly formulating "general recommendations" thereon was to be conferred on the existing Commission on Human rights and not on the new Human Rights committee. In other words, there was to be a dual system of implementation: interstate complaints would be considered by the new Human Rights Committee set up under the Covenant; periodic reports would be examined by the existing Commission on Human Rights provided for in the Charter.

This implementation system proposed by the Human Rights Commission was considerably revised by the Third Committee of the General Assembly in the next stage of the drafting process. The Committee accepted the idea of a permanent Human Rights

Committee but increased its membership from nine to eighteen. (The increase in membership was eminently reasonable since the membership of the UN had doubled since 1954). The members were to be elected by the states parties instead of by the International Court of Justice. Their term of office was reduced from five to four years. An article to the effect that the secretary of the Committee should be "a high official of the United Nations elected by the Committee" was deleted. The general view in the Third Committee was that "the best course of action was to make provisions similar to those applicable to other United Nations bodies." In so doing, the Third Committee diminished to a certain extent the degree of autonomy and standing which the Commission had wished to give to the Human Rights Committee. It retained the proposal for a system of reports, but decided that they should be examined by the new Human Rights Committee and not by the UN Human Rights Commission. The reporting system thus becomes the principal measure of implementation. The possibility (if interstate complaints was retained but made optional, applying only between states making a declaration recognizing the competence of the Committee to consider such "communications." This was supplemented by provisions for ad hoc conciliation commissions, if the parties to the dispute agreed.

As regards the possibility of petitions by individuals to the Human Rights Committee, it seemed at first that this would have greater chance of acceptance in the Third Committee in 1966 than in the Commission on Human Rights in 1954, since the Third Committee itself had provided for such a procedure (on an optional basis) in the Racial Discrimination Convention the previous year. However, national susceptibilities were to count for more than logic; because of the influence of the African states in particular, states were reluctant to oppose such measures for strengthening implementation of the Racial Convention, but a Netherlands proposal to include an optional provision for individual petition in the Covenant was not adopted. The Third committee decided that this procedure should be included in a separate Protocol to be annexed to the Covenant. In retrospect, this decision seems a wise one, because the inclusion of a procedure for individual petition in the body of the Covenant, even on an optional basis, would probably have rendered its ratification more difficult in a number of countries; even without this provision it took ten years to obtain the thirty-five ratifications necessary for the Covenant to enter into force. On the other hand, the Optional Protocol providing for the right of individual petition obtained a sufficient number of ratifications to enter into force in 1976 at the same time as the Covenant on Civil and Political Rights.

The Third Committee also deleted from the draft Covenant several articles designed to permit or encourage reference of various matters to the International Court of Justice, no doubt because the diplomatic representatives in a committee representing over a hundred states in 1966 had less respect for that august body than the small number of specialists who sat on the Commission in 1954.

The changes made by the Third Committee were accepted by the General Assembly when it approved the text of the two covenants on December 16, 1966.

The Human Rights Committee

Article 28 of the Covenant provides for the establishment of the Human Rights Committee, the principal organ of implementation of the Covenant on Civil and Political Rights. This contrasts with the Covenant on Economic, Social, and Cultural Rights, where no new body was created and reports on compliance are received by the Economic and Social Council.

The Human Rights Committee consists of eighteen members. Although they serve in their personal capacities (Article 26), not as representatives of any government, they must be nationals of states which are parties to the Covenant. They must be "persons of high moral character and recognized competence in the field of human rights"; consideration shall also be given "to the usefulness of the participation -of some persons having legal experience." The Commission's draft had proposed "some persons having a judicial or legal experience," but the Third Committee decided to delete the reference to judicial qualifications. The change, in fact, makes little difference, since "persons having legal experience" clearly does not exclude judges, and in any event, the clause is not mandatory.

Under Articles 29 and 30 of the Covenant, the members of the Committee are elected by secret ballot by the states parties at a special meeting convened for this purpose by the Secretary-General of the United Nations. Each state party may nominate not more than two candidates, who must be nationals of that state. The details of the election procedure are set out in Article 30. Article 31 provides that the Committee may not include more than one national of any one state and that consideration shall be given to the principles of equitable geographical distribution and representation of the different forms of civilization and principal legal systems .24 The term of office is four years, though at the first election, nine members are to be elected for only two years, in order to avoid a complete change of membership at any one time (Article 32). Members of the Committee are eligible for reelection (Article 29). Articles 33 and 34 deal with the possibilities of incapacity and casual vacancies. Article 35 provides that the members of the Committee shall receive emoluments from United Nations resources, thus emphasizing that they serve in their personal capacity. This principle is further emphasized in Article 38, which requires each member of the Committee to make a solemn declaration that he will perform his functions impartially and conscientiously. Article 36 provides that the Secretary-General of the United Nations shall provide the necessary staff and facilities for the functioning of the Committee.

The Covenant on Civil and Political Rights and the Optional Protocol entered into force on March 23, 1976, and the first meeting of the states parties to elect the members of the Committee took place on September, 20, 1976. At that election the principles of equitable geographical distribution and representation of the principal legal systems were in fact respected; five members were elected from Western Europe, four from Eastern Europe, two from Asia, three from Africa, one from North America and three from Latin America. The five Western Europeans were all from states which are parties to the European Convention, one of them being also a member of the European Commission of Human Rights; the three Latin Americans were nationals of states parties to the American Convention on Human Rights. Only seven members of the Committee were nationals of states which had ratified the Optional Protocol providing for the right of individual petition.

The early experience with the composition of the Committee underscores difficulties which have beset other UN bodies of "experts" serving "in their personal capacities." Unfortunately, some of the representatives had been, and often continue to be, government officials. That contradicts the intent of the Covenant: it not only makes it difficult for the members to devote the necessary time and attention, but also makes it less likely that they can perform their functions "impartially." The task of the Committee is difficult and delicate, and is not aided by subjecting any of its members to political pressures that are inevitable if Committee members are, or are seen as, representing governments.

Rules of Procedure

The first meetings of the Human Rights Committee, in 1977, were concerned with organizational matters, and, in accordance with Article 39 of the Covenant, settling its Rules of Procedure. Rule 2 provides that the Committee shall normally hold two regular sessions each year. The practice was established in 1977 of holding spring and summer sessions, alternating between New York and Geneva. Rule 3 deals with the possibility of special sessions, which may be convened by decision of the Committee, by decision of the Chairman in consultation with the other officers, at the request of a majority of the members, or at the request of a state party. In fact, it soon became apparent that the Committee would not be able to handle the volume of business which was likely to fall to it in the course of two regular sessions a year, particularly as the number of reports and individual communications increased and the interstate procedure entered into force. Indeed, in 1978 the Committee held three sessions and found that it was unable to complete its business for lack of time. At the fifth session (October/November 1978) the Committee decided that its work load would make three sessions a year necessary for the foreseeable future. Moreover, much preparatory work is necessary between sessions, which a number of members of the Committee who have other professional obligations find difficult to undertake. Nor can the Division of Human Rights in the UN Secretariat meet all the Committee's requirements. There is a strong case for making membership on the Committee a salaried occupation to which members could devote all their time.

The two most interesting points in the Rules of Procedure concerned the publication of the proceedings and the method of voting. It was agreed that reports, formal decisions, and all other official documents of the Committee and its subsidiary bodies should be documents of general distribution, unless the Committee should decide otherwise in any particular case; the periodic reports by states parties and additional information submitted by them should also be public documents. On the other hand, documents and decisions relating to interstate complaints under Articles 41 and 42 of the Covenant, and to individual communications under the Optional Protocol, should have only restricted distribution and remain confidential.

While Article 39 of the Covenant provides that the Committee shall establish its own rules of procedure, paragraph 2 stipulates that these rules shall provide inter alia (a) that twelve members constitute a quorum; and (b) that decisions be made by a majority vote of the members present. During the drafting of the Rules of Procedure, some members of the Committee referred to a tendency in recent years in various legal bodies (both inside and outside the United Nations) to adopt decisions on the basis of consensus; they urged that the Human Rights Committee should follow this method and thus "underscore the resolve of members to work harmoniously and in a spirit of cooperation." They added that "efforts had been made throughout history to incorporate moral principles into positive law. The Committee now had an opportunity to do so and should take advantage of it." The argument is a good one, but it is by no means clear that the Committee would accomplish this noble aim more effectively if consensus (practically implying unanimity) is usually required. Rather, the attempt to reach consensus is liable to water down the moral principles to a lowest common denominator.

Other members argued that, while consensus was desirable if possible, to establish a rule to this effect "might considerably restrict the Committee's power of decision-making" and would be inconsistent with Article 39(2b) of 'the Covenant. Finally, it was agreed to incorporate in Rule 51 the method of decision by a simple majority, but to add a footnote indicating that there was general agreement that the "method' of work normally should allow for attempts to reach decisions by consensus before voting. . . ."39 In the procedures for the consideration of communications under the Optional Protocol, it was provided that a summary of an individual opinion may be appended to the collective view of the Committee (Rule 94). The point provoked a good deal of discussion; some members from the Eastern European and Latin American countries opposed the provision for individual opinions (which would frequently be dissenting opinions), on the ground that they would weaken the opinion of the majority and the moral authority of the Committee. Other members of the Committee took the opposing view, referring to "the right of dissent" implied in Article 19 of the Covenant, and drawing attention to possible situations in which the Committee might simply be unable to agree on an important point. Rule 94, permitting a summary of an individual opinion, seems a reasonable compromise. This provision should prevent the Committee's work from being hamstrung by the search for unanimity and the corresponding possibilities of intransigence.

In 1979, after the tenth state had made a declaration under Article 41, bringing the interstate complaint regime into force, the Committee put into effect Rules 72 to 77 of its Rules of Procedure to govern such interstate complaints. In general, these merely follow the provisions of Article 41, notably that the Committee will consider communications only if both states have declared under Article 41, and all domestic remedies have been exhausted (or have been unreasonably prolonged). Rule 75 provides that the Committee shall examine communications under Article 41 at closed meetings, but the Committee may, after consultation with the states parties concerned, issue communiques, through the Secretary-General, for the use of the information media and the public. The Committee may, through the Secretary-General, request from either of the parties concerned additional information or observations in oral or written form and set a time limit for their submission. Under Rule 77 the parties have a right to be represented when the matter is considered by the Committee and to make submissions orally and/or in writing. The Committee shall adopt a report, in accordance with Article 41(lh), within 12 months of the notice bringing the matter to the Committee's attention, but the parties do not have a right to be present during the Committee deliberations concerning the adoption of the report. If the matter is not resolved to the satisfaction of the parties, the Committee may, with their prior consent, proceed to the conciliation procedure prescribed in Article 42.

These rules are sound, reasonable, and promising, and their promulgation did not meet with efforts to limit the Committee's powers. Doubtless they were helped by the fact that most of the members of the Committee were nationals of countries that had not submitted to this regime, and their governments were not threatened by it. The few members of the Committee from countries that had submitted to this regime were eager to see it work, and even their governments, having submitted to it voluntarily, were not disposed to try to frustrate or weaken it.

Reporting Procedures

The 1954 draft covenant had envisaged interstate complaints before the Human Rights Committee as the principal measure of implementation; a reporting procedure was added but it is clear that it was considered a less important and subordinate measure. In the final text of the Covenant, the position was reversed: the reporting procedure became the principal measure of implementation and the interstate procedure was made optional. Although that procedure went into effect in 1979, less than one-fourth of the parties to the Covenant have submitted to it. Therefore, reports by states parties and their examination by the Human Rights Committee are likely to be of cardinal importance and remain the principal means of implementation of the Covenant. Under Article 40 reports are to be presented within one year of the Covenant's entry into force for the state party concerned, and thereafter when the Committee so requests.

Many tend to doubt the value of reports by states on their compliance with their international obligations. Such reports will, of course, be compiled by national officials who have a natural tendency to give the best account they can of the situation in their own country; it is unlikely that they will draw the attention of an international body to any shortcomings or failures in their national record and report violations of human rights by their government or other organs of the state. Is there then, it is asked, any value in a reporting system?

The experience of other bodies, notably the International Labour Organization which has had the longest experience, shows that several elements are necessary to make a reporting system effective: the cooperation of governments in providing full information; the possibility of obtaining further (and perhaps critical) information from other responsible sources; the examination of the information thus obtained by independent persons who are not government officials; and the right of some organ or body taking part in the procedure to make suitable recornmendations about any necessary improvements in the law- or practice of the country concerned.

This emphasis on the need for independent scrutiny and on the power of recommending improvements is not dictated by prejudice, suspicion, or hostility toward particular governments. It results from the complex nature of modern society, the vast range of subjects with regard to which government action affects the lives of the citizens often beneficially, but not always so-and the huge apparatus of public administration engaged in implementing that action. Officials, even with the best intentions, make mistakes; occasionally, their intentions may leave something to be desired. The greater the centralization of power in the hands of governments, the greater is the need for effective safeguards to protect the rights of the individual. In how many countries are there laws and even constitutional provisions which are beyond reproach, yet administrative action fails to correspond? It is against such general considerations that we need to look at the reporting system established by the Covenant on Civil and Political Rights.

When the Third Committee of the General Assembly was discussing the measures of implementation of the Covenant in 1966, a group of nine Afro-Asian countries tabled an amendment calling for the insertion of a new article, which became, with little amendment, Article 40. It is the first article on procedures for implementation, coming immediately after the articles on the constitution and functioning of the Human Rights Committee; its adoption resulted in the deletion of the article on periodic reports proposed by the Commission on Human Rights. The general view appears to have been that this proposal represented a substantial improvement over the 1954 draft. "It was also stressed that, since the procedure of conciliation envisaged was to be purely optional, care should be taken to ensure the efficacy of the only means of implementation, namely, the reporting system."

Even this reporting system of limited efficacity was not accepted with general enthusiasm. In the early days, when reporting procedures were first discussed in the Commission on Human Rights, the objection was made that "any such procedure was contrary to the United Nations Charter, in particular to Article 2(7), and constituted a violation of national sovereignty." This extreme and illogical view, however, was fortunately not repeated in the Third Committee; indeed, in 1963 the Eastern European representatives, reversing their earlier position, indicated that they were prepared to accept a reporting system.

Of the four conditions enumerated above for an effective reporting system, the first, cooperation of governments in providing full information, is expressly required by the Covenant. It remains to be seen how well this will be achieved in practice though the early signs are reasonably encouraging. They are somewhat encouraging too as regards the other conditions—the possibility of obtaining further information, independent scrutiny, and recommendations for necessary improvement.

The Human Rights Committee has profited and learned from the experience of its earlier counterpart, the committee established under the International Convention on the Elimination of All Forms of Racial Discrimination. Article 8 of the Convention provides for the establishment of a Committee on the Elimination of Racial Discrimination (CERD) of eighteen independent experts. Article 9 of the Convention contains an undertaking of the state parties to submit reports 11 on the legislative, judicial, administrative or other measures which they have adopted and which give effect to the provisions of the Convention." The reports are to be submitted within one year of the entry into force of the Convention and thereafter every two years or on request. Article 9 also provides: "The Committee may request further information from the States Parties." It is clear that there is a rather close, but not complete, parallel between Article 9 of the Racial Discrimination Convention and Article 40 of the Covenant on Civil and Political Rights, and that the experience gained in the implementation of the former was likely to influence the practice and procedure of the new Human Rights Committee.

The Committee on the Elimination of Racial Discrimination has taken its task seriously and has succeeded in imposing its authority. With the approval of the General Assembly, it has adopted the practice of inviting states parties which have submitted reports to send a representative to take part in the committee proceedings when the report is under examination. Almost all states parties have accepted such invitations and in this way a constructive dialogue has developed between the Committee and the governmental representatives, who answer questions, afford explanations, provide additional information, and so on. This procedure has the additional advantage of permitting the Committee to indicate informally that a government is not fully complying with its obligations, without the necessity for a formal decision to that effect. The Committee appears to have established a basis of mutual confidence with governments (or the majority of them) which augurs well for its future work.

Obviously similar problems were considered as the Human Rights Committee engaged in settling its methods of work and drawing up its Rules of Procedure. The Committee quickly established its intention of following the practice of the CERD in two important respects; in requesting additional information from governments when required, and in inviting governments to send representatives to discuss their reports with the Committee and to answer questions. Of course, common sense requires such action, but some governments are so extraordinarily sensitive about anything in the nature of international examination of their human rights record-invoking arguments about national sovereignty and nonintervention-that it is a distinct achievement to get them to accept even these modest measures. One member of the Human Rights Committee argued that states had agreed to accept "a reporting procedure, not an investigatory procedure" and that once they have submitted a report they have no further obligation to cooperate with the Committee. The argument was even made that Article 40 of the Covenant does not contain an express provision like that in Article 9 of the Racial Discrimination Convention authorizing the Committee to "request further information from the States Parties," and that the Committee therefore should not make such requests. It is therefore a cause for satisfaction that this negative attitude has not prevailed.

As a result of these and other discussions, Rule 66 of the Rules of Procedure which contains the general provisions about the submission of reports, includes a provision that the Committee may inform states of its wishes as to the form and contents of their reports. - Rule 68 provides that representatives of the states parties may be present when their reports are examined and that such a representative "should be able to answer questions which may be put to him by the Committee and make statements on reports already submitted by his State, and may also submit additional information from his State." It is clear, then, that both the Rules of Procedure and the initial practice of the Human Rights Committee are conceived in that spirit of "constructive dialogue" which is so obviously necessary.

At its session in August 1977 the Committee formulated general guidelines about the form and contents of reports, asking that they be in two parts. The first part should describe briefly the general legal framework within which civil and political rights are protected, including information as to whether they are protected in the constitution or by a separate "Bill of Rights," whether the provisions of the Covenant are directly enforceable in internal law, and what remedies are available to an individual who thinks that his rights have been violated. The second part should deal with the legislative, administrative, and other measures in force to protect each right and should include information about restrictions or limitations on their exercise. The Committee also requested that it be informed of any significant new developments at any time.

At the same session, the Committee considered its first group of reports. In all cases a representative of the government concerned was present to answer questions and provide further information. Questions were put by members of the Committee on such subjects as: the relationship between treaty obligations and domestic law in proceedings before national courts, and whether an individual can claim annulment of a national law or measure in case of incompatibility; limitations on grounds of ordre public, and review of their compatibility with the Covenant; detention for political reasons; equality between the sexes; the prohibition of torture, and remedies available to victims of torture; limitations on freedom of expression, freedom of religion, freedom of assembly, and freedom of movement; the existence of minority groups and the rights accorded to them; the distinction between the treatment accorded to detained persons and to convicted prisoners; permissible length of detention; and others.

The early Annual Reports of the Committee to the General Assembly show that each report was examined carefully and in detail, usually over two or three days. Many searching questions were put to the representatives of the states parties. In some cases adequate answers were given on the spot. More often, detailed replies were promised at a later date. The effectiveness of the system will depend largely on the supplementary information provided subsequently and its careful scrutiny by the Committee.

The proper role of the Committee and the scope of its authority have been a subject of continuing debate. Some members of the Committee have stressed that under Article 40(4), the Committee's function was to exchange information and promote cooperation among states parties and respect for human rights. It was not to evaluate any state's compliance with the Covenant. The Committee could study the reports submitted by states, but any comments on the reports had to be "general," not about any particular state, limited to matters of common interest and addressed to all states.

Most members of the Committee, however, saw the Committee's role as one of promoting and ensuring compliance with the Covenant. Several members stressed that the Committee had the duty to scrutinize the reports received to ensure that the Covenant has been implemented, and that it should seek further information where necessary, in particular where the reports were not consistent with other information available to the Committee. The Committee should adopt a separate report on each state to be transmitted to that state relating to the fulfillment of its obligations. General comments to be included in the Annual Report would review the overall adequacy of the reports received, list difficulties in implementation and suggest solutions and propose possible amendments to the Covenant.

Despite these differing viewpoints, the Committee succeeded in adopting by consensus a draft statement on how it would proceed. The statement included principles for the Committee's guidance in formulating general comments and a list of subjects to which the general comments could be related, inter alia. The committee also confirmed its aim of engaging in a constructive dialogue with each reporting state on the basis of its periodic reports. It decided to request a second periodic report from states parties within four years of the time its first report was considered, and undertook to develop guidelines for these new reports. Before the Committee meets with the state representatives to discuss the second periodic report, a working group of the Committee would review the information received in order to identify those matters which it would be most helpful to discuss.

Two major problems were revealed early in the reporting system: the delay in reporting and the Committee's need for adequate time for detailed scrutiny. The importance of the first point should not be exaggerated; as a new system begins to operate, it is not surprising if a number of states (especially those with limited resources in their national administrations) fall behind the timetable. The second point is more serious. The Committee's falling behind is not surprising, since each report is supposed to cover the measures (constitutional, legislative, judicial, administrative, and other measures) designed to ensure the protection of twenty-two distinct rights and freedoms, many of them of great complexity, such as the right to liberty and security of the person (Article 9) and the right to a fair trial (Article 14). But if the Committee was behind in its work at the beginning when it had hardly begun to consider individual communications submitted under the Optional Protocol, and when the interstate procedure set out in Articles

41 and 42 was not yet in force, how will it manage in the future?

The second element in an effective reporting system is the possibility of obtaining further, and perhaps contradictory, information from responsible sources other than the governments. This is provided for in the systems established by the ILO for its international labor conventions and by the Council of Europe for the European Social Charter. The Covenant on Civil and Political Rights does not formally institute any similar arrangements. The nearest it comes to doing so is the provision in Article 40(3), introduced as an amendment by the United Kingdom in the Third Committee, which authorizes the Secretary-General of the United Nations, after consultation with the Committee, to "transmit to the specialized agencies concerned copies of such parts of the reports as may fall within their field of competence." Both the ILO and UNESCO have expressed their willingness to cooperate with the Human Rights Committee in this respect, and the appropriate provision has been included in the Rules of Procedure. It would be wise not to expect too much from these arrangements for consultation with the specialized agencies, because comparatively few of the rights protected by the Covenant on Civil and Political Rights relate to matters within the competence of the ILO and UNESCO; moreover, the specialized agencies do not possess a right to comment on states' reports and may do so only if specifically requested by the Committee (Rule 67(2)). ILO, UNESCO, FAO, and WHO have been invited to send representatives to attend the public sessions of the Committee, but their relationship to it still remains to be clarified.

One special source of additional material was used early. In considering the report of Chile, which painted a wholly favorable picture of the condition of human rights in that country, the Committee referred to resolutions of the General Assembly and the report of an Ad Hoc Working Group of the UN Commission on Human Rights that indicated flagrant violations of human rights by Chile. Members of the Committee used those resolutions and reports as the basis for criticizing the report in detail, challenging its assertions, and asking for further information, explanation, and justification. The representative of Chile, while responding to many of the questions, challenged the competence of the Committee to use the UN materials as a basis for questions. Those UN resolutions and reports, he argued, derived from complaints by states or by private persons. Since Chile had not agreed to submit to interstate complaints (under Article 41) or to private complaints (under the Protocol), using them to impugn Chile's report would be an indirect way to subject Chile to interstate or private complaints. It was not for the Committee or any of its members, the Chilean representative argued, to express any opinion as to whether Chile was complying with the Covenant: that would constitute a form of complaint by states or individuals to which Chile had not submitted. In his view, the Committee could not look beyond the report a government submitted and could make no allegations based on any other sources.

The Committee, however, rejected these objections, and, relying on the UN materials, found that the information -supplied by the report was insufficient and invited the Government of Chile "to submit a report in accordance with Article 40 of the Covenant and to furnish specific information on restrictions" imposed by Chile during the period of state of emergency. The representative of Chile replied that his government considered that it had complied with its obligations under the Covenant but, although it could not accept the preambular part of the Committee's statement, it was prepared to submit a new report as requested. After the Committee received a note from the Chilean

Foreign Minister, challenging the Committee's action "the Committee decided to inform the Government of Chile that the Committee expected to receive the supplementary report requested in accordance with Article 40."

In the Chilean case, the Committee was content to ground its challenges to a report on materials developed by UN bodies. There is no reason why the Committee must limit itself to UN sources only. From what other responsible sources could the Committee obtain information to supplement, or possibly contradict, the information furnished by governments? The answer which springs readily to mind is: the nongovernmental organizations having consultative status with the Economic and Social Council. There are several dozens of these organizations-of which perhaps the best known are Amnesty International, the International Commission of jurists and the International League for Human Rights-which have followed assiduously the work of the Commission on Human Rights for many years, brought relevant information to its attention, and often made useful suggestions. Unfortunately, certain governments have sought to restrict rather than encouarge the activities of NGO's and have even talked of withdrawing completely their consultative status. In these circumstances, the organizations have not been accorded any rights to lay information before the Human Rights Committee when it is considering the reports of governments. This is a real defect in the system. That does not prevent the NGOs from supplying information to members of the Committee in their individual capacity, but this is not the same as presenting information officially to the Committee itself. Moreover, some members of the Committee are particularly sensitive on this score and have objected to the fact that the Secretariat forwarded communications from an NGO; also, that one member of the Committee, in addressing questions to the representative of Czechoslovakia, was apparently using information not included in the government's report. There appears to be a tendency in the Committee to follow the practice of CERD whereby use may be made of all official publications but not of the reports of NGOs or of the press.

As regards the possibility of obtaining independent information, one must conclude that the situation is far from satisfactory. One cannot but hope that the members of the Committee will succeed in overcoming this difficulty, perhaps by the intelligent use of the right of any independent expert to do his own research work and to use such sources of information as are available to him.

The third requirement which we have postulated as necessary in any effective reporting system is the independence of the persons who examine the reports. As we have seen, the text of the Covenant is satisfactory in this respect; Article 28(3) states that the members of the Committee "shall be elected and shall serve in their personal capacity." This compares with "shall sit . . . in their individual capacity" in the European convention (Article 23), and "shall be elected in a personal capacity" in the American Convention (Article 36). What is perhaps more important are the provisions of Article 38 of the Covenant requiring each member to make "a solemn declaration in open committee that he will perform his functions impartially and conscientiously"; and of Article 35 that the members of the Committee "shall . . . receive emoluments from United Nations resources." Furthermore, Rule 16 of the Rules of Procedure reiterates the requirement of a solemn declaration of impartiality, while Rule 13 requires that the resignation of a member of the Committee must be in writing to the Chairman or the Secretary-General by the member himself, thus eliminating the possibility that a government might decide to remove a member of the Committee and notify the Chairman or the Secretary-General that he has resigned.

But if the text of the Covenant is adequate in this respect, it remains to be seen whether governments will in fact apply these provisions in the spirit in which they were drafted. Regrettably, similar guarantees of the independence of international officials have not always been respected in practice. One must hope that a greater measure of independence is allowed to members of the Human Rights Committee. What one would like to see is a categorical exclusion from the Committee (and from the European and American Commissions) of persons who are salaried national officials (particularly members of permanent delegations to the UN)-not because they are not usually of the highest integrity, but because their impartiality is that much more difficult to sustain when, for the greater part of their lives, their habit, and their duty is to act on the instructions of their governments, and when the prospects for their future careers depend on the goodwill and approval of their governments. It would be both logical and sensible to establish that a salaried national official position is incompatible with membership of an international organ whose members are required to serve in an independent capacity.

The fourth requirement of an effective reporting system is that the body that receives the report shall have authority to make suitable recommendations for any necessary improvements in the law or practice of the country concerned. In this respect the Covenant on Civil and Political Rights is sadly deficient. Under Article 40(4) and (5), the Committee proceeds as follows:

1. The Committee studies the reports submitted by the states parties.

2. The Committee draws up its own reports and transmits them with "such general comments as it may consider appropriate."
3. The Committee may also transmit these comments to the Economic and Social Council together with the reports of the states parties.
4. The states parties may submit to the Committee their observations on the latter's comments on their reports.

These procedures are deficient in several respects. The Committee is authorized to make "general comments" only. The term is not defined. It does not mean that these comments must be addressed to all parties and not to particular states. As drafting history makes clear, the Human Rights Committee may make recommendations to particular states parties. But they must be in general terms and not relate to individual cases, and cannot therefore focus attention on specific violations and bring influence to bear to remedy them.

Moreover, the states concerned are not required to take any action on the comments made by the Committee on their reports. They "may submit . . . their observations on any comments that may be made" or may ignore them completely. And unlike other reporting systems (for example, in the procedures of the ILO and the Council of Europe), the Committee's conclusions are not submitted to an authoritative political organ empowered to make formal and specific recommendations to the government concerned. One might have thought that the Economic and Social Council would fulfill this role. But there is no obligation for the Committee to submit its comments to ECOSOC. If the Committee does submit its comments to ECOSOC, there is no requirement that the governments concerned communicate to ECOSOC their observations on the Committee's comments. And there is no provision that ECOSOC is to pursue the Committee's comments with recommendations for necessary remedies.

In the light of these deficiencies, much will depend on the use which the Committee makes of the possibilities offered by Article 45, which provides that the Committee shall submit to the General Assembly, through ECOSOC, "an annual report on its activities." If the Committee uses this opportunity to draw attention to situations which it considers unsatisfactory but with regard to which it cannot obtain remedial action from governments, it may help to remedy the deficiencies in the procedure under Article 40. Quite properly, the Committee was cautious in its exercise of this power during the first few years, but it may become bolder as its influence increases.

It is not surprising that there are weaknesses and deficiencies in the reporting system instituted by the Covenant on Civil and Political Rights, since it is the product of the heterogeneous community of the United Nations, some of whose members oppose any system of international control at all. Seen in this perspective, the reporting system is a reasonable compromise. It will be a demanding challenge for the Human Rights. Committee to make it as effective as possible.

Proceedings between State Parties

Like other multilateral international agreements, the Covenant on Civil and Political Rights is an agreement among the states parties to it, creating rights and obligations among them. Since parties to an inter national agreement generally can enforce it against one another by appropriate remedies, it was natural that the Human Rights Commission, in proposing the establishment of a Committee to implement the Covenant, should contemplate permitting the

Committee to receive complaints by one state party alleging violation by another.

The implementing system envisaged in the 1954 draft of the Human Rights Commission involved the following stages: bilateral negotiations between complaining and respondent state; in the event of their failure, reference to the Human Rights Committee; the Committee would establish the facts' and make available its good offices with a view to a friendly settlement; in the absence of such a settlement, the Committee would draw up a report on the facts and state -its opinion on the question of violation; the report would be sent to the states concerned and to the Secretary-General for publication. The Committee then, was first to have a role of mediation and then, if that failed, a quasi-judicial role. The Committee would declare its opinion after proceedings of an almost judicial character; and while the opinion would not be binding on the parties, it would no doubt carry great weight.

Many of those responsible for this text would doubtless have preferred something stronger, probably a committee which, if mediation was unsuccessful, would have the power to reach a decision and not merely express an opinion; but (as happens so often in the United Nations) it was no doubt necessary to accept a weaker text as a compromise.

The Third Committee of the General Assembly, instead of strengthening the powers of the Human Rights Committee to deal with interstate disputes, did the opposite. Its most important change was to make Committee examination of interstate complaints an optional procedure. Thus, Article 41 of the Covenant provides: "A State Party . . . may at any time declare . . . that it recognizes the competence of the Committee to receive and consider communications to the effect that a State Party claims that another State Party is not fulfilling its obligations under the present Covenant." A separate declaration recognizing this competence, in addition to the act of ratification of the Covenant, is therefore required. Moreover, it is not sufficient that the state alleged to be responsible for a violation has made such a declaration. Communications can be considered by the Committee only if the complaining state has also done so. There must be (in a new sense) "equality of arms": only states which have agreed to expose themselves to this procedure have the right to use it against another state party. Furthermore, under Article 41(2), the procedure was to come into force when ten states made the necessary declarations, and that did not happen until 1979, thirteen years after the approval of the covenants by the General Assembly and nearly three years after the entry into force of the Covenant itself by the end of 1980, only thirteen of the sixty-five states parties to the Covenant had made the declaration provided for in Article 41. It is clear, then, that this procedure is not the principal measure of implementation provided for in the Covenant.

It is instructive to note the obligatory or optional nature of the systems of international control in the different human rights treaties. The European Convention on Human Rights (drafted in 1950, entered into force in 1953) makes the -procedure for interstate complaints obligatory for all contracting parties (Article 24) and the procedure of individual petition optional (Article 25). The UN Covenant makes both procedures optional, while the American Convention on Human Rights (drafted in 1969, entered into force in 1978) makes the procedure of individual petition obligatory for all contracting parties (Article 44) and the procedure of interstate complaints optional (Article 45). During the conference at San José, Costa Rica, at which the American Convention was drafted, it was explained quite frankly that human rights issues were inflammatory and that a system permitting interstate proceedings between American republics on such issues was politically dangerous; it was therefore considered prudent to make this an optional provision which states could accept or reject. No doubt similar considerations led the Third Committee of the General Assembly to a similar conclusion. As the Committee stated in its report, various factors of international tension and mutual suspicion still exist in the world, and it was unlikely that mandatory complaint procedures would be Widely accepted. It was believed that the adoption of an optional procedure would afford a satisfactory solution, and that with the passage of time "an increasing number of States Parties would no doubt accept the optional clause . . . and thereby give full effect to the system of implementation of the Covenant. One may hope that this optimism was not ill-placed. In any event, it is worth recording, and bearing in mind for the future, that the Third Committee itself recognized that the system of implementation would only be fully effective when the optional provisions of Article 41 are generally accepted. It is noteworthy that the Convention on the Elimination of All Forms of Racial Discrimination, adopted by the UN at about the same time as the Covenant, provides for interstate complaints, although the procedure has not been frequently invoked. In addition, there have been state-to-state complaints under the European Convention without devastating effect on relations between the countries involved.

The second way in which the Third Committee watered down the Commission's 1954 proposals was by taking away the Human Rights Committee's right to express an opinion on the question of violation. The procedure set out in Article 41 of the Covenant envisages, in the first place, bilateral negotiations between the two states concerned; if the matter is not thus settled and domestic remedies have been exhausted, either state may 'refer it to the Human Rights Committee, which must examine the question in closed meetings; the Committee may call for all relevant information and the states parties may be represented and make oral and written submissions; then, the Committee is to make available its good offices with a view to a friendly settlement of the matter, based on respect for human rights; finally, if this is not achieved, the Committee is required to submit a report which is to be confined to a brief statement of the facts, with the written or oral submissions of the states parties attached. The functions of the Committee in relation to interstate disputes are practically limited to establishing the facts, proposing its good offices, and exercising them if the offer is accepted. As certain representatives stated in the Third Committee, the Human Rights Committee is "no longer the same as the quasi-judicial body originally proposed by the Commission on Human Rights" but - more in the nature of a functional organ."

There is, however, another procedural possibility, presented by Article 42 of the Covenant. This provides that if a matter referred to the Committee under Article 41 is not resolved to the satisfaction of the states parties concerned, the Committee may, if those states consent, appoint an ad hoc conciliation Commission, which will in turn make available its good offices "with a view to an amicable solution of the matter on the basis of respect for the present Covenant." The Commission is to consist of five members who are nationals of states which have accepted the Article 41 procedure but not nationals of the states parties involved in the dispute. Article 42 deals with the composition, method of election and procedure of the Conciliation Commission; in particular, it provides that the information obtained by the Human Rights Committee shall be made available to the Commission, which may also call on the states concerned for further relevant information.

When it has completed its work, or in any event within a year of being seized of the matter, the Conciliation Commission is to draw up its report. If an amicable solution has been reached, the report will contain a brief statement of the facts and of the solution reached. If an amicable solution has not been reached, the report will contain a full statement of the facts and the Commission's view on "the possibilities of an amicable solution of the matter." Within three months of the receipt of the report, the states parties will indicate "whether or not they accept the contents of the report of the Commission" (Article 42[7c] and [7d]).

Though the relevant subparagraphs of Article 42(7) are not very clear, the text seems to give the Commission a real function of conciliation, making proposals for consideration and possible acceptance by the parties. This is rather more than merely having the Commission state "its views on the possibilities of an amicable solution of the matter." It would seem that this phrase in subparagraph (c) should rather be taken to mean that the Commission shall set forth "proposals for a possible amicable solution of the matter," because otherwise there would be little meaning in the requirement of subparagraph (d) that the state parties shall indicate "whether or not they accept the contents of the report of the Commission."

One may summarize by saying that in interstate disputes the function of the Human Rights Committee is one of good offices, while that of the Conciliation Commission is of good offices and perhaps conciliation; but neither function can be exercised except in relation to states both of which have made an express declaration accepting the competence of the Committee to exercise this function and, as regards the Conciliation Commission, have consented to its appointment.

Whether state complaints to the Human Rights Committee will play an important part in protecting human rights remains to be seen. The procedure has come into force but, as of 1980, has not been used. Most of the states that have accepted it are parties to the European Convention on Human Rights and will not normally refer to the UN Committee matters which could be considered by the European Commission of Human Rights. The American States, too, are more likely to use inter-American procedures. If "state-to-state" enforcement is to develop in other parts of the world it is also likely to happen in a regional context before regional commissions. In the past, the Communist states have made it clear that they will not accept this procedure, as they are opposed to the basic principle on which it rests.

The fact that the Covenant provides for "state-to-state" complaint to the Human Rights Committee, if only on an optional basis, has raised the question whether states parties to the Covenant may refer disputes about its interpretation or application to other procedures of international settlement (for example, to the International Court of justice). It has been argued that the Covenant is an international agreement like any other and states parties to it have the usual remedies available to states for breach of an agreement. It is relevant to observe that in Articlc 62 of the European Convention on Human Rights, the contracting parties agree that they will not avail themselves of other international procedures for settling disputes arising under the Convention, unless by special agreement concluded for the purpose. There is no corresponding provision in the UN Covenant. It can therefore be argued that no such limitation is implied in the Covenant. And as regards resort to the International Court of-justice this interpretation is supported by the very broad terms of Article 36 of the Statute of the Court.

On the other hand, some have argued that the intention of the states parties was to establish special procedures for dealing with any dispute which may arise about the interpretation and application of the Covenant and that it is only by means of these procedures-and subject to the conditions and limitations pertaining to them in the Covenant-that one state is entitled to question the action of another state concerning any matter arising under the Covenant.

As regards international judicial procedures, this problem may be largely academic, since the Court is not frequently used. What may be more important is the availability of the Covenant as a basis for diplomatic protection. Under traditional international law one state is entitled to "intervene" with another state for the purpose of protecting the rights of its own citizens, principally in cases of "denial of justice." After the entry into force of the Covenant on Civil and Political Rights, a good case can be made for holding that one state party is justified in exercising the right of diplomatic protection if another state party fails to ensure any of the rights protected in the Covenant, at least where a national of the complaining state is concerned. This would give a valid justification for one state party to secure the protection of the fundamental rights of its citizens when on the territory of another state party, even if the respondent state has not accepted the provisions of Article 41 of the Covenant. And some have argued strongly that, because a breach of the Covenant is involved, such "diplomatic protection" may be provided by any state party against any other state party even on behalf of the latter's nationals, although complaint to the Human Rights Committee is not available under Article 41.

Individual Communications

The real test of the effectiveness of a system of international protection for human rights is whether it provides an international remedy for the individual whose rights are violated.

In its classic conception, international law governs relations between states, and the individual has no place therein. His interests are supposed to be protected by the state of which he is a national and he has no locus standi before international tribunals or international organizations. In the second half of the twentieth century, however, certain inroads upon, or exceptions to, this classic doctrine have been established. Whether these inroads and exceptions are to be encouraged and further developed, or resisted and restricted, has been debated for thirty years; and the debate will no doubt continue for at least another generation. There is an immense literature on the subject, and there have been and will continue to be innumerable speeches about it in United Nations organs and elsewhere.

One's personal response to this issue may depend principally on one's conception of the role of the state in the modem world. If one believes that national sovereignty and the unrestricted power of the nation-state are, and should remain, the basic premises of political organization and of the law (both national and international), one will resist all attempts to permit the individual to challenge the authority of the state, in particular by the use of international remedies. If, on the other hand, one believes that the concept of the nation-state as developed in the last few centuries-and particularly in the nineteenth and twentieth centuries is not the summum bonum or greatest achievement of mankind, but merely one stage in a process of constant evolution, and that the state is made for man and not man for the state, then one will welcome and encourage all attempts to protect the individual against the abuse of power by the state. To put it another way: is one on the side of Machiavelli and Hobbes or of Locke,

Rousseau, and Bentham? Those who are heirs to the Bill of Rights, the American Declaration of Independence, and the French Declaration of 1789 will have no difficulty in answering this question.

To go from the general to the particular, in my view there are two practical arguments which are determinant. 93 The first is that the classic doctrine of international law simply does not work in the context of the protection of human rights. If an individual's rights are violated, this will in the great majority of cases be the result of acts by organs or agencies of the state of which he is a national. It is therefore nonsense to say that his rights will be championed by the state of which he is a national when that state is ex hypothesi the offender. Second, as is well known, the United Nations receives many thousands of communications each year complaining of violations of human rights throughout the world. Article I of the Charter states that one of the purposes of the United Nations is "to achieve international cooperation . . . in promoting and encouraging respect for human rights and fundamental freedoms for all . . . " and there are seven other references in the Charter to the functions of the United Nations and its organs in relation to human rights. If-as was at one time the case-the organization takes no action with regard to the communications it receives, this inevitably brings it into disrepute and shows that it is failing to fulfill one of its principal functions. Both common sense and the need to preserve the reputation of the United Nations, therefore, make it necessary to adopt a constructive and positive attitude to the question of access ' of the individual to international remedies, notably in the system of human rights protection which the UN has launched.

These considerations led to discussions which went on for many years in different UN organs about whether the Commission on Human Rights could take any action about communications from individuals and nongovernmental organizations complaining of violations. These discussions finally led to the adoption by the Economic and Social Council in 1970 of Resolution 1503, which authorized the Commission to examine "communications, together with replies of governments, if any, which appear to reveal a consistent pattern of gross violations of human rights." The procedure is complicated, involving a triple screening, and the results so far have been disappointing. It is outside the scope of this chapter to examine the Resolution 1503 procedure in detail; but its existence confirms a clear if timid recognition that the United Nations and the international human rights system cannot totally ignore individual complaints of violation of human rights.

There is also a third important argument for allowing individuals who believe that their rights have been violated to appeal to an international organ of control. If there is neither the possibility of state-to-state complaint nor a right of individual complaint, there is no meaningful vindication of individual rights beyond the general and indirect influences of the voluntary reporting system. If the international organ can be seized of interstate complaints, but there is no right of individual petition, aggrieved individuals will look for another government to champion their cause by bringing a case against the government of which they are nationals. Thus Greek citizens whose rights were violated by the military regime in their country in 1967 were led to appeal to the Scandinavian governments for help. It is obviously in the interest of peaceful relations between states that what is essentially an individual and national problem should be dealt with as such not transformed into an international dispute between states.

When the Covenant on Civil and Political Rights was being drafted, it became necessary to face squarely the question whether the measures of implementation to be provided in the Covenant should include the right of individual petition to the Human Rights Committee. Indeed, the Commission on Human Rights had been specifically instructed to examine this problem by the General Assembly when it approved the Universal Declaration in 1948. As we have seen earlier in this essay, in 1950 the Commission considered that the Committee to be established by the Covenant should be competent to consider interstate complaints but rejected the possibility of access by nongovernmental organizations and individuals." The issue was later reopened in the Third Committee of the General Assembly. In the explanatory paper on measures of implementation which he presented to the General Assembly in 1963, the Secretary-General summarized the history of the matter and the issues involved, and explained the procedures for handling individual communications which existed under the European Convention, the draft Inter-American Convention, and the Constitution of the ELO.

The Third Committee discussed the matter at length. After it had approved the two articles on interstate procedures (which became Articles 41 and 42) it considered the addition of a new article providing for the competence of the Human Rights Committee, on an optional basis, to receive and consider individual petitions-a text which was largely inspired by the corresponding provisions of the European Convention. Another proposal was aimed at limiting the functions of the Committee to the simple receipt and transmission of communications. A revision of the original amendment set out the procedure in greater detail and would have authorized the Committee, when examining individual communications, to "forward its suggestions, if any, to the state party concerned and to the individual." In the end, the debate turned on the question whether such a procedure should be included in the Covenant itself, on an optional basis, or in a separate protocol thereto, which would also be optional. It was decided by a very narrow majority to incorporate the right of individual petition in a separate legal text.

It seems regrettable that such an important measure of implementation should be altogether absent from the Covenant itself. On the other hand, its inclusion in the Covenant would no doubt have rendered more difficult the procedure of ratification in a number of countries. There is also perhaps a certain psychological advantage in the fact that the measure is included in a separate Optional Protocol, because this fact draws more attention to the existence of the procedure of individual petition than would be the case if it were set out in an article of the Covenant. The Protocol is now included separately in the list of United Nations treaties; ratifications are published and to some extent publicized; it is thus an object of greater attention than the optional procedure in Article 41 of the Covenant: One should not exaggerate, buton balance-nothing seems to be lost, and probably something is gained, by the fact that the Optional Protocol exists as a separate legal text.

Any state party to the Covenant which ratifies the Protocol thereby "recognizes the competence of the Committee to receive and consider communications from individuals subject to its jurisdiction who claim to be victims of a violation by that State Party of any of the rights set forth in the Covenant." Article 2 of the Protocol establishes that communications to the Committee may be submitted by "individuals who claim that any of their rights enumerated in the Covenant have been violated and who have exhausted all available domestic remedies." Article 3 provides that communications shall be considered inadmissible if they are anonymous, abusive, or incompatible with the provisions of the Covenant. Article 5(2) introduces a further precondition by providing that the Committee shall not consider a communication unless it has ascertained that the same matter is not being considered under an other procedure of international investigation or settlement. This rule is eminently reasonable in itself. But this paragraph seems to place on the Committee the positive obligation of ascertaining that the matter is not being examined under another international procedure-an obligation which may be difficult to fulfill-whereas it would seem sufficient to have provided that the Committee will not examine a communication if it is shown, by the respondent government or otherwise, that the matter is being examined under another international procedure.

The rule of exhaustion of domestic remedies is well known to international lawyers and is based on both justice and common sense. It is based on justice, because it would be unjust that the international responsibility of a state should be engaged on account of the action of one of its agents or tribunals when a national means of redress is available but has not been used. Equally, the rule is based on common sense, because it is in the general interest that an aggrieved person should make use of domestic remedies, when they are available, to right a wrong, rather than address himself to an international commission, court, or other tribunal. Access to the international organ should be available, but only in the last resort, and after the domestic remedies have been exhausted. Normally, this will mean that appeals against the acts of the executive branch of the government should be addressed to the national courts before being addressed to an international organ; equally, that appeals against decisions of inferior courts should be addressed to the higher courts and, if necessary and possible, to the Supreme Court or Constitutional Court, before being addressed to an international organ. Not only are the domestic remedies likely to be speedier and perhaps less expensive; in many cases they may be more effective, because a national court of appeal or Supreme Court can usually reverse the decision of a lower court, whereas the decision of an international organ does not have that effect, even though it will engage the international responsibility of the state concerned.

All this is on the assumption that domestic remedies are available and are effective. If no domestic remedies are available, clearly there is no need to have recourse to them before the applicant can address himself to the competent international organ. Equally, if domestic remedies are theoretically available but there is unreasonable delay on the part of national courts in granting a remedy, the applicant should not be penalized as a result.

A large proportion of the applications filed with the European Commission of Human Rights are declared inadmissible on grounds of non-exhaustion of domestic remedies. It remains to be seen whether the same will be the case with the Human Rights Committee.

Article 4 and the remaining paragraphs of Article 5 of the Protocol deal with the procedure of the Committee for dealing with individual communications. They shall be communicated to the state party concerned, which within six months must "submit to the Committee written explanations or statements clarifying the matter and the remedy, if any, that may have been taken by that State." Article 5(l) states that the proceedings shall be based on "all written information made available . . . by the individual and by the State Party concerned," which would seem to exclude oral hearings and information from other sources. Communications are to be examined at closed meetings and, under Article 5(4), "the Committee shall forward its views to the State Party concerned and to the individual." Finally, under Article 6 of the Protocol, the Committee will include a summary of its activities thereunder in its annual report to the General Assembly provided for in Article 45 of the Covenant.

From this brief summary it will appear that the procedure is not contentious, permitting argument by counsel, examination of witnesses and so on, nor is it an adjudication on the question of violation by the Human Rights Committee. Nevertheless, it marks a big advance over any measures of implementation Previously established by the United Nations. Much will depend on how the Human Rights Committee interprets its powers under the Protocol, particularly in forwarding "its views" to states parties under Article 5(4) and in reporting to the General Assembly under Article 6.

The Optional Protocol contains no separate provisions for rules of procedure, which means that the general provision of Article 39 of the Covenant on Civil and Political Rights applies also to action taken under the Optional Protocol, including the provision that twelve members shall constitute a quorum and that decisions "shall be made by a majority vote of the members present." The Committee Rules include a separate chapter on "Procedure for the Consideration of Communications Received under the Optional Protocol" (Rules 78 to 94).101 The first section (Rules 78 to 81) deals with transmission of communications to the Committee. The Secretary-General of the United Nations is the channel of communication. He is required to prepare lists of the communications received, with a brief summary of their contents, for circulation to the members of the Committee; the full text is available to them on request. A register of communications is to be kept. The Secretary-General may request from the authors of communications any necessary clarifications, particularly as regards the exhaustion of domestic remedies.

The second section (Rules 82 to 86) contains certain general provisions. Meetings at which communications are examined shall be closed (or private), but the Committee may issue communiques for the press and general public about its activities. The third section (Rules 87 to 92) deals with the admissibility of communications. The conditions of admissibility set out in the Protocol are repeated. The Committee may establish working groups of not more than five members to examine and make recommendations to the Committee about the admissibility of communications. The Committee or working group may request additional information relevant to the question of admissibility; a communication may not be declared admissible unless the state concerned has received a copy of it and has had an opportunity to comment.

Rules 93 and 94 deal with "Procedures for the Consideration of Communications," repeating essentially what is provided in Article 5 of the Protocol. Once a decision is taken that a communication is admissible, the state concerned and the individual are informed; within six months the state "shall submit . . . written explanations or statements . . . and the remedy, if any, that may have been taken by that State." These explanations and statements are to be communicated to the author of the communication for his comments. Finally, the Committee will consider the substance of the case "in the light of all the written information made available to it by the individual and by the State Party concerned and shall formulate its views thereon." These views will be communicated to the state concerned and to the individual.

There are two additions to what is specified in the Protocol Paragraph 1 of Rule 94 reiterates the Committee's use of working groups to make recommendations about admissibility, and paragraph

3 of Rule 94, in effect, permits dissenting opinions. Lengthy dissenting opinions will not be possible, however, because a member may only request that "a summary of his individual opinion shall be appended to the views of the Committee when they are communicated to the individual and to the State party concerned." Nevertheless, this is a useful addition which should strengthen the quasi-judicial character of the Human Rights Committee when exercising its functions under the Optional Protocol and should contribute to the development of its jurisprudence.

As of January 1, 1981, twenty-five states had ratified the Optional Protocol. The Committee's first Report to the General Assembly on its activities recorded the appointment of working groups to consider the admissibility of communications. Since the proceedings are confidential, information was not published about the identity of the applicants, about the nature of the alleged violations or about the states against which the complaints were lodged. The Committee's reports tell only the results of the procedural steps taken: decisions of inadmissibility; decisions to transmit communications to governments for their observations on admissibility; requests to applicants for further information, including steps to exhaust domestic remedies; and so on. 106 The Reports also give indications of the Committee's thinking on four topics: the standing of the author, the examination of complaints ratione temporis, the exhaustion of domestic remedies, and the problem of determining whether a matter is being examined under another international procedure of investigation or settlement.

In 1979 the Committee for the first time "forward[ed] its views to the State Party concerned and to the individual" (Article 5[4]) and made public what was, in effect, its first "judgment" on a private communication under the Protocol. The Committee had received a "communication" (Article 1) from a Uruguayan citizen alleging mistreatment of herself and three members ' of her family. Each had been charged with "subversive association" or "assistance to subversive association," and was allegedly detained 'without trial', held incommunicado, and tortured. The Committee brought the communication to the attention of the government of Uruguay (Article 4[1]). The government of Uruguay objected to the admissibility of the claim on the grounds that domestic remedies had not been exhausted, and that the alleged violations against the principal complainant had occurred before the Covenant entered into force for Uruguay. The Committee agreed that acts occurring before the Covenant's entry into force were beyond its jurisdiction. As regards violations alleged to have occurred after that date, however, the Committee found that no further domestic remedy remained. It decided also that the "close family connexion" permitted the author of the communication to act on behalf of the other victims. When, after six months (Article 4[2]), the government of Uruguay failed to give a satisfactory explanation of its actions, the Committee formulated its views on the basis of the facts as alleged. It expressed the view that the facts disclosed several violations of the Covenant, including: torture and detainment in unhealthy conditions contrary to Articles 7 and 10(l); imprisonment after a release order contrary to Article 9(l); failure to inform the prisoners of the charges against them contrary to Article 9(2); denial of a prompt and fair trial contrary to Articles 9(3) and 14; inadequate appellate remedies contrary to Article 9(4); imprisonment incommunicado contrary to Article 10(l); and denial of political rights contrary to Article 25. The Committee expressed the view that the government of Uruguay was obligated to "take immediate steps to ensure strict observance of the provisions of the Covenant and to provide effective remedies to the victims."

Relation to Regional Systems of Implementation

Any critical analysis of international systems for the protection of human rights must pose the question whether it is desirable or appropriate to have regional systems of protection in addition to the international system established by the United Nations. Are regional systems compatible with the universal system or are they likely to diminish its value and perhaps even undermine its effectiveness? In any event, how does the universal system relate and interact with regional systems?

As regards the compatibility of regional and universal systems, there is a good deal to be said on both sides of this question. On the one hand, it was possible in Europe to conclude a convention containing binding obligations and setting up new international machinery at a time when this was not possible in the worldwide framework; and though the UN covenants and the Optional Protocol are now in force, it is quite uncertain how many states will accept their optional provisions. It is likely that at least for a considerable period of time the European system will contain far more effective procedures than the universal system. Similar considerations would justify regional systems in' other parts of the world.

On the other hand, it can be argued that human rights appertain to human beings by virtue of their humanity and should be guaranteed to all human beings on a basis of equality, without distinction, wherever they may live. Discrimination on grounds of race, sex, religion, or nationality is forbidden both in the United Nations texts and in the regional conventions. Equally, there should be no distinction based on geography and differences between regions. The African and the Asian should have the same human rights as the European or the American.

The two points of view can be reconciled. Human rights are and should be the same for all persons, everywhere, at all times. In other words, the normative content of different international instruments should be, in principle, the same. There may, of course, be minor differences in formulation, due to differences in drafting techniques or in legal traditions, but the basic rights and fundamental freedoms should be the same for all. The yardstick is the Universal Declaration, which sets out, in the words of its Preamble "a common standard of achievement for all peoples and all nations." No regional system should be allowed to exist which is not consistent with the norms and principles set out in the Universal Declaration.

When we come to measures of implementation, however, the answer is different. While it is desirable that the most effective system possible should be established everywhere, it is a fact that this optimum system is not at present acceptable in all parts of the world. It is therefore reasonable to set up regional arrangements which differ from each other, provided that the rights to be protected are essentially the same as those established in the Universal Declaration. This was the approach adopted by the European Convention, in which the contracting parties expressed their determination "to take the first steps for the collective enforcement of certain of the rights stated in the Universal Declaration." Other regional systems are equally legitimate if they seek to enforce, by means of regional procedures which can be accepted by a group of states in a particular area, some or all of the rights proclaimed in the Universal Declaration.

The principle of regional settlement is quite consistent with the Charter of the United Nations. The Charter in Articles 33 and 52 recognizes the regional settlement of disputes and even requires members of a regional agency to "make every effort to achieve pacific settlement of local disputes . . . by such regional agencies before referring them to the Security Council "Moreover, the UN Covenant on Civil and Political Rights, in Article 44, recognizes that its provisions "shall not prevent the States Parties . . . from having recourse to other procedures for settling a dispute in accordance with general or special international agreements in force between them." Consequently, the existence of regional remedies is perfectly consistent with the Covenant. But the rights should be the same for all men and women everywhere.

Both the European Convention (and its First and Fourth Protocols) and the American Convention set out to protect the same rights and freedoms proclaimed in the Universal Declaration of 1948; both recognize this fact in their preambles, and many of the Articles in both instruments were inspired by the text of the Covenant on Civil and Political Rights or by its earlier drafts. At the same time, the system of international control in the two regional conventions is more developed and more effective than the UN system. The large majority of the parties to the European Convention have accepted the competence of the European Commission to receive individual complaints, as well as the jurisdiction of the European Court of Human Rights; the Committee of Ministers of the Council of Europe has authority to act on reports of the Commission and to supervise compliance with the judgments of the Court. The American Convention also established both a human rights commission and a human rights court and the Commission can automatically receive private complaints against any state party; if a judgment of the Court is not complied with, the Court may report the matter to the General Assembly of the Organization of American States.

The "coexistence" of the United Nations Covenant on Civil and Political Rights and regional human rights agreements is now a fact. In 1968, in response to an appeal from the Secretary-General of the UN, the Assembly of the Council of Europe called for ratification of the two Covenants and of the Optional Protocol "after having taken . . . the necessary decisions on the problems arising in connection with the coexistence of the European convention on Human Rights and the United Nations Covenants." It was clear that the member states of the Council of Europe wished to give favorable consideration to the ratification of the Covenants, which their representatives had taken a prominent part in drafting. At the same time, it was necessary for them to consider what problems, if any, would arise if they were to become parties to both instruments: were the same rights protected by both instruments and, if not, were the differences important; were the definitions the same and, if they were not, would this cause difficulties; would there be a conflict between the procedures of the United Nations and the Council of Europe; could the different procedures be used simultaneously or consecutively, and so on. It was decided to make a joint study of them in the framework of the Committee of Experts on Human Rights of the Council of Europe.

The experts submitted two separate reports: the first in 1968 on the coexistence of the two systems of control; 110 the second in 1970 on the differences in the enumeration and definition of the rights."' The conclusion of these studies was seen as an important step in permitting, or at least facilitating, ratification of the Covenants by member states of the Council of Europe.

The study made by the Committee of Experts on Human Rights led to two conclusions about the measures of implementation set out in these two treaties. As regards interstate complaints or "communications," member states of the Council of

Europe should normally use the procedures provided for in the European Convention for their disputes inter se, in accordance with the principle of regional settlement of disputes before having recourse to United Nations procedures. But they should agree to accept the United Nations procedures for cases which may be brought against them by non-European states.

As regards individual applications or "communications," the governing consideration should be to secure the most effective protection of individual rights. The individual applicant should be free to choose his forum and apply either to the European Commission or to the United Nations Committee, in accordance with his own judgment about where he has the best chance of success. Once he has put in an application either in Strasbourg or in New York, however, he should not be allowed, if he is unsuccessful in one forum, to make a second attempt in the other, unless he has made an honest mistake. It should not be possible to appeal-or to appear to appeal-from the European Commission to the United Nations Committee, or viçe versa. The European Convention in Article 27(lb) apparently excludes the possibility of submitting to the European Commission a case previously submitted without success to the United Nations Committee, but the Protocol, Article 5(2a), bars the Committee from considering a communication only while it is "being examined under another international procedure." The Committee of Ministers therefore recommended to member governments that when ratifying the Optional Protocol they should make a declaration or reservation to the effect that, while they accept the competence of the Human Rights Committee to consider communications from individuals, they interpret Article 5(2a) to mean that a communication is inadmissible if the same matter is being examined or has been examined under another international procedure of investigation or settlement. Contracting parties to the European Convention which have ratified the Covenant have for the most part made a declaration or reservation to this effect.

Article 5(2a) of the Optional Protocol imposes on the Human Rights Committee the obligation of ascertaining that the same matter is not being examined under another international procedure; in practical effect that means the European Commission of Human Rights or the Inter-American Commission on Human Rights. In order to discharge this responsibility, the Committee has made arrangements for the exchange of information with the two regional Commissions, and has expressed its appreciation of their "most helpful cooperation." 112 Furthermore, the Committee has decided that the international procedures referred to in Article 5(2a) are for examination of individual petitions, and that the procedures established by the Economic and Social Council under Resolution 1503 are not included, since they refer to "situations which appear to reveal a consistent pattern of gross violations of human rights" and such a "situation" is something different from individual communications. The new procedures established by UNESCO in April 1978 for handling communications from individuals relating to matters within the competence of that organization would seem to be within the compass of Article 5(2a), but the question has not been considered.

As regards the comparison of the rights and freedoms protected in the UN Covenant and the European Convention, the Committee of Experts of the Council of Europe concluded that there were fifteen provisions in the Covenant which involved more extensive obligations than those contained in the European Convention, but that in many of these cases the national law of member states was already in conformity with those obligations. The implication would seem to be that it was not necessary for the European states to hesitate unduly about accepting the obligations contained in the Covenant. There is, generally speaking, a greater similarity between definitions of the rights in the American Convention on Human Rights and those in the Covenant. This is not surprising, because the American Convention was concluded in 1969, when the text of the UN Covenant had been available for three years. It is significant that the member governments of the Organization of American States decided to continue with the drafting of their own regional convention even after the conclusion of the UN Covenants in December 1966.

It is perhaps premature to attempt to reach any firm conclusions about the relationship of the UN procedures to regional systems of implementation when the Human Rights Committee has been in existence only since 1976 and the American Convention on Human Rights in force only since 1978. Nevertheless, we can assert with some confidence that there is no incompatibility or objection in principle to the idea that universal and regional systems of implementation should coexist, provided that the conditions indicated are respected, and that measures of consultation and exchange of information between the Human Rights Committee and the Regional Commissions will occur on a continuing basis. A good start has evidently been made in establishing such arrangements. We may be reasonably confident that they will develop harmoniously in the future and thus facilitate the task-and contribute to the success of the work-of all the three organs concerned. Indeed, it is legitimate to hope that, with the passage of time, we may see the establishment of regional commissions on human rights in other parts of the world, in which case their relationship with the UN Committee could follow the pattern already established by the regional commissions in Europe and the Americas. All will have a common objective: in the words of the Universal Declaration, "to secure the universal and effective recognition and observance" of the rights proclaimed therein.

6

Enforcement of Fundamental Rights Under Indian Constitution

The United Nations Charter is the first international document having an objective of Promotion Of Human Rights and Fundamental Freedoms. In its early days, the UNO, its Economic and Social Council, and the Human Rights Commission. Worked on the notion that the International Bill of Right should have a declaration of general principles, having moral force and a separate Covenant having legally binding force on those states which ratified it, and the mode of their implementation. Thus came into existence the Declaration of Human Rights adopted by the General Assembly, December 10, 1948. The Declaration has influenced many states drafting their Constitutions having these rights as part of their Constitution, and therefore enforceable by municipal courts.

However, the Declaration does not have the force of law, though its moral influence is substantial. The Declaration is not even a multilateral treaty.

The international community finally decided to have two Covenants, one on Civil and Political Rights and the other on Economic, Social and Cultural Rights. Two Covenants were necessary as it as felt that civil and political rights could be secured immediately, whereas enforcement of economic, social and cultural rights could only be achieved progressively, depending upon the available resources of each state. The Covenant on Economic, Social and Cultural Rights came into effect on January, 3, 1976 as by then 35 States have ratified it. The Covenant on Civil and Political Rights came into force on March 23, 1976 when the like number of States have ratified it.

The first optional protocol also came into force on March 23. 1976. It needed ratification by 10 states for coming into force.

A State which has ratified the Covenant on Civil and Political Rights has obligation to secure these rights, to its people. Article 2 of the Covenant runs:

> Each State Party to the Present Covenant undertakes to respect and to ensure to all individuals within its territory and subject to its jurisdiction the right recognized in the present Covenant, without distinction of any kind, such as race, colour, sex, on, Political or other opinion, national or social birth of other status.
>
> Where not already provided for by existing legislative or other measures, each State Party to the present Covenant undertakes to take the necessary steps, in accordance with its constitutional Processes and with the provisions of the Present Covenant, to adopt such legislative or other measures as may be necessary to give effect to the rights recognized in the present Covenant. Each State Party to the present Covenant undertakes:
>
> (a) To ensure that any Person whose rights or freedoms as herein recognized are violated

> shall hive an effective remedy, notwithstanding that the violation has been committed by Persons acting in an official capacity;
>
> (b) To ensure that any Person claiming such a remedy shall have his right thereto determined by competent judicial, administrative or legislative, authorities, or by any other competent authority provided for by the legal system of the State, and to develop the possibilities of judicial remedy;
>
> (c) To ensure that the competent authorities shall enforce such remedies when granted.

On the other hand, a State ratifying the Covenant on Economic, Social and Cultural Rights merely acknowledges its responsibility to promote better living conditions to its people and other rights under the Covenant. Article 2 of the Covenant runs:

> Each State Party to the present Covenant undertakes to take steps, individually and through international assistance and cooperation, especially economic and technical to the maximum of its available resources, with a view to achieving progressively the full realization of the rights recognized in the present Covenant by all appropriate means, including particularly the adoption of legislative measures. The State Parties to the present Covenant undertake to guarantee that the rights enunciated in the present Covenant will be exercised without discrimination of any kind as to race, colour, sex, language religion political or other opinion national or social origin, poverty, birth or other status.
>
> Developing countries, with due regard to human rights and their national economy may determine to what extent they would guarantee the economic rights recognized in the present Covenant' to non-nationals.

The instrumentalities for the implementation of the Covenant provisions are:

(a) Human Right Committee,

(b) Periodic Reports, and

(c) Conciliation Commission.

The purpose of the Covenant is to persuade the States so far as possible to enact suitable legislation so that human rights could be enforced by the municipal courts of each state-party to the Covenants. Mostly human rights are violated by the States. The objective of Covenants is to protect the individual from such excesses.

Implementation Provisions under the Covenants

For the implementation of the provisions of the Covenant on Civil and Political. Rights, the main instrumentality envisaged is the Human Rights Committed. The procedure for constituting Human Rights Committee is that each State Party nominates its two nationals who are persons of high moral character and recognized competence is the field of human rights. Consideration should also be given to the usefulness of his having some legal comptence. Out of the persons so nominated by the State parties, eighteen members are elected by secret ballot. The human rights committee consists of eighteen members.

A member of the Committee is eligible for re-nomination.

At least four months before the date of each election of the Committee (other than an election to fill a vacancy) the Secretary-General of the United Nations is required to address a written invitation to the Staff-parties to the Covenant to submit their nominations for membership of the Committee within three months. Thereafter a list in alphabetical order of all the persons so nominated with an indication of the State parties, to which he belongs is prepared and submitted to the State parties not later than one month before the date of election. The Secretary-General is required to convene a meeting of the State parties to elect members to the Human Rights Committee. At such meeting two-thirds of die state parties will constitute a quorum. Those persons who obtain largest number of votes and an absolute majority of the votes of the representatives of the State-parties present and voting will be declared elected. The Committee should not include more than one national of the saw State. At the same time consideration has to be given to equitable geographical distribution of membership and to the representation of the different forms of civilization and of the principle legal systems. The initial election should take place not later than six months after the date of entry into force of the Covenant. [Article 30(l)].

The term of the Human Rights Committee is four years. The members are eligible for re-election provided they are nominated by State-Parties to the Covenant. However, the term of half of the members of the first Committee would expire at the end of two years after the first election. The refiring nine members will be chosen by lot by the Chairman of the Committee.

The elections for the new Committee will be held in the same manner as of the first Committee.

In the event of a seat failing vacant on account of the death or resignation of a member of the Committee or on account of his removal by the unanimous opinion of other members, the Chairman is required to inform the Secretary-General of the United Nations. Thereupon the Secretary-General will declare the seat vacant and the process for the election to the vacant seat will be started provided the term of the member to be replaced does not expire within six months for the declaration of the vacancy. The member of the Committee so elected will hold office only for the remainder of the term of the member who had vacated the office.

The members of the Committee will be entitled to such remuneration from the United Nations on such terms and conditions as the General-Assembly may decide.

The meeting of the Committee are to be held at the headquarters of the United Nations or its office at Geneva.

Necessary staff and facilities for the effective functioning of the Committee will be provided by the Secretary-General of the United Nations. The Committee elects its own officers for a term of two years. They may be re-elected.

Twelve members constitute the quorum of the Committee arid' all decisions of the Committee, are taken by a majority vote of the members present.

The Committee will formulate its own rules of procedure.

Before entering upon his office, each member will make a solemn declaration in open Committee that he will perform his functions impartially and conscientiously.

The members of the Committee are entitled to all facilities privileges and immunities of experts on mission for the United Nations as laid down in the Convention on Privileges and Immunities of the United Nations.

Reporting Procedure

Under the Covenant the State parties have an obligation to submit reports on the measures they have adopted to give effect to the human rights envisaged under the Covenant and the progress made in the enjoyment of these rights. Such reports are to be made within one year of the entry into force of the present Covenant and thereafter whenever the Human Rights Committee requests a state-party to submit its report. All reports are to be initially submitted to the Secretary-General of the United Nations who is required to transmit them to the Committee for consideration. Such Reports should indicate the facts and difficulties, if any, relating to implementation of the Covenant provision.

The Human Rights Committee considers such reports and transmits its comments and observations to the State-parties concerned. The Committee may also transmit to the Economic and Social Council these comments along with copies of the report it has received. The State-parties to the Covenant may also submit to the Committee observations or any comments of the committee.

The Secretary-General of the United Nations may, after consultation with the Committee, transmit to their specialized agencies concerned copies of such part of the report as may fall within their field of competence.

Inter-States Complaints

A state-party may at any time declare that it recognizes the competence of the Committee to receive and consider Communication to the effect that a state-party is not fulfilling its obligations under the Covenant. However, such communications can be received and considered only if submitted by a State-party which had made a declaration recognizing the competence of the Committee to do so. The procedure for considering an inter-state complaint is:

(a) If a State-party to the present Covenant considers that another State-party is not giving effect to the provisions of the present Covenant, it may, by written communication, bring the matter to the attention of that State-party. Within receiving state shall afford the State which sent the communication, the receiving state shall afford the State which sent the communication an explanation or any other statement in writing clarifying the matter, which should include, to the extent possible and pertinent, reference to domestic procedure and remedies taken, pending or available in the matter.

(b) If the matter is not adjusted to the satisfaction of both State-parties concerned within six months after the receipt by the receiving State of the initial communication, either shall have the right to refer tile matter to the Committee, by notice given to the Committee and to the other state.

(c) The Committee shall deal with a matter referred to it only after it has ascertained that all available domestic remedies have been invoked and exhausted in the matter, in conformity with the generally recognized principles of international law. This will not be so where the application for the remedies is unreasonably prolonged.

(d) The Committee shall hold closed door meetings when examining communications under this article.

(e) Subject to the provisions of sub-paragraph (c), the Committee shall make available its good offices to the State-parties concerned with a view to a friendly solution of the matter on the basis of respect for human rights and fundamental freedoms as recognized in the present Covenant.

(f) In any matter referred to it, the Committee may call upon the State parties concerned, referred to in sub-paragraph (b), to supply any relevant information.

(g) The State parties concerned, referred to in sub-paragraph (b), shall have the right to be represented when the matter is being considered in the Committee and to make submissions orally and/or in writing.

(h) The Committee shall, within twelve months after the date of receipt of notice under sub-paragraph (b), submit a report,

(i) If a solution within 'the terms of sub-paragraph (e) is reached, the Committee shall confine its report to a brief statement of the facts and of the solution reached,

(ii) If a solution within the terms of sub-paragraph (e) is not reached, the Committee shall confine its report to a brief statement of the facts. The written submissions and record of the oral submissions made by the State Parties concerned shall be attached to the report.

In every matter, the report shall be communicated to the State-parties concerned.

A declaration made by a state-party may be withdrawn at any time by notification to the Secretary-General of the United Nations. But such a withdrawal will not prejudice the consideration of any matter which is subject of a communication already transmitted.

At the first instance, the Committee established direct contact with the parties concerned and tries to get resolved matters by mutual dialogue. The communications of the complaining state should be brought to the notice of the party against whom complaint has been made. The latter should send a reply within three months. The reply should contain an explanation of the complaint-matters, the domestic remedies already availed of, or still available. Then both the parties may adjust the dispute to their mutual satisfaction within three months. If the dispute remains unsettled even then, then either party may refer the matter to the Human Rights Committee. The Human Rights Committee would look into the matter only when all domestic remedies have been exhausted. The Committee would make available its good offices for amicable settlement of dispute to both the parties. The Committee would seek relevant information on the dispute from both parties. The parties may submit the information orally or in writing within a period of six months. The parties have the right to he heard. Thereafter the Committee would prepare its report and send it to both the parties. The report should include a brief summary of facts its recommendations and comments of the Committee.

If the dispute remains unresolved even then, the Covenant provides that the Committee may constitute an ad hoc Conciliation Commission with the consent of both the parties for the amicable solution of the dispute. The ad hoc Conciliation Commission will have five members. The selection of these members is to be made by the parties with their mutual consent failing which the Human Rights Committee will elect by secret ballot within two-thirds majority vote of the Committee five persons from among its members. The members should not be nationals of the parties at dispute, and they should also not be members of the States which are not parties to the Covenant or of a state-party which has not made a declaration under Article 41. These members will act in their individual capacity. The Commission will elect its own Chairman and frame its own rules of procedure. The meetings of the Commission should he held either at the headquarters of the United Nations or United Nation's office at Geneva. However, meetings may be held it some other convenient place as the Commission may determine in Consultation with Secretary-General of the United Nations and the Stale-parties concerned. The

Commission has to be provided with the information collected by the Human Rights Committee. The Commission may also call upon the parties to supply any other relevant information.

After fully considering the matter but not later than twelve months after having being seized of the matter, ad hoc human rights commission is required to submit to the Chairman of the Committee a report for communication to the concerned state-parties. In the event the Commission is riot able to complete its deliberations within 12 months, it would confine its report to a brief statement on the status of its consideration of the matter. If a solution is reached, the Commission's report would confine itself to a brief statement of facts and of the solution reached. If solution is not reached, then the Commission would embody its findings on all' questions of fact relevant to the issue between the State-parties to the dispute, and its view on the possibility of an amicable solution of the matter. The Report of the Commission should also 'contain the written submissions and a record of oral submissions made by the State-parties to the dispute. Thereafter within three months of the receipt of the Reports the State parties should inform , the Chairman of the Human Rights Committee whether or not they accept the contents of the Report of the. Commission.

The State parties to the dispute would share equally all the expenses of the Commission.

The Human Rights Committee should submit its annual report to the General Assembly through the Economic and Social Council.

Optional Protocol to the International Covenant on Civil and Political Rights

Under the Covenant on Civil and Political Rights it is only the State who have locus stand to file complaint or communication as the complaints are designated. The individual has been conferred such a right under the first Optional Protocol to the Covenant on Civil and Political Rights. An individual may now lodge a complaint against a state violating human rights under the Covenant.

However, such a complaint can be lodged only against a State party to the Covenant. Article 2 of the Protocol runs:

A State Party to the Covenant that becomes a party to the present protocol recognizes the competence of the Committee to receive and consider communications from individuals subject to its jurisdiction who claim to be victims of a violation by that State Party of any of the rights set forth in the Covenant. No Communication shall be received by the Committee if it concerns a State Party to the Covenant which is not a party to the present protocol.

An individual who claims (hat any of his rights enunciated in the Covenant has been violated and he had exhausted all available domestic remedies may submit a written communication to the Human Rights Committee for consideration. No anonymous communication will be entertained. Similarly, a communication which the Committee considers to be abuse of the right of submission of such communication will not be entertained. The same would be fate of a complaint which is incompatible with the provisions of the Covenant.

Once a communication against a state is entertained the Human Rights Committee would bring it to the attention of the alleged delinquent Stale. Such a Stale would submit to the Committee its explanation clarifying the matter and the remedy, it any within six months.

Thereafter the Human Rights Committee would proceed to consider communications in the light of all written information made available to it by both the parties. The Committee will consider such communication only after ascertaining that the same matter has not been examined under another procedure of international investigation or settlement and after ascertaining that the individual complaint had exhausted all domestic remedies available to him.

The Committee will consider the entire matter in closed door meetings and thereafter will communicate its views to the individual complainant and the State concerned.

In its annual Report, the Human Rights Committee will include a report of its activities under the protocol.

If should be noticed that the Protocol all along uses the expression communication- and not complaint. Though virtually Communication is nothing but a complaint. It should also be noticed that the Committee does not render "decision." Even the word "recommendation" has not been used. The expression used is "views."

One may say what is the value of mere "views" when Committee is not competent even to make its recommendation much less to render a decision. Its views are not binding on the state concerned. The Human Rights Committee includes these -views- in its annual report. This means that the activities of the alleged delinquent state will come before the international community. It will certainly gather public opinion. The delinquency of the State will come under the gaze of everybody. All states will know that the delinquent state is not adhering to the provision of the Covenant.

In our submission, the greatest relevance of this provision is that an individual can expose the delinquent state before the international community and people. In our submission even if no direct benefit accrues to the individual addressing a communication to the human rights committee about abuse of human rights, -the greatest gain is that individual has got locus standi to come before international forum.

Implementation of the Human Rights under the Covenant on Economic, Social and Cultural Rights

We have seen earlier that there is the marked difference in the process of implementation of human rights under the two Covenants. While Article 2 of the Covenant on Civil and Political Rights lays down that "each state part to the Covenant 'undertakes to respect and ensure to all individuals human rights under the Covenant, the Covenant on the Economic, Social and Cultural Rights merely lays down that each state party to the Covenant undertakes to take steps progressingly to achieve the implementation of human rights under the Covenant.

Reports

The mode of implementation of the Covenant provisions is, what may be called, "Reporting Method." This has been indicated in Articles 16 to 23. The Parties to the Covenant, the Human Rights Commission and the Economic and Social Council have to submit reports.

Firstly, the State-parties to the present covenant have to submit reports on the measures adopted and progress made by them 'in achieving the observance of the Human Rights to the Secretary-General of the United Nations. The Secretary-General will then transmit these reports to the Economic and Social Council for consideration in accordance with the provision of the Covenant. Copies of the report or pail thereof will also be send to the specialized agencies by the Secretary-General so far as relating to any matter falling within their area of responsibility.

The State-parties are to submit their reports in stages, in accordance with a programme to be established by the Economic and Social Council. Such programmes are to be chalked out by the Council within one year of the coming into force of the Covenant. The Reports of the States should indicate factors and difficulties, affecting the degree of fulfilment of obligations under the Covenant.

Article 18 stipulates that the Economic and Social Council may make arrangements with the specialized agencies in respect of their reporting to it on the progress made in achieving the observance of the provisions of the present Covenant falling within the scope of their activities. These reports may include particulars of decisions and recommendations on such implementation adopted by their competent organs.

The Economic and Social Council may also transmit to the Human Rights Commission for study and general recommendation or for information the report concerning human rights submitted by the State-parties to the Covenant.

On the recommendations of the Commission on Human Rights the States and the specialized agencies may submit their comments to the Economic and Social Council.

The Economic and Social Council is empowered to submit its report to the General Assembly with recommendations of general nature and a summary of the information received from states and specialized agencies on the measures taken and the progress made in achieving general observance of the human rights recognized by the Covenant. The Council may also bring to the attention of other organs of the United Nations, their subsidiary organs and specialized agencies concerned for furnishing technical assistance on any matter arising out of the reports; made by the

State and others which may assist such bodies in deciding on the advisability of international measures likely to contribute to tile effective implementation of the Covenant provisions.

One may tend to be sceptical on the enforcement of human rights by the reporting method. However, one should not forget that implementation of economic, social and cultural rights very much depends upon the economic progress of a state. The reporting method tends to Promote the observance of the obligations undertaken under the Covenant at least in some measures. It certainly does strengthen international co-operation among the states. No one will deny the limitation of the reporting method. The method itself suffers from infirmities. There is lack of co-ordination among the States and various organs and agencies of the United Nations. But the Covenant does recognize and tend to promote international responsibility for providing assistance in the promotion of human rights.

Remedial Fundamental Right Under the Indian Constitution

One

The enumerated and guaranteed fundamental rights would be no more than paper tigers, if the right to enforce fundamental rights is not made a fundamental right itself. It is the remedial fundamental fight which gives teeth to all fundamental rights. Article 32, which enshrines the remedial fundamental right has been described as "the cornerstone of the democratic edifice," as "the protector and guarantor of fundamental rights," or as the "qui vive." It has been said repeatedly that it is the duty of the courts to guard the remedial fundamental fight and to protect it 'zealously and vigilantly.' Article 32 guarantees the right to move the Supreme Court by appropriate proceedings for the enforcement of the fundamental rights guaranteed by Part III of the Constitution. Clauses (1) and (2) of Article 32 run as under:

(1) The right to move the Supreme Court by appropriate proceedings for the enforcement of the rights conferred by this part is guaranteed.

(2) The Supreme Court shall have power to issue directions or orders or writs including writs in the nature of habeas corpus mandamus, prohibition, and certiorari which may be appropriate for the enforcement of any of the rights conferred by this part.

Article 32(4) lays down that this fundamental right cannot he suspended except as otherwise provided by the Constitution, Articles 358 and 359 provide for the suspension of certain fundamental rights during the period of promulgation of Emergency. Under Article 226 also the fundamental rights can be enforced by moving the High Courts. Other rights can also he enforced under Article 21.6.

We would proceed to discuss (i) enforcement of the fundamental rights in part two, (ii) various writs in part three, and (iii) suspension of the fundamental rights during a proclamation of Emergency in part four of this part of the Chapter.

Two

ENFORCEMENT OF FUNDAMENTAL RIGHTS: ARTICLE 32 CLAUSES (1) AND (2)

Who can Invoke the Jurisdiction?

The general rule is that any person natural or artificial whose fundamental right is violated can invoke the jurisdiction of tile Supreme Court under Article 32. The infraction of the fundamental right of the petitioner is the condition precedent for moving tile court under

Article 32. A person who is not interested in the subject-matter of the order has no locus standi to invoke the Jurisdiction of the court. However, actual infringement of the fundamental right need not be proved a petition would be even if there is an imminent danger of the infraction of a fundamental right. A shareholder has no right to enforce the fundamental right of the company since the company possesses a distinct personality than that of a shareholders, unless the infraction of the right of a company also involves the infringement of the right of the petitione. In Maganbhai Ishwarbhai Patel v. Union of India, the petitioner challenged the Indo-Pakistan Agreement under which a part of Rann of Kutch was agreed to be transferred to Pakistan. He challenged the agreement on the ground that once that area was ceded to Pakistan his fundamental right of going or residing there would be violated in future. 'The Supreme Court observed that a petition would not lie merely on the basis of mere apprehension of infringement of a fundamental right but the Supreme Court nonetheless agreed to bear this petition as the court found that the right of the petitioners who claimed infraction of fundamental right had some temporary and almost ephemeral connection.

It is in the case of a writ of habeas corpus that a petition can be filed by a person whose fundamental right is infringed on by any other person on behalf of an imprisoned or defained person.

Public Interest Litigation

The rule of locus standi has undergone a fundamental change. In public interest litigation any person or organization may move the Supreme Court if a breach of fundamental right of any person or group of persons is alleged. In the words of Bhagwati, J:

> The narrow confines within which the rule of standing was imprisoned for long yews as a result of inheritance from the Anglo-Saxon system of jurisprudence have been broken and a new dimension has been given to the doctrine of locus standi which has revolutionized the whole concept of access to justice in a way not known before it.

The learned judge added that having regard to the peculiar socio-economic conditions prevailing in India where there is considerable poverty, illiteracy and ignorance, obstructing and impeding accessibility to the judicial process, it would result in closing the doors of justice to the poor and deprived sections of the community if the traditional rule of standing evolved by Anglo-Saxon jurisprudence that only a person wronged can sue for judicial redress were to be blindly adhered to and followed and it is therefore, necessary to evolve a new strategy by relaxing this traditional rule of standing in order that justice may become easily accessible to the lowly and the lost. Thus, the present position is that wherever a person or class of persons to whom legal injury is caused or legal wrong is done who by reason of poverty disability or socially and economically disadvantageous position, is not able to approach the court for judicial redress any member of the public or any public organization may move the court on his or their behalf for judicial redress. But it is necessary that the individual or organization who moves the court for judicial redress is acting bona fide with a view to vindicating the cause of justice and not for personal gain or private profit or out of political motivation or some other oblique consideration.

It may now be taken to be established that wherever a person or class of persons to whom legal injury is caused or legal wrong is done mid who, by reason of poverty, disability or socially or economically disadvantageous position is not able to approach the court for judicial redress, any member of the public any public organization may move the court on his or their behalf for judicial redress. In such cases the court may he moved by any member of the public by addressing a letter drawing the attention of the court to such legal injury or legal wrong, and the court would set aside all technical rules of procedure and entertain the letter as a writ petition on the judicial side and take action upon it. In S.P. Gupta v. Union of India, Bhagwati, J., observed:

> The court has to innovate new methods and devise new strategies for the purpose of Providing access to justice to large masses of People who are denied their basic human rights and to whom freedom and liberty have no meaning.

The law seems to have crystallized in this: whenever there is a Public injury caused by an act or Omission- of the State or public authority which is Contrary to they Constitution or the law, any member of the public acting bona fide and having sufficient interest can maintain an action for redressal of such public wrong or public injury. The strict rule of standing which insists that Only a person who has suffered a specific legal injury, can maintain an action for judicial redress is relaxed and replaced by a broad rule which gives standing 10 any member of the public who is not a more busybody or a meddlesome interloper but one who has sufficient interest in the proceedings. In the absence of a machinery to effectively represent the public interest generally in courts, it is necessary to liberalise the rule of standing in order to provide judicial redress for public injury arising from breach of public duty or from other violation of the constitution or the law by allowing public spirited persons and organizations to move the court and act for a general or group interest, even though, the)-may not he directly injured in their own rights. It is only by liberalising the rule of locus standi that it is possible to effectively Police the corridors of power and prevent violations of law. The oppression might be financial commercial corporate or governmental.

Bangalore Medical Trust v. B.S. Muddappa, provides an apt illustration. The question was: whether a private nursing home with modem facilities and sophisticated instruments is more conducive to the public interest than a park as it was stressed that even if the conversion of the site suffered from any infirmity Procedural or substantive the High Court should have refrained from exercising its extraordinary jurisdiction and that also in favour of those residents many of whom did not have their houses around the park and thus could not be placed in the category of persons aggrieved. It was also emphasised that the hospital with research centre and even free service being more important from social angle the inhabitants of the locality could not be said to stiffer any injury much less substantial injury. The Supreme Court said that a private nursing home could neither be considered to be an amenity nor it could be considered improve over necessity like a public park. The exercise of power in conversion of public park into Private nursing home therefore was contrary to the purpose for which it is conferred under the statute.

Thus the public interest litigation is essential for maintaining the rule of law furthering the cause of justice and for acceleration the pace of realization of the constitutional objectives.

Of course what is sufficient public interest to give standing to a member of the public would have to be determined by the court in each individual case. It has of necessity, to be to the discretion of the court.

The limitation of the doctrine of public interest litigation have been spelled out in Judges Transfer case. These are:

(a) If the individual or organization moving the court for judicial redress is not acting bona fide with a view to vindicating the cause or justice but for personal gain of private profit or out of political motivation or some other oblique consideration the court should not allow itself to be activised at the instance of such person and must reject his application. In the words of Tulzapurkar, J. Those who move the Court should not be wayfarers interlopers officious interveners or busy-bodies without any interest or concern of their own in the subject-Matter.

(b) Ordinarily, this jurisdiction may be confined to cases where legal wrong or legal injury is caused to a determinate class or group of persons or the constitutional or legal rights of such determinate class or group of persons is violated and the court should not as far as possible, entertain cases of individual wrong or injury at the instance of a third party, where there is an effective legal aid organization which can take care of such cases.

(c) The distinction between locus standi and justiciability should be kept in view and thus it is not every default on the part of the state or public authority that is justiciable. Mr. Justice Bhagwati cautions that the court must take care that it does not over-step the limits of its judicial function and trespass into the areas which are reserved to the executive and the legislature by the Constitution. Mr. Justice Venkataramiah cited two instances in which court will not interfere, viz., questions of international relations, and national security.

(d) Where there is a public injury by the act or omission of the state or a public authority but such act or omission also causes a specific injury to an individual or to a specific class or group or individuals, and if the latter, who are primarily injured, do not maintain any' action, the member of the public who complains of a secondary public injury cannot maintain the action, since granting of relief in such cases could mean foisting a relief on the person or specific class or group of persons primarily injured which they do not want.

Breach of Fundamental Rights

The question whether public interest litigation can be initiated in the Supreme Court where no breach of fundamental right is involved came before the court in People's Union for Democratic Rights v. Union of India. The Supreme Court answered the question in the negative. But, then what is breach of fundamental rights has to be looked at in a broader perspective. In the construction of Asiad Games complex, the Union of India, Delhi Development Authority, and Delhi Administration were involved. These authorities had given construction work to several contractors who had hired contract labour. The contract labour was hired through agents known as jamadras. Through these Jamadars, workers were brought to construction site from different parts of the country. The Union for Democratic Rights alleged:

(a) That workers were not paid the minimum wage (the minimum wage was fixed at Rs. 9.25 per day and out of it the Jamadars deducted Re. 1 as their commission), which was clearly a violation of the Minimum Wage Act.

(b) That in the payment of wages discrimination was

made between man and woman, and women workers were paid only Rs. 7.00 per day and the balance of Rs. 2.25 was retained by the *Jamadars, this was clearly a violation of Equal Remuneration Act,* 1976.

(c) That children below the age of 14 were employed which was a violation of the Employment of Children Act, 1938 as well as Article 24 of the Constitution.

(d) That amenities and facilities as laid down in the Contract Labour (Regulation and Abolition) Act, 1970 were not provided and thus it was a clear violation of the several provisions of the Act.

(e) That amenities and facilities as laid down in the Inter-State Migrant Workers (Regulation of Employment and Conditions of Service) Act, 1979 were not provided which was a clear violation of the provision of the Act.

The Union of India and other authorities in their reply denied the violation of any of the aforesaid provisions by the contractors. However, the Union of India did admit that the Jamadars were probably making some deducations out of the wages paid to the workers. As to the employment of children below the age of 14. It was asserted by the Union of India and other authorities that the Children Act. 1938 was not applicable to construction workers. The court observed that it was unfortunate that the Union and the State Governments have not made applicable the Act to the construction works clearly a hazardous occupation, despite the fact that India is a party to Covenant No. 59, adopted by the ILO which prohibits child labour. However. Article 24 of the Constitution lays down that no child below the age of 14 shall be employed to work in any factory or mine or engaged in any other hazardous employment. This was clearly a violation of Article 24. As to the violation of the provisions of the Inter-State Migrant Workmen (Regulation of Employment and Conditions of Service) Act. 1979 was concerned the Union of India averred that since the Rules under the Act were not finalized the Act was not enforceable in Delhi. The court observed that it was unfortunate that rules have not been finalized but nonetheless, those provisions of the Act whose enforcement did not require framing of the Rules were certainly enforceable. Bhagwati. J., observed:

> So far as the rights and benefits conferred upon migrant workmen under the provision of sections 13 to 16 of the Act are concerned the responsibility for ensuring such rights and benefits vests not only on the contractors but also on the Union of India, the Delhi Administration, and DDA who is the Principal employer in relation to the construction work entrusted by it to the contractors.

The court observed that allegation relating to violation of the provision of the Equal Remuneration Act, 1946 is in effect and substance a complaint of breach of the principle of equality before the law enshrined in Article 14. Similarly, allegation regarding non observance of the provisions of the Contract Labour (Regulation and Abolition) Act, 1970 and the Inter-State Migrant Workers (Regulation and Employment and Conditions of Service) Act, 1979 was in effect and substance a complaint relating to violation of Article 21. It is now the established view that Article 21's guarantee of the right to life is not confined to physical existence but also included within its scope and ambit the right to live with basic human dignity and the state could not deprive any one of this right because no procedure by which such deprivation might be effected could ever be regarded as reasonable fair and just. Since these statutes are nothing but the recognition of this aspect of the fundamental right to life any violation of any of the provisions of the Acts is in effect a violation of this fundamental right.

Relating to breach of Minimum Wage Act, 1948, the court observed that the statute was nothing but an effort to implement the fundamental right relating to "prohibition of traffic in human beings and forced labour." The words used in, Article 32(l) are: "begar and other similar form of forced labour." Bhagwati, J., very cogently argued that payment of wages less than the minimum wages is nothing but another form of forced labour. The learned judge observed:

> It may therefore be legitimately presumed that when a person provides labour or service to another against receipt of remuneration which is less than the minimum wage, he is acting under some force or some compulsion which deprives him to work, though he is paid less than what he is entitled to receive.

Thus it would appear that a public interest petition will lie in the Supreme Court wherever there is a breach of any social legislation, since social legislations are passed to ensure fundamental rights for the weaker sections of society the tight which are usually denied to them. It is submitted that a writ petition will also lie whenever there a breach of any law which is passed in pursuance to any Directive Principle of State Policy since the Directive Principles are as much fundamental part of the Constitution as are the fundamental rights.

Over-burdening of the Court

The over-burdening of the already over-burdened courts by the public interest litigation is a spacious argument and should not deserve attention. This argument has been put forth repeatedly as if this is only cause for mounting arrears in the Supreme Court. This is far from being true. The public interest litigation in the Supreme Court is only a fraction of total number of cases filed in the Supreme Court. It is not even one per cent of the total number of cases filed in the Supreme Court. Further, should the doors of the highest court be closed to the poor because this adds up to the arrears of pending cases? Are the door of the court open only to those who can afford to file regular petitions? When the rights of the rich to exploit the poor is upheld by the Supreme Court it is praised, applauded and acclaimed for Its boldness and courage and its independence and fearlessness, but in the words of Bhagawati. J.:

> If the fundamental right of the poor and helpless victims of injustice is sought to be enforced by public interest litigation the so-called champions of human rights frown upon it as waste of time of the highest court of the land, which, according to them, should not engage itself in such small and trifling matters.

The Province of PIL: Some Illustrative Cases

The public interest litigation's province has become very wide. By virtue of Article 32, the Supreme Court has been able to widen the horizons and intervene whenever injustice is caused or being caused by state action or by lack of it and has tried to help the poor, hapless and helpless people who have no means to approach the Supreme Court or who do not know whom to approach. Thus, whether it is blinding of under-trial prisoners or flesh-trade or languishing children in jails or poor homes pitiable situation in so-called women's home which have become virtual brothers, protection of pavement and slumdwellers, payment of minimum wages or equal pay for equal work freeing of bonded labour protection of environment and ecology and the like have found a sympathetic judicial forum in the

Supreme Court, and the Supreme Court has not hesitated in taking appropriate action. Here we would take two illustrative cases.

Protection of Environment

Rural Litigation and Entitlement Kendra v. State of U.P., led to the closure of a certain lime stone quarries on the ground that these quarries were a great hazard and were affecting the ecology of the area adversely. H.C. Mehta v. UOI, resulted in the closure of tannaries which were polluting Ganga.

Mukti Sangarsh Movement v. State of Mah., sought to prevent reckless exploitation of river running through some parts of Maharashtra which, was adversely affecting its bed due to reckless quarrying of its sand, while F.K. Hussain v. Union of India, sought to prevent lowering of underground water level on account of its reckless withdrawal by electric pumps.

Flesh Trade and Child Abuse

It is a common knowledge allover the world that many blooming teen-aged girls are being sold in flesh trade, market. The vice of child, too, is well known. The irony is that the Prevention of Immoral Traffic Act, 1988 has been used to arrest the prostitutes but not pimps, landlords, and visitors to brothels. Sheela Barse's investigation revealed that from 1980 to 1984 not one pimp or landlord was arrested under the Act though 1,351 prostitutes were.

Vishal Jeet v. Union of India, brought to the notice of the Supreme Court the miseries of women and children being exploited for sex which is becoming an organized industry. The devadasi and jogin tradition is utilized to give legitimacy to the sex industry. It has been congently argued that Article 23 and clauses (e) and (g) of Article 39 mandate on the Indian State to prevent child-abuse and traffic in human beings—use of women and children for immoral purposes is nothing but traffic in human beings. The Supreme Court issued the following directions to all State Governments and Union Territories: (i) law enforcing authorities to take speedy action under the law in eradicating child prostitution, (ii) to set up a separate advisory committee consisting of secretary, social welfare department secretary of law department, sociologists, criminologists, members of women's organisations, members of the Indian Council of Child Welfare and members of social organisations. This committee would suggest remedies for the eradication of child prostitution and devadasi and jogin tradition: (iii) to take steps in providing adequate rehabilitative homes manned by well-qualified and trained social workers, psychiatrists and doctors. Besides the union government was directed to set up committees to evolve welfare programmes to he implemented on the national level for the care, protection and rehabilitation of young, fallen victims and make suggestions for the amendment of the existing law.

Judicial Predicament and Public Interest Activism

Today, the province of public interest litigation has widened so much that every injury, every grievance is sought to he brought under it, so much so that executive is finding it difficult to cope with it and finding ways to evade directions of the courts. Judiciary too is trying to restrain its activism. It is declining to issue directions in policy matters. Thus judiciary is in a predicament: how far it could go and where it should not. This has been so well expressed by Prof. Parmanand Singh that we cannot resist the temptation of quoting him extensively. He says:

> Public Interest Litigation (PIL) has today become a byword judicial involvement in social political and economic affair the Indian society and state. Through legal activism, the judges

> are seeking to take a leading part in prescribing the goals of a society and new patterns of behaviours so that critical social are remedied, the inadequacies in the body politics ire recti and the hopes and aspirations of the masses are satisfied. Over years PIL activism is fast moving into new arenas, arousing heightened expectations from the judges that they are available to provide relief from all kinds of miseries, oppressions misfortunes. Artocities on the scheduled castes, criminalisation politics, corruption in public life, custodial violence, for prostitution and child-abuse, environmental pollution and a horde of other issues are attracting remedial attention of the courts. The judges are asked not only to vindicate the governmental commitment to the welfare of the poor and the repressed but also to maintain communal harmony, social control and social peace, preserve rule of law and prevent the decline in public morality. In addition to this, everyday we are witnessing that anything and everything can be a subject matter of PIL. Thus, the right to work, shelter, low cost housing, pure drinking water, minimum income, food, pollution free environment and a horde of other basic human needs are claimed as guaranteed legal rights.

At the game time it is painfully apparent that the political economy emerging in India ever since Independence has only resulted in the formation of new social ' classes of land owning prosperous farmers, traders, money-lenders, wealthy politicians, bureaucrats and other dominant classes who are controlling the social and economic institutions and cultural networks and are promoting the capitalists path of development. The contemporary social economy is encouraging the barbarity of "primitive accumulation" of early capitalism, by legal proliferation of contract mafias, education mafias, religious mafias and other dominant groups who are powerful enough to manipulate political power for accumulation of economic power. In other words the structure of political economy has provided enormous resources as well as legal and normative value system favourable to these new social classes. The logic of hectic-profit chase by the emerging new prosperous economic classes has accelerated the process of pauperisation, loss of purchasing power, and mass unemployment.

Territorial Jurisdiction

Under Article 32 the Supreme Court has very wide jurisdiction. Any order, direction or writ issued by the Supreme Court under Article 32 can be issued not merely anywhere in India but also beyond the territorial limits of India to all those authorities which are functioning inside or outside India under the control of the Union Government. Article 142 lays down that the decree and orders of the Supreme Court are enforceable throughout the territory of India. But, it is submitted, this limitation does not apply to orders, directions and writs issued under Article 32: if an authority abroad is under the control of the Government of India, an order, etc., can be enforced by passing suitable orders against the Government of India.

Against Whom a Writ, etc., Lies

An order, direction or writ, issued under Article 32 lines against the Government of India or State Government or against any authority under the power or control of the Government of India or any State Government. Since fundamental rights are enforceable against the State. Article 12 defines "State" as "the Government and Parliament of India and the Government and the legislature of each of the States and all local or other authorities within the territory of India or under the control of the Government of India." In Electricity Board, Raj. v. Mohan Lal, the Supreme Court held that "other authorities will include all authorities created by the Constitution or statute and on whom powers are conferred by law, and it is not necessary that the statutory authority should be engaged in performing the governmental functions. Thus bodies created for promotion of education or economic interest of the people would be such authorities. The Rajasthan Electricity Board was held to be such an authority. Indian Airlines, Corporation v. Sukhdeo Singh, and U.P, State Warehousing Corporation v. C.K. Tyagi, took the view that a corporation set up by a statute is not an "authority" since only those come under "authority" which exercise governmental or quasi-governmental functions. These decisions have been overruled by the Supreme Court in Sukhdeo Singh v. Bhagat Ram. The majority by four to one, held that the term "other authorities" under Article 12 was wide enough to include every authority created by statute and functioning within the territory of India or under the control of the Government of India. It was held that the Oil and Natural Gas Commission, Life Insurance Corporation, and Industrial Finance Corporation are such authorities and, therefore, orders, directions and writs can be issued against them.

In Ujjain Singh v. State of U.P., the Supreme Court held that a writ, etc., could riot be issued against a quasi-judicial authority on the sole ground that the Provisions of the Act or the term of notification issued thereunder had beef, violated. But in the following cases writ, order, etc., are maintainable against the quasi-judicial authorities, (a) when statute or rules framed thereunder are ultra vires and any action taken thereunder is violative of a fundamental right, (b) when such authority acts without jurisdiction or assumes jurisdiction wrongly and an action of such authority is violative of any fundamental right, and (c) if the action of the authority is procedurally ultra vires, such as when there is a violation of principles of natural justice. Hidayatullah, C.J., summed up the rule thus: a person has -a right 'to move the Supreme Court under Article 32 when an action is taken under an ultra vires statute or when the action is without jurisdiction though the statute is intra Vires or when principles of natural justice are violated. But no action would lie where error of law of fact is committed in exercising jurisdiction founded on a valid law. In cases coming before the 44th Amendment, it was held that whenever an illegal tax affected the fundamental right to property under Article 3 1(1) an action under Article 32 would lie. After the abrogation of Article 31 by the 44th Amendment this would not be so.

No Writ can be Issued against High Courts

The Supreme Court has expressed the view that judicial adjudications, orders and decrees by themselves do not violate fundamental rights. In Sridhar v. State of Maharashtra, the Supreme Court was called upon to determine whether an order of the High Court prohibiting the publication of the testimony of a witness in newspaper violated the fundamental right under Article 19(l)(a)? It was held that no writ could be issued against a High Court. Whether or not an adjudication by a High Court suffers from any infirmity can be considered only in an appeal.

Petitions

Whenever a breach of fundamental right is alleged by the legislature or the executive, the jurisdiction of the Supreme Court can be invoked. But if the enforcement of a fundamental right is not involved Article 32 is not available. Thus the breach of the right of freedom of trade and commerce guaranteed under Article 301, or v; any other right, or legality or illegality of an executive action or ultra viresness of a statute, cannot be questioned under Article 32 if breach of a fundamental right Is not Involved. For these matters, the jurisdiction is conferred on the High Court under Article 226. But the validity of a law can be challenged under Article 32 if, it involves a question of enforcement of any fundamental right.

For the enforcement of the fundamental rights, the procedure under Article 32 is by "appropriate proceedings" which means that a petition has to be filed on the original side of the Supreme Court. This is sometimes called "the extraordinary original jurisdiction" of the Supreme Court. The appropriateness of the proceedings would depend upon the particular writ or order which a petitioner claims and it is in that sense that the right has been conferred on the citizen to move the Supreme Court by appropriate proceedings." Since the jurisdiction under Article 32 is extraordinary, the Supreme Court has very wide discretion in matter of providing remedy for the enforcement of fundamental rights. The right under Article 32 is itself a fundamental right. No fetters can be placed on this right. It was on this reasoning which led the Supreme Court to strike down its own rule providing for security from the petitioner. But this does no(mean that the Supreme Court cannot regulate the procedure. It has the power to make rules which will govern the procedure and practice for the filing of petitions under Article 32.

In early cases the Supreme Court expressed the view that if a petitioner made out a case under Article 32, the Supreme Court had no discretion. It must grant an appropriate writ or order in favour of the petitioner: it Was the duty of the Supreme Court to do so.

Article 32(2) specifically mentions five types of directions, Orders, writs, viz., habeas corpus, mandamus, prohibition, quo warranto and certiorari. The Supreme Court has power to issue any one of these as well as to frame any with or order or direction which it may consider appropriate in a given case. In the words of Mukherjea. J.: "We can make an order or issue, writ in the nature of certiorari (or any order or direction or writ) in all appropriate cases and in appropriate manner, so long as week keep in view the broad and fundamental Principles of the exercise of jurisdiction in the matter of granting such writs in English law. However, It would be correct to say that once the breach of a fundamental right is established the Supreme Court has no discretion in the matter and 'must award appropriate relief. The following, propositions may be taken as well established:

A. The write order or direction under Article 32 to issued as a matter Of Course once a violation of a fundamental right is established and technical rules applicable to suits like the provision of section 80, Civil Procedure Code are not applicable to Proceedings under Article 32.

B. But this general rule does not imply that the Supreme Court is required to ignore and trample under foot all laws of Procedure, evidence, limitation, res judicata and the like. The court is not bound to grant relief:

   (i) When Petition contains misleading and inaccurate, statements, or it would be against public policy to accept such a petition.

   (ii) When petition is barred by resiudicata.

   (iii) When petition is barred by laches.

C. The existence of an alternative remedy does not bar the jurisdiction of the Supreme Court under Article 32.

D. The existence of the concurrent jurisdiction of the High Court under Article 226 does not bar a person who alleges violation of a fundamental right to approach the Supreme Court directly.

Jurisdiction of the High Court under Article 226

Under Article 226 the High Court has concurrent jurisdiction with the Supreme Court in the matter of granting relief in cases of infraction of fundamental rights, though the High Courts exercise jurisdiction in case of any other right too. This does not imply that a person who alleges violation of a fundamental right must first approach the High Court. One can approach the Supreme Court directly. That this is so has been very cogently stated in Romesh Thapar v. State of Madras, thus: "that Article 32 does not merely confer power on this court, as Article 226 does on the High Court, to issue certain writs for the enforcement of the rights conferred by Pan III or for any other purpose as part of its general jurisdiction. In that case. It would have been more appropriately placed among Articles 131 to 139 which define that jurisdiction. Article 32 provides a guaranteed remedy for the enforcement of those rights and this remedial right is itself made a fundamental right by being included in Part 111. This court is thus constituted as the protector and guarantor of fundamental rights and it cannot, consistently with the responsibility so laid upon it, to refuse to entertain applications seeking protection against infringement of such rights."

The High Courts under Article 226 exercise much wider discretion than the Supreme Court exercises under Article 32. The High Courts have held that they would refuse to exercise jurisdiction, inter alia. If there is an adequate alternative remedy. If there are laches. If the conduct of the petitioner is reproachable, if interest of justice does not require a writ to be granted, if the petition involves disputed questions of fact or if granting of the writ would be futile. But it seems that these considerations would apply only when the High Courts grant relief "for any other purpose," and riot for the enforcement of fundamental rights. Seervai rightly holds the view that it would not be a judicial exercise of the discretion to refuse a writ for the enforcement of fundamental rights on a ground on which the Supreme Court could not refuse a writ under Article 32.

Existence of Alternative Remedy

The Supreme Court has repeatedly held that the existence of an alternative remedy did not bar the jurisdiction of the court to grant relief under Article 32. However, in some cases the Supreme Court has observed that it might exercise its discretion to refuse to grant relief when an alternative remedy is available since extraordinary remedies should not replace the ordinary, remedies. It is necessary that the alternative remedy is equally convenient, beneficial and effective. It is not so, it cannot be regarded as an adequate alternative remedy. When it is question of enforcement of a fundamental right, it appears that in most cases the alternative remedy is not adequate and therefore the Supreme Court and the High Courts rarely refuse to grant relief on the ground of the existence of alternative remedy. When the jurisdiction of the High Court is invoked in other matters, it takes into account the existence of an alternative remedy as a ground for refusing relief. But the, rule of existence of alternative remedy is a rule of policy, convenience and discretion rather than of law.

Petition Barred by Laches

No statute of limitation (such as the Indian Limitation Act) applies to petitions under Articles 32 and 226. But this does not mean that relief can be sought under these articles at any time. Hidayatullah, C.J., rightly observed that there was no lower or upper time limit for entertaining petitions under Article 32, but there was the overriding qualification that a party seeking this extraordinary remedy must come to the court with the utmost despatch. This means that each petition has to be determined on the basis of its own facts and circumstances, But beyond this, the Supreme Court has expressed conflicting views. In some cases, it has been held that the Limitation Act might be applied by analogy. In Kaminikumar v. State of W.B., the court observed that there was no inexorable rule and when justice required there was no period of limitation. In some cases the period of limitation prescribed for appeals had been suggested in some cases a view had been expressed that no petition should be allowed after one year. But all these views need not be discussed here in they stand superseded by the Supreme Court decision in R.S. Deodhar v. State of Maharashtra. The court observed that the doctrine of laches was not a rule of law, but a rule of practice based on sound and proper exercise of the discretion, and them, wax no Inviolable rule that whenever there was delay, the court must necessarily refuse to entertain the petition. 'This court which has been assigned the role of a sentinel on qui vive for the protection of fundamental rights cannot easily allow itself to be persuaded to refuse relief on the jejune ground of laches delay or the like," the present writers are in respectful agreement with the view. The implication of this decision is that the court will decide each case on its facts and circumstances as to whether or not the petition should be rejected on the ground of unreasonable delay. It is submitted that the rules evolved under section 23(l)(d), Hindu Marriage Act, 1955 which deals with delay in matrimonial petitions could be a good guide to Articles 32 and 226.

Petition Barred by res judicata

It is now established rule that the doctrine of res judicata applies to petitions under Articles 32 and 226. The doctrine of res judicata seeks to regulate the manner in which the remedial fundamental right can he asserted in a court of law, A petition under Article 32 is not maintainable if the petitioner has obtained a decision on merits on the same mailer in a petition under Article 226. Like the doctrine of laches the doctrine of res Judicata is based on considerations of public policy and is not a technical rule of procedure. The public policy requires that the finality should attach to binding decision of courts of competent jurisdiction and that the individuals should not he made to suffer the odium of the same kind of litigation to be brought over and over again. The doctrine of res judicata lays down that if a matter has been decided on merit between the parties, then the same parties cannot agitate the same question over agains A person cannot move successive writ petitions on the same cause of action. Thus where an order assessing a tax was once challenged by a petition and dismissed by the court after considering the case on merits, then the petitioner cannot challenge the assessment of the same tax by another writ petition even though the petition alleges some new grounds of challenge. But if order of assessment challenged by successive writ petitions do not relate to the same years, the petition is maintainable. The doctrine of constructive res judicata also applies (constructive res judical mews that a ground ought to have been taken but was not in fact taken is tantamount to ground taken). The principle is the same namely, there should be an end to litigation and that a person should not be vexed, twice in respect of the same subject matter. This also means that a person must elect as to whether he wants to file a petition under Article 32 or Article 226. If a petition is dismissed, neither another writ petition, nor a suit on the same subject is maintainable.

Withdrawal of a petition has the same effect. A writ petition is also not maintainable against an order passed by the High Court in a revision petition; in such can, even an appeal may not be entertained. The doctrine of res judicata obviously does not apply if the matter is not decided on merit.

The doctrine of res judicata obviously does not apply to a writ of habeas corpus. Even if the petition is dismissed by the High Court on merit, a fresh petition to the Supreme Court is maintainable.

Petition Barred on Account of Misconduct or Bad Conduct of Petitioner

The equitable principle of one who comes to equity must come with clean hands applies to the writ jurisdiction under Articles 32 and 266. If a petitioner is guilty of bad faith, fraud or improper conduct in respect of matter relating to controversy the petition may be refused, improper conduct may be precedent or subsequent to the filing of the petition. If the affidavit filed by the petitioner is not candid and does not state the facts fairly but states them in such a way as to mislead and deceive the court the petition may be dismissed. In Daulal Singh v. Dy. Commr., Karnal. where the petitioner himself unlawfully invoked the jurisdiction of a tribunal, the court observed that they could not be heard to say that the tribunal had no jurisdiction when the selfsame jurisdiction is invoked by the opposite party it was held that conduct of the petitioners was such as to disentitle them for any relief under Article 226.

Disputed Question of fact may not Bar Petition

If a prima facie case of violation of a fundamental right is made out the petition will not be barred, even if its determination involves an inquiry into disputed questions of fact.

A Writ will not be Issued if it would be rutile

The court will not issue a writ, order or direction if its granting will be futile. Thus it would be futile to issue a writ of mandamus against a Returning Officer directing him to accept the nomination paper which he had rejected, since, despite the writ, it was open to an, election tribunal to take the view that the nomination paper was rightly rejected. Similarly, it has been held that there was no use granting a writ in respect of a liquor licence granted to a third person without authority of law where the contract would be terminate within days. or to order reinstatement to an office from which the petitioner could be removed by a higher authority.

Can a Remedy under Article 32 be Directly Pursued in the Supreme Court

Before 1989, it was the confirmed view that for the enforcement of any fundamental right a person could directly approach the Supreme Court. But in P.N. Kumar v. Municipal Corporation of Delhi, the Supreme Court expressed the view that the citizen should first go to the High Court and if not satisfied he should approach the Supreme Court. The Supreme Court laid down the following guidelines:

(1) The scope of Article 226 is wider than Article 32. The parties should first seek relief in the High Court and should come to the Supreme Court in appeal only.

(2) Hearing of the case at the level of High Court is more convenient to the parties. It saves lot of time.

(3) The High Court has its own traditions. They have eminent judges, whose capacity should be utilised.

(4) Every High Court has a good Bar. There, eminent lawyers with wide experience, handle different kinds of cases. They know history of every legislation in their State.

(5) The Supreme Court has no time to decide cases pending before it for the last 10 to 15 years, with the present strength of judges it will take more than 15 years to dispose of all pending cases.

(6) If the cases are filed in the High Court, the task of Supreme Court acting as an original court which is time-consuming can be avoided.

(7) If cases which may be filed in the High Court are filed in this Court it would effect the initiative of the High Courts. We should preserve the dignity, majesty and efficiency of the High Courts. The taking over by this court the work of High Court may undermine the capacity and efficiency of the High Courts and should be avoided.

(8) The time saved by this court by not entertaining the cases which may be filed before the High Courts can be utilised to dispose of old matters in which parties are crying relief.

In our submission, the views expressed by the Supreme Court are not in conformity with the values enshrined in the constitution and with rule of law. The rationale behind the Supreme Court decision is that the ever increasing load that is placed on the Supreme Court by arrears of cases would be thereby reduced. In our submission it is not the citizen to be blamed for the mounting arrears of cases, but the executive which tramples over the rights of citizens with impunity and arrogance. It is hoped that the Supreme Court would confine this judgment to live in archives only.

Three

The Writs

The remedial fundamental right contained in Article 32 can be brought into action, by what may he compendiously called, the writ jurisdiction of the Supreme Court and High Courts. Under Article 226 the High Courts have power to issue orders directions or writs including writs in the nature of habeas corpus, mandamus, prohibition, certiorari and quo warranto for the enforcement of the fundamental rights as well as for "any purpose," including the enforcement of any other legal rights.

With the enshrinement of a Chapter on Fundamental Rights in the Constitution, it was necessary corollary to provide for a quick and inexpensive remedy for the enforcement of fundamental rights. We drew from the English law and found the prerogative writs were peculiarly suited for the purpose. Article 32 makes if a fundamental right of any person who alleged violation of a fundamental right to seek the remedy through these writs. In the States' sphere similar power was conferred upon the High Courts. Power was conferred upon the High Courts of not merely issuing these writs, etc., for the enforcement of fundamental rights, but, also for the enforcement of any other legal right.

Although these writs have been borrowed from English law, we need not get bogged down by the and technicalities and precedents of English law, though with a view to having a proper perspective, we may keep in view the broad and fundamental principles of the writ jurisdiction of English law.

Mandamus

In English law, "the writ of mandamus is a high prerogative writ of a most extensive remedial nature, and is, in form a commanding from the High Court of Justice directed to any person, corporation, or inferior court, requiring him or them to do some particular thing therein specified which appertains to his or their office and is in the nature of public duty, its purpose is to supply defects of justice: and accordingly it will issue, to the end that justice may be done, in all cases where there is a specific legal right and no specific legal remedy for enforcing that right." This description of mandamus has been accepted by the Indian Courts. A writ of mandamus is in the nature of a command issued by a court of law asking a public authority to perform a public duty which it is bound to perform, or to refrain from performing a particular act which it should not perform. For instance, if a tribunal is bound to decide a matter and it refuses to decide mandamus could be issued to it directing it to decide the matter. A mandamus lies to compel the performance of an obligatory duty imposed by law. Thus a mandamus would lie to compel an Income-tax Officer to carry out the direction given to him by the Income-tax Appellate Tribunal. It also lies to restrain an authority which acts without the authority of law or contrary to law or in excess of the authority conferred by law or acts mala fides. Thus, mandamus was issued to Government restraining it from giving effect to a notification cancelling a reference made to an Industrial Tribunal since it had not authorized to do so by law, or against a court or tribunal which acted in excess of jurisdiction or failed to exercise jurisdiction or committed error apparent on the face of the record. A writ can be issued quashing the order of the tribunal, and directing it to hear and determine the matter according to law, or restraining it from giving effect to its order. For issuance of a mandamus the following conditions should be fulfilled:

(i) The petitioner must have a legal right to Compel

the public authority to do or refrain from doing something.

(ii) Mandamus is ordinarily issued against a public authority and not against a private body or individual but if private body has public duty to perform mandamus may be issued against it.

(iii) Mandamus is meant to secure the performance of a public or statutory duty in the performance of which the petitioner has sufficient legal interest.

(iv) Mandamus does not lie where the performance of the public duty is discretionary, but if the authority is under a duty to exercise discretion, mandamus lies to compel the authority to exercise that discretion.

Who can Seek Mandamus

A petition for the issuance of a writ of mandamus must show that he has a legal right to compel the authority to do or refrain from doing something. This is subject to what we have stated under the head public interest litigation." In other words the petitioner must have a right to compel performance of some public duty on the part of the respondent. Thus a mandamus will not lie where the petitioner's contention is that a man junior to him in service had been appointed when in fact the junior so appointed was qualified, and the petitioner had no qualifications for the post. A petition will lie against the respondent only when he has a duty of public nature, whether created by the Constitution, statute or common law and not if the duty is of a private nature even if the respondent is a public body. Contractual obligations cannot be enforced through mandamus, but mandamu; will lie if the public authority acts in an arbitrary and unlawful manner even where right arises under contract. Mandamus will lie to restrain a public authority from acting under a law declared unconstitutional.

Mandamus is not available to enforce a purely money obligation under a civil liability, but an order to pay money may be passed against a public authority if monetary obligation arises under a statute. Mandamus would, thus, lie to prevent the authority from realizing illegal tax.

It is necessary that before approaching the court the petitioner must have made a demand on the authority concerned and the latter must have refused to concede it. The refusal to concede the demand may be inferred from the conduct. The demand of the right on the part of the petitioner is not a men matter of form; it is a matter of substance. An evasion or shelving of a demand is tantamount to denial.

Against Whom Mandamus may be Claimed

In State of J. & K. v. A.R. Jakki, the Supreme Court said that a writ of mandamus cannot be issued to the Legislature to enact a particular legislation. Nor can direction be issued to executive to frame rules as the same, is also a legislative action. The ordinary rule is that mandamus ties against a public authority or person holding a public office or a public corporation or inferior court to perform a public or statutory duty imposed upon it by law. In Sohan Lal v. Union of India. mandamus was issued against the Union of India to restore possession to the petitioner when he (a displaced person) was evicted in contravention of the express provision of the Public Promises (Eviction) Act. At one time this was a strict rule Thus, an application for Mandamus will not lie against a company for an order of reinstatement to an office which is essentially of a private character, nor can such an application be maintained to secure performance of obligations owed by a company towards its workmen or to resolve any private dispute. In Praga Tool Corporation Y. Immanual. Shelat. J., observed that mandamus was an order which was made against a person directing him to do some particular thing specified in the order which appertained to his office in the nature of a public duty and as a company is a non-statutory body incorporated under the Companies Act, had neither a statutory nor a public duty imposed on it by a statute in respect of which enforcement could be sought by a mandamus, nor did the workers have any corresponding legal right of enforcement of any such statutory or public duty. This restrictive meaning is no longer tenable. In several cases it has been held that a writ may he issued against a private body. If the duty cast upon it is of a public nature. Of these cases. Vaish College Society v. Lakshmi Narain, is the most instructive. The main question before the court was: could mandamus lie against the Managing Committee of a private, college affiliated to a University (statutory body) against its order terminating the service of a teacher'? Although teachers were appointed in the college under contract a statutory duty was cast upon the Managing Committee while appointing a teacher under Meerut University Act. In the words of Asthana. J., "when non-statutory bodies perform non-statutory functions their acts will not be subject to judicial review by the court but when they perform statutory functions, there is no valid reason why it should not be held that their actions will be amenable to judicial review by the court inasmuch as non-statutory bodies when performing statutory functions will be nothing else than instrumentalities acting under the statute which imposes duty upon it affecting the right of third persons and parties."

A writ would lie against a judge, including the judge of the High Court against his administrative actions.

Sharif Ahmed v. Regional Transport Authority. takes the law of mandamus a step further. It lays down that mandamus can be issued against an authority asking it to perform its ministerial functions. The shortened facts of the case are: The Transport Appellate Tribunal directed the Regional Transport Authority to issue state carriage permit to those persons who complied with all the conditions laid down for the issuance of the permit. The petitioner complied with all the conditions. However, before the permits were issued, the State Government issued a notification changing its policy and directed the RTA not to issue permits. Subsequently, certain changes were made in the law retrospectively. The Supreme Court observed that once the Transport Appellate Authority had directed the RTA to issue the permit, the consideration of the applications for grant of permit was no longer pending before it; what remained pending was a mere ministerial act to be performed by the RTA. When the Government changed the law there was nothing pending before the RTA expect "that in the physical sense a paper containing a permit was not actually issued." Since it did not issue the permit, it failed in its legal duty in not implementing the order of the Appellate Tribunal. The court felt that it was just and proper to grant the writ of mandamus. Untwalia. J., observed that the RTA had merely a ministerial duty to perform and the minor discretionary element given to it for finding out whether the terms of the order had been complied with or not was enough to deter the court from characterising the function as ministerial.

A writ of mandamus does not lie against a legislature or a subordinate legislature (like a municipality) to prevent it from enacting a law in violation of the Constitution or asking it to pass a particular law.

When Performance of Public Duty is Discretionary, no Mandamus Lies

A writ of mandamus cannot he issued to compel all authority to perform its discretionary duty. In State of

M.P. v. Mandawar, Rule 44 of the Fundamental Rules conferred a discretion to grant dearness allowance at a particular rate. The court held that mandamus could not be issued. The administrative instructions which have no statutory force cannot be enforced by mandamus.

But if the authority is bound to exercise its discretion the mandamus lies. A mandamus can be issued to an authority to compel the exercise of discretion though not to compel it in the manner in which it has to be exercised. A mandamus lies where the discretion is exercised on irrelevant or extraneous considerations or where the exercise of discretion is delegated to someone else or where its exercise is declined. But where the discretion has been exercised in good faith the court would not intervene: it is not the function of the court to substitute their wisdom and discretion for that of the persons to whose judgment the matter is entrusted by the law.

Certiorari and Prohibition

In the modem law the horizon of certiorari has been much widened. At one time it was the confirmed view that the writs of certiorari and prohibition lay only to control judicial or quasi-judicial acts. Today it is established that these writs lie to control the administrative act also if there is a duty on the person or authority acting administratively to act fairly. The landmark English decisions propounding this view are Ridge v. Baldwin. and in re H.K. (An infant). and the leading Indian decisions are A.K. Kraipak v. Union of India, and Maneka Gandhi v. Union of India.

In the modem law certiorari is issued to quash the decisions of a court or quasi-judicial tribunal or an administrative body of having a duty to act fairly or in accordance with the principles of natural justice when it has assumed jurisdiction which it does not possess or where the order passed by it contains an error of law apparent on the face of the record. Prohibition issues in similar circumstances to restrain the court tribunal or authority which threatens to assume or has assumed a jurisdiction not vested in it or acts in contravention of any law including the principle of natural justice, before the conclusion of proceedings. The courts have often said that in certiorari jurisdiction the courts do not Supplant but only supplement. In Halsbury's Law of England, the writ of certiorari is defined as the writ which "issues out of a superior court and is directed to the judge or other officer of an inferior court of record. It requires that the record of the proceeding in some cause or matter pending before such inferior court shall be transferred to the supreme court to be there dealt with In order to ensure that the applicant for the writ may have a more sure and speedy justice.- Prohibition is defined as a writ "issuing out of the High Court of Justice and directed to an inferior court which forbids such court to continue proceedings therein excess of its jurisdiction or in contravention of the law of the land." These definitions have been accepted by the Indian Courts. Both the writs are issued practically on the same grounds. The main distinction between the two is that prohibition lies before the court or tribunal has completed its proceedings or delivered the judgment or passed the order, while certiorari lies where proceedings have been completed or a judgment delivered or an order passed. Sometimes both the writs lie in the same cause, a petitioner may pray that the inferior court or tribunal should be prohibited from proceeding further in the matter and that the case be transferred to the superior court.

Who Can Seek these Writs

Any person who alleges that in his case the inferior court or any other authority or person having the duty to act judicially or the duty to act fairly is acting without jurisdiction, or in excess of jurisdiction or in violation of principles of natural justice or fair play can maintain a petition for the issuance of the writ.

In a petition for *certiorari* or prohibition, the petitioner must slaw all material facts of the case and should not suppress or mis-state any material facts.

Against whom, Certiorari and Prohibition Lie

In the modern law the writ of certiorari or prohibition lies not only against the inferior courts or quasi-judicial tribunals or bodies, but also against any person, body or authority having duty to act judicially or fairly. These writs do not lie against private domestic tribunals or bodies or persons even if they are required to act judicially or fairly. It seems that the writ would lie against in arbitrator appointed under section 10-A. Industrial Disputes Act. Certiorari also lies to determine questions affecting the fundamental rights.

In earlier cases, the Supreme Court stuck to the formulation made in the English case, viz., writ would issue to anybody or person having legal authority to determine questions affecting the rights of an individual and having duty to act judicially but which acts in excess of its legal authority. Kania. C.J. observed ". . . when the law under which the authority is making a decision itself requires a judicial approach, the decision will be quasi-judicial." The italicised words should be, noted. This thesis was further elaborated in Nagendra Nath Bora v. Commr. of Hill Div., where Sinha, J., observed that whether an authority had an obligation to act judicially must determine in each case on an examination of the relevant statute and the rules framed thereunder.

In the early Indian cases, the courts considered two questions: (a) whether the authority is a tribunal, and (b) whether authority is required to act judicially.

In Associated Cement Co. v. P.M. Sharma. the court was concerned with the fact whether [tic State Government exercising appellate jurisdiction under the Punjab Welfare Officer (Recruitment & Condition of Service) Rules., 1952 was a tribunal and in Shri Bhagwan v. Ram Chandra, whether there was violation of natural justice when Government did not hear the parties in the exercise of its revisional jurisdiction. In both cases court gave an affirmative answer. In Sadhu Singh v. Delhi Admn., the detenu challenged his preventive detention on the ground that he was given no opportunity to make a representation against his detention when his case was reviewed under Rule 35-A, Defence of India Rules. The court held that the detention and its review were purely administrative acts and not subject to certiorari. This case has been overruled in P.L. Lakhanpal v. Union of India. The Supreme Court held that when the authority reviewed a -detention case, it was required to act objectively. With this decision the modern trend was set in motion. Then came the crucial decisions in State of Orissa v. Binapani Devi. which held that the principles of natural justice must be followed even in respect of administrative or executive acts. Shah, J., observed: "But the decision of the State could be based upon the result of an enquiry in a manner consonant with the basic concept of justice. An order by the State to the prejudice of person in derogation of his vested right may be made only in accordance with the basic rules of justice or fair-play." The rule that a party to whose prejudice an order is intended to be passed is entitled to a hearing applies alike to judicial tribunals and bodies of persons invested with authority to adjudicate upon matters involving civil consequences. Duty to act judicially would, therefore arise from the very nature of the function intended to be performed: it need not he shown to be superadded. In this case the Department was engaged in the task of determining the age of a Government servant.

The decision in A.K. Kraipak v. Union of India. has put a stamp in this view. In this case person sat on the selection board in which he was a rival with other candidates though at the time of his own selection he withdrew but continued to sit when his rivals were interviewed. He was selected and his rivals were left out. It was a case of violation of the second limb of the principle of natural justice, viz., disqualification by interest and bias (the first requirement of natural justice is that no one should be condemned unheard). Hedge, J., observed:

> The dividing line between an administrative power and a quasi-judicial power is quite thin and is being gradually obliterated. For determining whether a power is an administrative power or a quasi-judicial power one has to look to the nature of the power conferred the person or persons on whom it is conferred the framework of the law conferring that power, the consequences ensuing from the exercise of that power and the manner in which that power is expected to be exercised. In a welfare state like ours it is inevitable that the organ of the State under our Constitution is regulated and controlled by rule of law. The concept of rule of law would lose its validity if the instrumentalities of the State are not charged with the duty of discharging their functions in a fair and just manner. The requirement of acting judicially in essence is nothing but a requirement to act justly and fairly and not arbitrarily or capriciously.

The court observed that reaching a just decision was the aim of both quasi-judicial and administrative enquiries. An unjust decision in an administrative enquiry will have more far-reaching effect than a decision in a quasi-judicial enquiry. The court held that today natural .justice has more than two rules (as it was understood in the past). It means:

(i) No one shall be judge in his own cause,

(ii) No one shall be condemned unheard, and

(iii) Inquiries must be held in good faith without bias and not arbitrarily and unreasonably.

Modem concept of natural justice has a few more subsidiary rules. Today it is no longer correct to say that principles of natural justice apply only to the authority which is required by the law under which it functioned to act judicially. Often it is not easy to draw the line between administrative enquiries and quasi-judicial enquiries.

The decision in Maneka Gandhi v. Union of India goes a step further. In this case the passport of the petitioner was cancelled without giving her any reasonable opportunity of being heard. Bhagwati. J. observed:

> Although there are no positive words in the statute requiring that the party shall be heard yet the justice of the common law will supply the omission of the legislature. The principle of audialteram partem which mandates that no one shall be condemned unheard is part of the rule of natural justice.

His Lordship further observed.

> The law must now be taken to be well settled that even in an administrative proceeding, which involves civil consequences, the doctrine of natural justice must be held to be applicable.

In the civil service examination candidates were required to write their roll number, on the space provided and at no other place. For the breach of this condition, the PSC decided that answer-book should not be evaluated. No opportunity of hearing need be given to the candidate. The order was quashed.

When does Certiorari or Prohibition Lies

It seems to be now settled that a writ of certiorari or prohibition would lie in cases where the tribunal or the authority:

(a) refuses to exercise jurisdiction,

(b) acts without jurisdiction,

(c) exercises jurisdiction by erroneously deciding facts necessary to confer jurisdiction,

(d) exercises jurisdiction by taking into consideration irrelevant and extraneous matter, or

(e) makes an error of law apparent on the face of the record.

Want of jurisdiction may arise on several counts, It may be on account of the fact that the tribunal has no jurisdiction over the subject matter of the enquiry or from absence of some preliminary proceedings such as omission to serve notice, or the tribunal may not be properly constituted or the law which conferred jurisdiction on the tribunal is unconslitutional. In Ambika Mills v. Bhun, the court found that the construction placed by the tribunal on the two clauses of the agreement between file Mill-owners' Association and Textile Labour Association was patently and manifestly erroneous. The court observed: "It is not a case where two alternative conclusions arc possible: it is a case of plain misreading of the two provisions ignoring altogether the very object with which the two separate provisions were made."

"The error apparent on the face of the record" does not mean mere error of law such an error which is manifest and apparent. Certiorari does not lie to correct an error of facts. The Certiorari jurisdiction is not an appellate jurisdiction. But finding of fact based on no evidence, or where the tribunal erroneously refused to admit admissible evidence or material evidence, or has erroneously admitted inadmissible evidence which led the tribunal to reach conclusion which it had, tantamounts to error of law and certiorari lies. But the finding of fact cannot be challenged merely on the ground of inadequacy of the evidence.

The jurisdiction of the certiorari has been extended to such an extent that was probably not contemplated originally. The courts now hold that the violation of natural justice includes the violation of duty to act fairly. (This aspect of the matter we have already discussed). The courts have repeatedly said that the concept of natural justice is flexible, and what amounts 'to violation of natural justice will vary from cam to case. In Hiranath, certain students were expelled from the College after an inquiry. Allegations against them were that they, being quite naked, entered the compound of the Girls' Hostel and even went outside the rooms of some girl students and tried to pull them out. The inquiry was conducted by a Committee of teachers constituted by the Principal of the College. The inquiry was challenged on the ground that the statements of the girl students were recorded in the absence of the accused, the girl students were not called for cross-examination to test their veracity, and a copy of the report of the Inquiry Committee was not supplied to them. Rejecting these contentions the Supreme Court observed that the requirements of natural justice were not static, these vary from case to case. The court observed that inquiry into the incident involved some delicacy, the police could not be called in, because the police investigation would have frightened the girl students and they might not have cooperated: an open inquiry was not feasible as the girl students would not have ventured to make their statements before the accused for fear of future harassment: (since-the college was not in a position to give protection to them outside the college and hostel premises); and for these very reasons a copy of the report was not given to the accused, The court held since the college stood in the capacity of loco parents to the girls staying in the hostel, it was necessary to hold the inquiry, and the type of inquiry held and the investigation made was only course open to the college as the accused were informed of the charges against them and were accorded adequate opportunity to defend themselves. There was no violation of natural justice or fairness.

We had already reviewed A.K. Kraipak v. Union of India, which is a case of bias. The principles of natural justice require that a prosecutor cannot be a judge; nor can a person be a judge in his own case; and the adjudicator should have no interest in the subject matter of adjudication either.

It is also part of the principle of natural justice that the accused should be given a fair hearing. It is of repeated adage that no one should be condemned unheard. But this does not mean that there should be oral hearing or adherence should he made to all the rules and the principles of the Evidence Act. What is required is that the accused should be given adequate opportunity so that the can explain his conduct, should be given adequate time to prepare his defence, and should be allowed to lead evidence in his defence.

Ordinarily, the evidence should be recorded in his presence and he should be allowed to cross-examine the witness. But this is not a hard and fast rule. Hiranath and State of J&K v. Bakshi Gulam Md. provides an exception to this rule and illustrates the flexibility of the rules of natural justice.

Representation through the lawyer is not part of natural justice.

Habeas Corpus

The fundamental right to personal liberty can he rendered nugatory if there does not exist the writ of habeas corpus which secures the instant release of a person detained unlawfully. The writ of habeas corupus is an order issued by the court calling upon the detainee to bring the detenu before the court and to let the court know on what ground he is detained and if no legal justification is shown the detenu is released forthwith. The writ of habeas sub jiciendum, as it was originally named, proved to be very speedy and effective legal remedy to secure personal liberty. The person to whom the writ is directed must at the return of the writ, produce in open court the body of the party so committed or restrained, and must certify the true cause of imprisonment within three days after such return the court must proceed to examine and determine whether the cause of such commitment appearing upon the return :s just and legal or not, and must deliver bad or remand the prisoner accordingly, under penalty or treble damages forfeitable to the party aggrieved. In England, the right to habeas corpus was secured firmly through several statutes. The Habeas Corpus Acts of 1640, 1679 and 1816 are important landmark statutes. The Habeas Corpus Act, 1862 laid down that the writ of habeas corpus could be issued out of the jurisdiction.

In India the writ of Habeas Corpus is pail of the remedial fundamental right under Article 32, and the High Court also have the power to issue it under Article 226. It can be issued for the release of any person who is detained unlawfully. A detention is unlawful if it is not in accordance with law, or the procedure established by law has not been complied with, or detention is not under a valid law, (invalidity may be because it infringes a fundamental right or legislature passing it has exceeded its authority or has no authority or has contravened Article 22). A detention would also be unlawful if the detaining authority exceeds its authority or abuses it or exercises it mala fide.

Who can Seek Habeas Corpus

The right to seek the writ of Habeas Corpus obviously belongs to the person who has been detained unlawfully. But it may happen that a prisoner or detenu is not in a position to make the application. Keeping such a situation in view, the law accords the right to apply for the writ on any of his relation or friend. This happens in those cases where a prisoner i,, denied the facility to file the writ or is not in a position to do so. Thus a child in unlawful detention may not be in a position of applying for the writ. It may happen that a child so detained has no legal guardian or the legal guardian is not capable of acting or does not act, an application may be made by a relation or friend.

Againt whom Petition for Habeas Corpus Lies

Under Article 32 a petition is maintainable only when a breach of fundamental right is alleged and if question of violation of the fundamental right under Article 21 does not arise petition is not competent. Under Article 32 petition is not available against a private person who is alleged to have unlawfully detained the petitioner. But a petition for Habeas Corpus under Article 226 is maintainable in all cases of unlawful detention and against any detainee whether a private person or Government or any of its departments or authority. Where conflicting claims for custody of a child are made, the court has power to inquire into them and award the custody to the proper person.

Habeas Corpus Jurisdiction is Remedial and not Punitive

The purpose of the habeas corpus is to secure the

release of a detenu from unlawful detention and not to punish the detainee. In Kedar Nath v. State of Punjab, the court observed that writ of habeas corpus was meant to determine the legality or illegality of the detention and not for punishing the detainee. This principle has very important consequence. Thus in habeas corpus proceedings the court has to consider the legality of the detention on the date of hearing. If on the date of hearing it cannot be said that the aggrieved party has been unlawfully deprived of his personal liberty and his detention is contrary to law a writ of habeas corpus cannot be issued. In Tajik Hussian v. State of J and K a person who was convicted by a court martial for criminal misappropriation of money and sentenced to a term of imprisonment applied for a writ of habeas corpus questioning the correctness of sentence. The court observed that in habeas corpus proceedings the correctness or otherwise of a conviction could not be questioned the court could go only into the question of jurisdiction of the court martial or whether it was properly constituted or whether some such illegality or irregularly was committed as would go to the root of the jurisdiction of the court. This principle also means that if at the time of the hearing the detaining authority has superseded its earlier unlawful detention order with a fresh order which is free from defects the writ would not lie. In Anwar v. State of J & K, it was held that a foreigner who had entered India secretly and was detained could not seek the writ of habeas corpus as his detention was not illegal. In Kanu Sanyal v. Distt. Magistrate. the court observed that in habeas corpus proceedings the court might examine the legality of detention without the detenu's production before it. Bhagwati, I., observed, ". . . it is not necessary to go through the idle formality of requiring him to be produced before the court and that it would be sufficient and appropriate instead to examine the validity of the detention without having him brought before the court."

Preventive Detention and Habeas Corpus

A preventive detention, too, can be challenged by a writ of habeas corpus under Article 32 or Article 226. The main question that the court considers in preventive detention cases is whether the detention is prima facie legal or not. But the correctness or otherwise of the detention order cannot be challenged, nix means that a detenu has to establish infringement of Article 21 or Article 22.202 In a petition for habeas corpus by a detenu the affidavit in reply to the petition must be that of the District Magistrate who had passed the detention order or some responsible officer who had personally dealt with the case.

Successive Applications for Habeas Corpus

Under English law before the decision in In re Hastings (No. 2) and in In re Hastings (No. 3), a person was free to apply for a writ of habeas corpus from judge to judge and from court to court. In re Hastings (No. 2) and lit re Hastings (No. 3) lay down that successive writ applications could not be moved from one division to another, since there was only one High Court (in England). This view was followed in India, in In re Prahlad Krishna Khurana. and court held that once an application was rejected by a judged or division of the High Court, another application could not be made to another judge or another Bench of the High Court. Chagla. C.J., observed that this would not cause any hardship Io the petitioner as he could directly approach the Supreme Court under Article 32 by way of appeal under Article 136. Thus the court applied the doctrine of constructive res judicata to habeas corpus proceedings. It is submitted that Seervai rightly says that the doctrine of constructive res Judicata should not be applied to the petitions of habeas cot-pus. Thus a second petition should lie to the same division or judge or to another division or judge of the High Court in case a petition is supported by fresh evidence or is made on some other ground. The petition should not be barred even if these grounds and evidence could have been taken in earlier petition, since "it would be contrary to public policy to apply the principles of constructive res judicata to the liberty of the subject and to allow an illegal detention to continue."

7

Human Rights: Global Responsibilities

Can one cogently speak of an international "community" whose commitment to human rights is justified by a principle of integrity? Dworkin's important insight that individuals might not agree about precisely what is required by justice, fairness, or due process (Tenet III supra) while still remaining bound by a community consensus embodied in their political institutions (Tenet V) is extendable to the global human rights context.

That there is an emerging transnational human rights "culture," as evidenced by proliferations of international guidelines and codes of conduct, is hard to deny. We may, however, expect continued disagreement about precisely what is required (and feasible) with respect to realizing human rights standards. Yet it seems reasonable to suppose that at least the outlines of a transnational community constituted by a shared allegiance to a core scheme of principles generated by human rights is currently in place. Dworkin speaks of an individual's obligations as having been instituted by a scheme of common principles which arise from the historical fact that his community has adopted that scheme, which is then special to it, not the assumption that he would have chosen it were the choice entirely his. In short, each accepts political integrity as a distinct political ideal and treats the general acceptance of that ideal, even among people who otherwise disagree about political morality, as constitutive of political community.

In the international arena, so far as human rights obligations are concerned, not only individuals, but also corporations and nation-states are to be counted as members of a "political community" in this sense.

The legal status of international human rights norms is indeterminate and uncertain. Attempts to give necessary and sufficient conditions for the concept of law, whether it be that of domestic, international, or human rights law, are of little help in answering puzzling yet pressing questions such as the following: How are the appropriate texts of various human rights identified by courts? What fixes the meaning of human rights in such texts? How do United States courts render interpretations about the weighing, scope and applicability of specific human rights in particular cases? What roles do international consensus and acceptance of human rights standards play in human rights adjudication? Are there any objective grounds for preferring one interpretation of human rights law to another in controversial cases? Answers to these sorts of questions simply cannot be deduced in an all-or-nothing fashion from general philosophical conclusions about whether international law really is or is not 'law.'

Likewise, the realist analyses of law harboured the mistaken hypothesis that law is merely a fiction relativized to moral and cultural values. The realists wrongly assume that all legal meaning is made up out of whole-cloth. Thus, having rejected the positivist and realist portrayals of international law has cleared the air for inquiring into the above questions with a fresh conception of international human rights law, I will be setting the stage in this chapter for testing whether the law-as-integrity model is a satisfactory paradigm for the human rights obligations of nation-states, individuals, and multinational corporations.

The integrity model's approach to treating issues of legality as "interpretive questions seems promising because so many of the central issues involved in contemporary human rights adjudication are highly controversial. They pose hard cases, to follow Dworkin's terminology. Integrity suggests that in resolving such hard cases, courts will be rendering decisions which will, as far as possible, fit with the relevant existing sources of law. Where the rules from such sources do not clearly dictate a result, integrity assumes that courts will fashion decisions with the assistance of general principles which are presupposed by, or which serve to justify, the extant institutional material.

Initially, we will examine some significant human rights decisions of United States courts. An advantage of selecting domestic adjudications of human rights as an interpretive context for the present study is that the context places human rights squarely within the scope of the three central paradigms of legal philosophy (positivism, realism, and integrity) which are directed at the law of domestic courts. A further advantage of this context is that it facilitates discussion of human rights in a practical way by centering debates around real adjudicative issues which federal courts will be confronting with increasing frequency in future.

In the latter part of the twentieth century, significant portions of the Universal Declaration of Human Rights and other international human rights documents, have developed into both conventional and customary law binding, at least in principle, on all nations. Indeed, in the past decade or so in particular, United States courts have played a leading role in developing, and in some instances, enforcing, this body of international human rights law.

In article VI, section 2, the United States Constitution refers to international law by providing that "all Treaties made, or which shall be made, under the Authority of the United States, shall be the supreme Law of the Land; and the Judges in every State shall be bound thereby, any Thing in the Constitution or Laws of any State to the Contrary notwithstanding. Pursuant to this provision, the only one in the Constitution which addresses the relation of international law to municipal law in domestic courts, a self-executing treaty proclaimed by the President, or a non-self-executing treaty when implemented by Congress, will supersede all inconsistent state And local laws. In addition, under the so-called "last-in-time" rule, a self-executing treaty will supersede prior inconsistent federal laws.

Although the other principal -source of international law, customary international law, is not treated in the text of the Constitution, the Supreme Court has held that it is "part of our law, and must be ascertained and administered by the courts of justice of appropriate jurisdiction, as often as questions of right depending upon it are duly presented for their determination." Since customary international law has the same status as treaty law it supersedes all inconsistent state and local laws and, theoretically, it supersedes prior inconsistent federal laws and international agreements. [A]s in the case of treaties, American courts will give effect to the obligations of the United States under customary international law; at the behest of affected private parties, courts will prevent violations of international law by the States or by lower federal officials."'

The idea that all human beings are entitled to at least some basic human rights stems from the traditional law of nations pertaining to State Responsibility for Injuries to Aliens. Eventually a body of law grew up around state practice and various arbitral decisions in the nineteenth and early twentieth centuries which bound all states to an international minimum standard" of procedural and substantive justice with regard to the treatment of aliens. The "minimum standard" required that aliens be treated in accordance with ordinary standards of civilization, and was interposed by the United States to protect its own citizens overseas in cases involving extended imprisonment, arbitrary expulsion, and cruel and inhuman punishment,

In 1945 the United States signed the United Nations Chartat, including the human rights provisions in articles 55 and 56, thus expanding the scope of its adherence to the "international minimum standard' for all human beings, instead of just for aliens, Moreover, by being a signatory to other international human rights documents including the Universal Declaration of Human Rights, the American Convention on Human Rights, and the United Nations Covenant on Civil and Political Rights, the United States made further commitments to the fundamental civil and political rights provided by those documents.

Regarding domestic interpretations and applications of international human rights norms as contained in human rights texts, it has only been in recent decades that United States courts have been deployed as part of customary or conventional international law. Since the United Nations Charter was ratified by the United States government, it is the supreme law of the land. Article 1(3) of the Charter sets out as one of the United Nations central aims the attainment of cooperation among nations "in promoting and encouraging respect for human rights and for fundamental freedom for all without distinction as to rue, sex, language, or religion.' According to article 55(c) the United Nations is obligated to advance "universal respect for, and observance of, human rights and fundamental freedoms for all without distinction as to race, sex, language or religion. And pursuant to article 56 the members of the United Nations "pledge themselves to take joint and separate action in cooperation with the Organization for the achievement of the purposes set forth in Article 55."

According to Poster *v. Nielson*, the legal status of such human rights provisions of the United Nations Charter in the domestic context depends on whether the provisions were intended by their authors to be self-executing." In the words of a court which followed this approach, [i]t is only when a treaty is self-executing, when it prescribes rules by which private rights may be determined, that it may be relied upon for the enforcement of such rights."' However, the *Nielson* approach, as with other such attempts to divine the actual framers' intent (this is discussed in more detail in the next chapter) is misled. Looking at the documents of the San Francisco Conference which instituted the United Nations in 1945, one scholar notes that "Nothing . . . indicates that the framers even considered the direct legal impact of the human rights clauses on the domestic law of the members. .6

Consequently, it has been suggested that the intent of the parties to an international treaty is irrelevant to the issue of self-execution. As one commentator has said:

The intent of the parties to an international treaty is relevant only to the question of whether private individuals shall have the right of protection in domestic courts against violations of a treaty provision. Whether this result is to be achieved by legislation or by the treaty itself is a question of constitutional law and not within the purview of the intent either of all parties to the treaty or of a particular ratifying power.'

American courts have ruled consistently that human rights clauses of the United Nations Charter are not self-executing. In Sei Fujii v. California, a part of the California Alien Land Law (which provided that land transferred to an alien ineligible for citizenship escheated to the' state) was invalidated by the District Court of Appeals of California on the ground that it violated the nondiscrimination clauses of article 55(c) of the Charter.' This judgment was affirmed by the California Supreme Court, though on the basis that the state law was violative of the fourteenth amendment's equal protection clause. In dismissing the District Court's rationale, the Supreme Court noted that it saw noting in articles 55 and 56 that would show that these provisions were intended to become rules of law for the courts of this country upon the ratification of the Charter. The language used in Articles 55 and 56 is not the type customarily employed in treaties which have been held to be self-executing and to create rights and duties in individuals. . . . [Articles 55 and 56] lack the mandatory quality and definiteness which would indicate an intent to create justiciable rights in private persons immediately upon ratification.... The humane and enlightened objectives of the United Nations Charter are, of course, entitled to respectful consideration by the courts and legislatures of every member nation, since that document expresses the universal desire of thinking men for peace and for equality of rights and opportunities. The Charter represents a moral commitment of foremost importance, and we must not permit the spirit of our pledge to be compromised or disparaged in either out domestic or foreign affairs. We am satisfied, however, that the

Charter provisions relied on by plaintiff were not intended to supersede existing domestic legislation, and we cannot hold that they operate to invalidate the alien land law.'

Other cases have indicated that the principle of nondiscrimination of article 55(c) is not a legal norm for domestic tribunals. Thus, in Camacho v. Rogers, a federal district court held that "the very wording of Article 55 shows that it *is* not intended to be self-executing, 10 Moreover, another district court *in Diggs* v. Dent stated that although the Charter places international duties on the United States government, it found that

> [T]reaties do not generally confer upon citizens rights *which* they *may* enforce in the courts. It is only when a treaty is "self-executing" that individuals derive enforceable rights *from* the treaty, without *further* legislative or executive action . . . . The provisions *of* the Charter for the United Nations are not self-executing and do not vest any of the plaintiffs with any legal rights which they may assert *in* this court."

The Diggs ruling was affirmed by the United States Court of Appeals for the District of Columbia. That court held that any obligation placed on the United States by the Charter "does not confer rights on the citizens of the United States that are enforceable in court in the absence of implementing legislation.""

The "skeptical" approach to the legality of the human tights clauses of the United Nations Charter has come under attack by several writers. In addition, since the issues raised in *Fijii* have not been appealed to the United States Supreme Court, strictly speaking, it remains unsettled whether the Charter's human rights provisions are in fact self-executing.

Advance arguments against the various aspects of the excessively skeptical interpretation embodied in the

Fijii opinion. The skeptical view, as has been shown, limits the construction of the human rights clauses in the Charter to the actual intent of the framers of the Charter. However, in actual practice, the Judiciary typically does, and indeed often must, go beyond actual intent in construing, e.g., constitutional provisions. At present it should be noticed that one can plausibly analogize the domestic approach to the interpretation of constitutional law to the interpretation of international human rights law, and specifically with respect to the ism of interpreting self-executing rights provisions. This proposal is advanced in the following passage:

> Section I of the Fourteenth amendment ... is "self-executing" in the sense that courts apply the Due Process clause or the Equal Protection clause without legislative implementation. But note, on the other hand, that Section 5 of that amendment gives Congress the power to enforce it "by appropriate legislation." That is, the same text at once constitutes applicable 'law" upon which private parties may rely in litigation, and provides a basis for federal legislation."

Another aspect of the skeptical position taken in *Fujii* is the claim that the human rights provisions of the Charter fail to constitute valid legal obligations for domestic courts because of their apparent vagueness and indefiniteness. But that objection cannot stand. The human rights provisions of the Charter are actually no more vague or indefinite than a host of well-established constitutional and statutory formulas which courts routinely apply. Perhaps more importantly, however, since the adoption of the Charter, a number of international human rights documents have arisen which give a good deal more content to articles 55 and 56. For example, the Universal Declaration of Human Rights embodies an extensive array of some very specific human rights the United Nations considers fundamental. In addition, the International Covenant on Civil and Political Rights has contributed significantly to an increasing international consensus concerning the concept of human rights.

A further dimension of the *Fujii* approach which is suspect is its lumping together of all of the various human rights provisions in the Charter without regard for differences in degree of international consensus and support for the separate provisions. Thus, even if it were true that some of the provisions in articles 55 and 56 were so general as to not be self-executing, It simply does not follow that all such human rights norms share the same fate. The latter view is held by a number of legal scholars who, citing the Advisory Opinion of the International Court of Justice in this Namibia am, maintain that the nondiscrimination provision Clause of article 55(c), at least, is generally binding an all stated.

The continued viability of the *Fujii* case has been called into question by cases which suggest that the United States Supreme Court, may in future overturn that decision. In People of Saipan ex rel. Guerrero v. United States Department of Interior, the 9th Circuit Court of Appeals formulated an alternative test for deciding whether a treaty is self-executing. Guerrero involved a challenge to the execution of a low alleged to be violative of the United Nations Trusteeship Agreement Over Micronesia. Finding that the agreement afforded "Judicially enforceable rights" the court stated that

The extent to which an international agreement establishes affirmative and judicially enforceable obligations without implementing legislation must be determined in each can by reference to many contextual factors: the purposes of the treaty and the objective# of its creators, the existence of domestic procedures and institutions appropriate for direct implementation, the availability and feasibility of alternative enforcement methods, and the immediate and long-range social consequences of self- or non-self-execution."

Pursuant to the Guerrero standard, it is certainly arguable that articles 55 and 56 are self-executing provisions. Even if determining the actual intentions of the 'creators of the Charter vis a vis the issue of self-execution is futile, there are other indicia of the objectives of the Charter, For example, article 1(3) sets out as among the central purposes of the Charter that of "promoting and encouraging respect for human rights and for fundamental freedoms for all without distinction as to race, sex, language, or religion." Because the "alternative enforcement methods" referred to in the Guerrero test are not yet fully developed in the international arena, a failure of domestic courts to interpret the human rights clauses of the Charter as self-executing will likely allow the perpetuation of international human rights violations.

Another case which could eventually provide a grounding for a Supreme Court reversal of *Fujii is Diggs v.* Shultz," which involved a challenge to the Byrd Amendment under United Nations Security Council Resolution 232. Although the Court of Appeals for the District of Columbia found that the Byrd Amendment prevailed under the "last-in-time" rule, it rejected the lower court's judgment that the plaintiffs lacked standing for the action. This ruling is significant in that it opens the way for plaintiffs to challenge, without dismissal for lack of standing, statutory violations of treaty obligations by the United States, and in so doing present test cases premised upon the theory of the self-executing nature of human rights provisions,

Customary International Human Rights Law

Traditionally, treaties have formed the dominant part of international human rights law. Nevertheless, customary law is becoming a significant factor in the development of international human rights norms. This is particularly noteworthy since customary law is binding on all states and not only the parties to an individual treaty, as some classical views held.

For example, Oppertheim maintained that conventions and treaties only establish contractual rights and duties for participating parties." This "limited contract view is premised on a peculiarly narrow conception of the legal effect of contracts.

But there are significant differences between standard municipal contracts and international treaties and conventions which make the restrictive contract view dubious. Municipal contracts are typically intended to the exclusive to the parties themselves. Do the signatories of human rights treaties intend its provisions to be limited only to *themselves* in the case of universalized human rights standards such a restrictive reading of the *parties*' intent would be seriously mistaken.

Another traditional view of international custom alleges that specific human rights provisions in treaties eventually "gel" into customary international law over time. A variant of this position adds the requirement that actual practices of nations in acquiescing to the provisions are needed as evidence of this selling into customary law.

But what constitutes the sort of empirical evidence necessary for interpreting customary practice? The traditional non-selling approach cannot settle all issues in interpreting custom, must actual violations of human rights provisions first occur and then be halted voluntarily by a non-signatory nation in deference to the treaty provisions for the Selling to become effective? Must the signatory nations make a demand on the non-signatory nation in accordance with the treaty provision? If so, then their demand would come from the treaty provision itself, in which case it already has antecedent legal effect, which is what the norm-gelling view denies.

A third approach holds that multilateral treaties and conventions automatically" pass into international law since they are *ipso facto* customary law themselves binding on non-signatory nations. But if that in true, then controversy would still erupt in the process of interpreting those human rights provisions. Suppose a dispute arises about what the parties intended a provision in a convention to mean. Do they intend a human rights provision prohibiting sets of torture to be universally generalizable or do they intend it to be exclusive to themselves? Perhaps the plain meaning of the language in the provision is not dispositive. In that case the *travaux preparatoires* could be looked at to determine their intent, Positivists such as D'Amato think that the intent of the parties in such cases provides the rule of recognition for identifying what the law is. But a specific intent found in the travaux preparatoires may not cover all the issues raised in it difficult case either. In fact, a court might find that the best interpretation of a human rights provision requires disregarding the specific intentions of the parties altogether. It is hard to we how that kind of an interpretation of the law could be based on a rule of recognition.

In the law of the United States today, although customary international law is not referred to in the Constitution, it is the "law of the land' which must be interpreted and applied when appropriate for rendering &judicial decision." The question of precisely which human rights are constitutive of customary international law is obviously of critical importance when domestic courts must render judgments on the basis of that law. The assertion that the Universal Declaration of Human Rights is a part of customary international law has been a continuous source of controversy. When the Declaration was adopted, the United States maintained that insofar as it was not a treaty, it did not establish international legal obligations." A contrary view, however, has been gaining increasing allegiance among international legal commentators, international resolutions," and judicial opinions." Perhaps one of the more ambitious claims that various portions of the Declaration evidence customary international human rights law was advanced before the International Court of Justice in the context of the Hostages Case. In its memorial, the United States discussed the existence of fundamental human rights norms in the international community as follows:

> . . .[R]ecognition of the existence of certain fundamental human rights has spread throughout the international community. The existence *of* such fundamental rights for all human beings, nationals and aliens alike, and the existence of a corresponding duty on the part of every State to respect and observe them, are now reflected, inter alia, in the Charter of the United Nations, the Universal Declaration of Human Rights and corresponding portions of the International Covenant on Civil and Political Rights.

In view of the universal contemporary recognition that such fundamental human rights exist ... Iran's obligation to provide the most constant protection and security' to United States nationals in Iran includes an obligation to observe those rights.'

Although the doctrine of *the Paquete Habana* indicates that insofar as the Universal Declaration manifests customary international law it is, in principle, enforceable in domestic courts as the law of the land, efforts to implement that law before 1980 typically were dismissed. However, in 1980, the case of *Filartiga v. Pena-Irala'* broke new ground in the implementation of customary international human rights law in domestic courts.

Filartiga involved a wrongful death action based on acts of torture committed by the Inspector General of Police in Paraguay against Joelits. Filartiga, a citizen *of* Paraguay. The United States Court *of* Appeals for the Second Circuit applied the Alien Tort Claims Act, which gives federal courts jurisdiction of lawsuits by an alien in tort for violations of the law of nations.

The court construed the apposite tort as a violation of international human rights law rather than only the law of Paraguay, The court interpreted international law as establishing a right not to be tortured by officials of one's own government. Because the plaintiffs did not allege that their claim arose out of a treaty to which the United States was a party, the jurisdictional issue under the Alien Tort Claims Act involved whether torture is violative of the "law of nations,' that is, customary international law. This interpretation included a finding of international consensus on the prohibition of torture sufficient to render the right not to be tortured a universalizable human rights norm. In relevant parts of its opinion, the court argued that "[t]orture is viewed with universal abhorrence; the prohibition of torture by international consensus and express international accords is clear and unambiguous; and 'for purposes of civil liability, the torturer has become—like the pirate and the slave trader before him—hostis humani generis, an enemy of all mankind.' In addition, the court stated that "[i]f the courts . . . are to adhere to the consensus of the community of humankind, any remedy they fashion must recognize that this case concerns an act so monstrous as to make its perpetrator an outlaw around the globe.'

Included in the sources of international law upon which the court based its decision was article 5 of the Universal Declaration. The Chief Judge indicated that the right to freedom from torture "has become part of customary international law, as evidenced and defined by the Universal Declaration . . . which states, in the plainest of terms, 'no one shall be subjected to torture.'

The *Filartiga* court did not refer to any ultimate empirical test of validity for international law in reaching its decision. Granted, the court initially looked to empirical textual sources of international and domestic law. The court noted, for instance, that torture was prohibited by the following legal documents: the Paraguayan Penal code, article 337; the American Convention on Human Rights, of which Paraguay was a signatory; and the Declaration on the Protection of All Persons from Being Subjected to Torture.

But the court had to justify its interpretation that the tight not to be tortured, expressed in these texts, was a universalized legal right that would apply to a government's torture of one of its own nationals. In making this determination, the court did not, as D'Amato's thesis suggests, consult a rule of recognition for international law; rather, it advanced an interpretation about the scope of applicability of a specific human right based ultimately on a theory of international consensus about that norm.

It might be objected that the *Filartiga* court interpreted the right not to be tortured as universalizable on the basis of an empirical finding of international consensus for that proposition. This consensus, then, might be construed as just the sort of rule of recognition that deny exists for settling human rights cases. But that would be a bad account of the meaning of the court's decision. The court did not consult a global Gallup poll. Indeed no such empirical test for international consensus could definitively resolve the matter. Questions such as the following would remain unanswered: Now much international consensus would suffice? Would unanimity be required, or would a majority or a plurality consensus among nations do?'

Clearly, the Filartiga court's finding of consensus makes more sense as an authoritative interpretation of what international legal scholars term custom. But this claim seems to raise a new difficulty. For if I am right in claiming that custom fails as a rule of recognition for international human rights law, how is custom identified and what is its role in validating human rights interpretations?

Filartiga is highly significant not only in its holding that torture is a violation of the customary international law of human rights, but in its engendering of other suits predicated on international human rights law." However, cases decided after Filartiga indicate, as Chief Judge Kaufman himself advocated in a *New* York Times article, that the Filartiga ruling is limited in scope, and ought not to be taken as an authoritative determination that every human right contained in the Universal Declaration has become a part of customary international law actionable in United States courts.

One limitation on the use of the law of customary international human rights arose from Fernandez v. Wilkinson, which involved an indirect application of that law in ascertaining a Cuban refugee's protection under domestic law.

Fernandez began with an I.N.S. determination that a member of the "freedom flotilla" from Cuba was ineligible for admission to the United States due to a past conviction of a crime involving moral turpitude. Pending the proceedings for Fernandez's deportation, he was detained in a federal penitentiary without bail and without having been charged with or convicted of a crime in the United States.

Our review of the sources from which customary international law is derived clearly demonstrates that arbitrary detention is prohibited by customary international law. Therefore, even though the indeterminate detention of an excluded alien cannot be said to violate the United States Constitution or our statutory laws, it is judicially remedial as a violation of international law.

Accordingly, the Fernandez district court ruling employed customary international human rights law in order to further enhance rights existing under domestic law from federal statutes and the Constitution.

The Court of Appeals for the Tenth Circuit offered a somewhat different approach by interpreting the apposite federal statutory law to mandate termination of the alien's detention. As to the role of customary international law, the appellate court stated that the relevant federal statutory law was harmonious with the former in the sense that its construction of the statutory provisions was "consistent with accepted, international law principles that individuals are entitled to be free of arbitrary imprisonment." Thus the court of appeals placed primary emphasis on its construal of domestic law, while acknowledging the supporting" role of customary international human rights law in that construal.

Another case which represents a qualification of *Filartiga* is In re Alien Children Education Litigation, involving the right to free elementary school education. The can originated with a challenge to a Texas statute which withheld free primary education to children of undocumented aliens. The court noted that documents such as article 26(1) of the Universal Declaration, as well as like provisions in a number of international human rights sources, evince an emergent right to free elementary education in customary international law. However, the court found that at the present time such a right was merely an important international goal" which fell, short of acquiring the status of customary international law.

It is arguable that even if international human rights law is not "directly incorporated' into domestic law via self-execution of human rights clauses of the United Nations Charter and through rules of decision from customary international law, it is nevertheless "indirectly incorporated" in the sense that it assists courts in their normative exegesis of statutory and constitutional provisions. Thus, domestic courts sometimes look to international human rights law as a basis for normative argumentation against the validity of inconsistent state or federal laws, while denying that such incongruity per se is sufficient to automatically invalidate the domestic law.

This approach was taken in a concurrence to the United States Supreme Court decision in Oyama v. California, when it ruled that a provision of the California Alien Land Law was unconstitutional. Finding the state law violative of the fourteenth amendment, a pair of justices declared that the Alien Land Law's "inconsistency with the Charter, which has been duly ratified and adopted by the United States, is but one more reason why the statute must be condemned." In addition, various court opinions have alluded to the Universal Declaration in support of the position that economic and social rights ought to be expanded.

Fundamental Human Rights Obligations of Multinational Corporations

In contrast to fundamental human rights such as freedom from torture, which are properly addressed to nation-states and individuals in the sense that they impose obligations on the addressee not to deprive the claimant of the right, there are a number of fundamental rights which are properly addressed directly to multinational corporations (though they are also addressed to nations). One of the most important of these rights in terms of evolving legal doctrine is the right to freedom from employment discrimination.

The United Nations has declared that all nations should strive to achieve nondiscrimination in employment. And in the World Labour Report, issued by the International Labour Organization, the following recommendation was given:

There are three major priority areas for action in the future: (1) women's work should be perceived in even more countries as an essential component of the development process; (2) special measures should be taken to ratify and implement under national legislation ILO and United Nations standards, especially on equal employment opportunities, equal pay for equal work, working conditions, job security and maternity protection; and (3) there is a need to formulate national policies to accelerate the creation of productive and equal employment opportunities for women so as to enable them to participate more fully in economic growth and social progress.'

Provisional Analysis

This portion of the chapter has allowed me to develop an empirically-based interpretive context centered around adjudication which facilitates discussion of the legality of international human rights beyond the constraints imposed by traditional philosophical analyses. A number of interpretive questions emerge from the foregoing exposition of international human rights law.

First, it was seen that as yet unresolved issues surrounding intent via a vie the self-executing nature of the human rights provisions in the United Nations Charter will dictate how the judiciary -- in particular the United States Supreme Court - will treat future cases.

Second, it remains to be seen how domestic courts will view customary international law in the wake of Filartiga and the post-Filartiga case law.

Thus, the nature and extent of the legality of international human rights norms, as interpreted by domestic courts, is a highly technical, interpretive matter which is still being formulated by the judiciary.

A number of objections might be raised against my exposition of the body of human rights adjudications so far. First, it might be argued that such judicial decisions represent an inappropriate attempt to use the rhetoric of human rights as a vehicle for resolving what are essentially international political matters, as a legal matter instead. A more appropriate response to alleged mistreatment of a foreign national by his or her own country would be through diplomacy or appeal to public opinion, such an objection might hold. Second, someone might object that this body of law at best is evidence of parochial norms which have legal effect only within the borders of the United States. Thus, such judicial decisions are in no way representative of international human rights law, much less of universal human rights norms. A third objection might claim that the parochial norms of other nations on similar cases involving similar issues might conflict with the decisions of U.S. courts.

The legal systems of other countries may not recognize the fights that U.S. courts declare to be human fights. The same may be said of an internationally-instituted tribunal charged with deciding human rights issues. It might reach different conclusions altogether about the substance of the human rights at issue. Thus, the overall integrity of human rights adjudication, when faced with the possibilities of such differing interpretations, is called into doubt.

8

Human Rights Development

Against the single background condition of secure and procedurally regularized legality, the first step toward human rights is worked out in terms of the problem of political freedom. The dynamics of human rights history present the problem of political freedom as a practical one rather than as a philosophic one, yet it is the pragmatic c vocabulary of the philosopher John Locke which we can use for a definition. Political freedom is the-condition-of "not being subject to the inconsistent, uncertain, unknown,, arbitrary will of another man does this problem have to do with the back of a secure legal system stipulated above? Unfortunately, Locke's fictional "social contract" ideas obscure the prior necessity for legal security if the problem of political freedom is to be managed. The tie between legal security and political freedom lies in the fact that in the liberal tradition the chief institutional solution to limiting the use of power has historically relied on balanced power wrapped up in the stipulations of legal limits. It is a problem of setting legitimate limits to domination.

Max Weber defines "domination" as the probability that certain specific commands (or all commands) will be obeyed by a given group of persons. He hastens to add that in order to achieve a measure of uncoerced compliance, such domination must be legitimate. It must be believed to be rightful. The establishment of political freedom demands that countervailing power be used to check government absolutism. The problem is tied in with a critical shift in patterns of legitimacy. When old equilibrium points in a traditional society change and a new balance of social forces is institutionalized by legal checks on power, prevailing beliefs about rightful authority are strained. A profound transformation in the legitimacy of restrained power is set in motion, even though such a transformation rubs against the grain of prevailing opinion in older traditional societies. Where social structure is popularly attributed to divine plan, moral sanctions are gratuitously seen as sufficient to punish a tyrannical ruler. In such a traditional social order, no opposition short of treason could seriously arise between the objectives of the common individual and those of the rules of the community. In a traditional society, even where natural law doctrines are invoked against abusive power, it may not be the individual and government that are opposed, but the ruler and eternal moral order.

Normatively diffuse and particularistic in application, traditional late medieval legal systems were so encumbered by religiosity and privilege as to forestall any but the most modest human rights developments. Most importantly, in the middle ages, where the social organization of feudalism was concerned, no clear distinction was discernible between the "private person" and the "public individual." When this differentiation was made in the age of the Reformation, the process of responding to the problem of political freedom was launched on an ideological plane. The private person sought not a new legal definition of his status as a public individual, and still less, political power. He sought assurance of his private existence: to be secure in the family unit by being unencumbered with excessive taxation and by being left alone in religious (and therefore ideological) matters.

Achieving this kind of accommodation between the "private person" and those in power entailed a crisis of political legitimacy growing out of two outmoded features of traditional society First, the essential norms and guiding principles of the older established legal order were anchored in transcendental standards-difficult to define and even harder to apply. Second, these-systems generally lacked universal norms applicable to the whole society rather than to a few of its segments, estates, or classes. The process of overcoming these structural features of earlier politico-legal systems-the process of responding to the problem of political - freedom, can be illustrated by historical reference to seventeenth century France and England. Although different results issued in, each of the two countries, the dynamic process of achieving political freedom was initiated in both cases by intolerable acts of royal absolutism. Some descriptive detail is in order.

The precipitous issue in France was the St. Bartholomew's Day Massacre of 1572 involving the slaughter of thousands of Huguenots. The event hardly disposed of French Protestantism, but it did result in sharp political divisions among Catholics. Opposed to those who applauded the bloodletting, there developed a politically active group of French intelligentsia, administrators, lawyers, and publicists who made common cause for reform. Called "*les politiques*," they criticized the royally sponsored program, while at the same time proclaiming their patriotism and Catholicism. Above all, they feared that national division would result from the centrifugal forces of religious fighting and royal family rivalries among les grands-the highest ranking nobbles and royal princes (notably including some Calvinists). The pamphlets of les politiques were among the first widely distributed tracts to promote religious toleration.

In England, the question of whether the law reflected merely the king's pleasure and command reached a critical point during the first half of the seventeenth century. The solution of parliamentary supremacy was painfully affected by revolution but eventually worked out in a framework of legality.

The Problem of Legal Guarantism

What is the relationship of the individual to the government, the place of the citizen in the system of political rule? This is the problem at the core of the second phase of human rights development. Changing socioeconomic conditions impel the individual to see his legal status in a new light. Economic advances motivate the individual to seek adjustments that will bring legal facts into line with socioeconomic and political circumstances—to bring his citizenship role into line with emerging middle class social roles. The German term for civil liberties linguistically reveals these interconnected roles in the word 'Burgherrecht," or "middle-class citizen rights."

Significantly, the quest for juridically fixed claims which the individual can make against government arose side by side with the growth of the middle class inured to an ideology of intolerance to arbitrary power. Acquiring economic resources, members of the middle class sought a marginal share of power and protection by some measure of legal recognition in the form of declarations of rights and privileges. The need, in some such form, to redefine the status of the individual as the institutions of agrarian feudalism declined was made unavoidable principally on account of critical changes affecting the individual in the distribution of material goods. These changes necessitated revised standards for the role of (1) the individual, and (2) the role of government.

(1) The assertion of property rights was the lynchpin which joined the individual's new economic role with his citizenship role as a public individual. Critical to the development of a postfeudal economy was the uneasy competition between monarch and merchants for the control of capital. Under feudalism, the network of distribution was tied to the landed sovereignty of the king; thus the system permitted compensatory privileges and stipends to the king's outlying landed agents for their efficiency in extracting goods and services from reluctant subjects. But to the commercially successful "third estate"-on the rise during the seventeenth and eighteenth centuries-material rewards followed accomplishments in the control and management of capital. With the beginning of mercantile banking and trading success for the propertied (but sometimes unlanded and usually untitled) middle class, the system of material goods distribution began to place a new premium upon ability and achievement. Legal entitlements protecting these values would have to replace the privileges attending the feudal structure of personalized property then giving way to exchange, commerce, and trade. The press of tax obligations sensitized the middle class to the need to use law as an instrument to protect the rights of private property. Thus eighteenth century jurists and publicists portrayed property as a natural right, representing the individual's field of action consonant with marketplace behaviour. Only in his economic role as owner of property could the individual approach self-sufficiency and thereby resist the overstepping of others and the encroachments of the state. On this understanding, property rights were given the highest priority among the revolutionary French declarations of

the rights of man, not only those of 1791 and 1795, but also the more radical declaration of 1793.

In addition to the problem of harmonizing the economic and political roles of the individual, the relation of these roles where government was concerned also underwent scrutiny and change. In the eighteenth century, from Spain to the German principalities, rulers advanced extravagant claims of divine right in ideological defence of the new efforts at centralized absolutism. In opposition, Enlightenment philosophic literature contributed to the case, not only for political freedom, but also for religious toleration and even broader civic liberties. A revolutionary novelty in the resulting ideology of natural law was the emphasis placed on the legal nature of the sphere of liberty, and the consequent insistence on government respect and protection of rights. In the lofty terms of the French Declaration of the Rights of Man and of the Citizen: "The aim of all political association is the protection of the natural and imprescriptible rights of man: liberty, property, security, and resistance to oppression." With the business of government thus radically redefined, the individual could get on with his private business. In terms less philosophic than those of the Declaration the need, as perceived economically, was for a system of rule strong enough to guarantee the legal underpinnings for private investment, and yet not so strong as to interfere greatly with the free decisions of men willing to risk their money and careers in the enterprise of commercial ventures.

Since the eighteenth century inception of guarantism, the techniques of enforcing individual rights, on the one hand, and the standards to be applied, on the other, have been the subject of comparison from one country to another. In 1789, La Fayette, who was then recently returned from America, read to the National Assembly the text of Jefferson's

Declaration of Independence and the Virginia Bill of Rights. Mirabeau, who was rapporteur of the drafting committee, was known even earlier to have called upon the Dutch people to resist the domination of Austria, and to frame a "list of rights which belong to you as men." Thus there was a cross-fertilization of interest, in guarantism among France, Holland, America, and elsewhere. Georg Jellinek has attempted to show that the French Declaration copied American documents which, in turn, ideologically grew out of Puritan conceptions largely inspired by Luther. French scholars, on the other hand, have dismissed both American and Germanic paternity for their classic Declaration, insisting that it was derived primarily from the European literature of the French Enlightenment.

As sterile as the debate over the origin of French guarantism may seem, it does point to an empirical social phenomenon often associated with institutional innovation, the demonstration effect. Foreign observers, noting successful innovation, seek to emulate its success in their own countries. For example, the French Declaration became a model of constitutional legislation widely adopted elsewhere. That reliance helps to explain why, despite national diversities, the list of basic rights and chartered freedoms in Europe have many commonalities. The development of human rights in the Netherlands (since 1798), in the German states (1818-1850), in Belgium (1831), Switzerland (1848), Italy (1848), and Austria (1867) were based on the French tradition.

The problem of defining the legal status of the individual extended to other countries besides France and America partly because of the "demonstration effect" associated with the apparent success of France and America. The prominence of France in world affairs made notice of its example unavoidable, and the suppressed hopes of colonial areas for national sovereignty made of the American example a carefully studied lesson in achieving independence. In both countries, the demonstration of success in legally defining the status of the individual supplied widely noted solutions to the complex problems of transforming demands previously voiced as moral aspirations into declarations and legislation that promised to shape legal reality. On the grounds that legal formulations reflect social content and not just rhetorical imitation, it should be noted that French and American models also have been followed elsewhere because, the socioeconomic conditions associated with efforts to create new political structures extended to other areas as well. For example, as sovereigns became financially dependent upon the support of a growing middle class, the need for, legal change became more pressing. The political context of change in Franco-casting off an over-bearing absolute monarchy-was different from that in America-achieving independence from a colonial master. But the underlying socioeconomic processes associated with these goals had a common basis. Involved was the critical economic problem of altering the distribution of goods and services from a basis of feudal status and privilege in France, and of imperial prerogatives and colonial exactions in America, to the freer market conditions sought by the developing middle class and independent landowners in both countries. From the economic plateau of a strong bargaining position vis-i-vis government, these groups could define and demand from government a set of liberating legal guarantees matched to their interest. For many French revolutionaries, the goal of the Declaration was not only to clarify the status of the citizen and lend dignity to the claims associated with being a man, but addition ally to elevate ability and achievement as values that helped to structure the newly rationalized system of material and service distribution.

The Problem of Equality Rights and Participation

The promotion of new standards of political and civil rights was worked out in nineteenth century Europe and America in terms of a drive toward democratization. Liberal democracy involves a system that is supposed to ensure that public officials are fairly chosen by the masses of voters casting equally weighted secret ballots in more or less competitive elections which involve public consideration of issues and candidates. Behind this composite of specifications lies a lengthy historical process which has resulted in electoral systems gradually and haltingly exposing government to widespread political participation.

As new segments of the population are given entree to the political process, their influx into the system creates strains on existing legal institutions. New interests and new issues arise in association with broadened participation. In particular, the issue of citizenship equality and civil rights becomes an important part of the adaptation required of the legal system to ensure the peaceful expansion of participation. The developmental link between political and civil rights lies in the fact that debate over democratization results not only in exploring alternative electoral arrangements, but also in politicizing issues relating to the legitimacy of social inequalities. The underlying theme of civil rights problems, legal equality, is an issue frequently introduced into political debate as competing elites vie for electoral arrangements favourable to their respective constituent groups.

The suggestion that civil rights issues are genetically connected to the working out of democratic electoral standards may be illustrated by reviewing five such standards as analysed by Stein Rokkan. First is the protection of the citizen's act: voting is made accessible to those who qualify consistent with a system of voting secrecy and protection against vote buying, tampering, and fraud. Second is the universality of access to the ballot: all accountable adults not in confinement for crimes or mental incapacity are given the vote, however peripheral their concern for public affairs. In the process of moving toward this objective, the inequality of excluded groups increasingly becomes the topic of debate as irrational exclusions are challenged on a group-by-group basis: the poor; aliens; racial, ethnic, linguistic, and religious minorities; the educationally deprived; women; and youth. Third is the weight of ballot influence (the "one person-one vote" problem): each vote cast counts as an equal unit of electoral influence. This standard is achieved only through the process of attacking geographical discrimination and politically 'sensitizing the electorate to the unfairness inherent in unequal schemes of representation such as rotten boroughs, and systems of legislative-malapportionment. Fourth is the problem of organizational capacity: groups are assured the legal competence to nominate political candidates consistent with the legal standards for terms and qualifications of elected public officials. As this electoral standard is recognized, contention focuses on the lack of equal access to the political process-the economic barriers which are inherent in the costs of electioneering, and the invidious discrimination against candidates and would-be voters. Fifth is the modem problem of the public's control over public policy: interelection safeguards (such as lobbying and campaign finance restrictions) are set out to ensure some degree of continued public influence over policy-making and its execution. Inherent in this problem is the politically advantaged status of monied elites whose influence on policy is disproportionately inflated compared to that of the common man.

The histories of political systems moving toward these standards of liberal democracy present an amazing array of responses to the task of giving the people a voice in government. In liberal theory, the desirable sociopolitical order is that which relies on the least possible coercion, which allows the free play of spontaneous social forces, and which ensures controls on government. To the extent that these ideas reflected ideological commitments on the part of prevailing elites in early nineteenth century England, France, and America, they created a political environment conducive to expanding civic participation. More fundamentally, however, whether these benevolent standards of the liberal democratic order could be implemented depended upon a larger process of stabilizing the revolutionary ferment from which ideas of individual liberty had been born. With the expansion of society in terms of the formation of new postfeudal classes and commercial interests which had demonstrated their capacity to use violence against royal crowns and colonial masters, a new political problem crucial for the development of human rights emerged. The problem, in terms of competing social groups and classes, was to isolate conflict, manage it, and noncoercively to routininze it. The problem generated a lengthy process involving critical changes in political participation and equal citizenship rights. The problem of routininzing conflict depended for its resolution on expanding political participation because the related institutions of representation supplied the needed forums into which new social groups could be drawn as they began to express their demands. The routinization of conflict also followed a path of legal development whereby civil rights were defined in terms of minimum standards of equality for members of various groups (such as aliens, religious and racial minorities, and women) and a beginning was thereby made toward regularizing procedures for the settlement of intergroup discord on a premise of equality.

At the opening of the nineteenth century, democratic elections and equal citizenship rights existed nowhere. American merchants and landowners shifted their position from acceptance of de facto autonomy to the insistence on consent in taxing policy. In the absence of vestigial feudal social barriers, broadened political participation developed first in America. English aristocrats moved from a defence of their feudal privileges to their own active inclusion in the decision making associated with limited monarchy. Extended participation was slow to follow. The dominant elite of landed and *haute bourgeoisie* French (with Bonapartist and restoration interludes) eschewed the claims of absolute monarchy in favour of their own participation in the workings of republican constitutionalism. The new assertion of American ex-colonials for self government on the one hand, and the claims of English and French privilege to control government on the other, gradually gave way to democratic demands for political participation broadened from an exclusive to a mass middle class base. In England, France, and America, the earliest implements of democracy—parliamentary privilege, electoral accountability, and political representation—were at first constructed by the upper classes for their own use in governmental participation. They were gradually, and grudgingly redistributed to groups clamoring for inclusion and equality. These aspirations broke out in the bourgeois revolution of 1830 in France and in revolutions in 1848 in western and central Europe where efforts to stamp out Jacobinism were often successful. Acceptance of reform so as to avoid the more threatening danger of violent conflict was variously from country to country subject to multiple pressures. But in France, England, and America, two forces in particular helped to shape civil and political rights development: stress in the dynamics of social stratification and elite competition.

Taking wealth, prestige, and power as the indicators of social status, it is clear that the forces affecting change from country to country vary considerably. Nevertheless, stratification systems in countries with high levels of industrialization have more in common with one another than do systems in countries with low levels of economic development. Simon Kuznets has shown that, in the early stages of industrial development, disparities in income between social extremes tend to grow, while progress in economic development has the effect of bringing the mean, median, and mode of income distribution closer together." In his analysis in Social Origins of Dictatorship *and Democracy,* Barrington Moore sheds additional light on the relationship between early industrial development and nascent democracy.' He argues that at the beginning stages of democratic development, the social divisions associated with the commercialization and modernization of the countryside are critical. Where the commercial impulse among the landed aristocracy is quite weak, the continuation of a peasant economy (as in provincial France) or a plantation system (as in the American South) serves as an impediment to the expansion of political and civil rights. Moore stresses that where agriculture has not undergone commercial' modernization, the need of the elite to hold the political levers which keep labouring forces on the land is incompatible with concessions to broadened participation and equality rights.

The predominance of rural over town areas precludes the development of urbanization, industrialization, and the spread of literacy which are all precursors of the expansion of political participation and egalitarianism. In France and the American South, where status reversal was inflicted upon the landed upper classes, resistance to liberal reform was particularly strong. But long-term trends worked in the direction of more equality. Once economic development was underway, expanding technology resulted in improved labour productivity and wages. The related demand for higher levels of skills within the work force had an equalitarian effect upon social stratification because of increasing emphasis placed upon education and literacy. Modest rearrangement in income distribution prompted increased pressures toward broadened participation is well. Thus political rights and issues associated with equality developed side by side with industrial development. The fact that the system of social stratification in France centered on class and religion tended to link the struggle for participation with issues of taxation, group associational rights, economic and labour policy, and church-state problems. The French artisans who joined forces with republican groups in the streets of Paris in 1830 sought not only some remedy to unemployment, but also demanded voting rights as a way of gaining respect from other elements of society. In the United States, the Civil War abolished the institution of slavery and introduced a deeply divisive element of racial stratification into the struggle for civic involvement. Because of the basic colour divisions characteristic of American social stratification, the quest for democratization gained association with issues of sectionalism, ethnicity, civil rights, and educational policy. The fourteenth and fifteenth amendments to the U.S. Constitution were adopted not only to assure the elimination of voting discrimination based on race, but also to guarantee black political participation as a symbol of newly achieved equal citizenship status and civil rights.

In contrast to rural France and the American South where the landed upper classes resisted the liberalization of political participation and equality rights, the English gentry and landed Whigs of the nineteenth century became a part of democracy's entering wedge. There the move toward extending political power was especially associated with the issue of achieving social status. Leadership for the Reform Bill of 1832 came from Whig aristocrats with commercialized farms, manufacturing interests in the industrializing provinces, and family ties to the banking centre of London. Their views reflected a tradition (predating the Puritan Revolution) of opposition to royal bureaucracy and alliance with the upper ranks of town dwellers. Fearful of the example of the Paris barricades of 1830, which reformed the franchise monopoly of the great landlords, the Whigs passed the Bill over the protest of the House of Lords. The Reform Act improved voter equality by abolishing the worst of the rotten boroughs. While it enhanced the representational position of industrial, commercial, and financial groups, property qualifications remained restrictive, notwithstanding some relief in 1867. Urban and rural voters were treated unequally until the Reform Acts of 1884-85, and universal suffrage was not fully adopted until 1919.

The problem of Positive Rights Policy

In times past, ecclesiastical almsgiving and the security reinforced by the extended family supplied the mantle of protection to individuals for basic bodily needs. But under the pressures of industrialization and the consequent adversities of unemployment, sickness, and old age, modem man tends to rely for support upon larger secular associations. The need for safeguards against the unexpected may be met by distributing financial risks among members of private associations: insurance funds distribute benefits to subscribers by the criterion of need; government-supplied security entitlements proliferate in the welfare state. By himself, the individual cannot always obtain employment, adequate education, sufficient medical care, and continuing wages upon retirement from the work force.

Positive rights promise such aid and shelter from jeopardy. They are designed to protect the individual from the economic stress that would otherwise by caused by a suspension of income and to ensure to him needed medical care. Private insurance and employer-employee financed pension plans may be widespread, but increasingly the most important of security entitlements flow from government. Of course, the methods of extending such protection vary greatly from country to country, and everywhere are subject to the contingencies of changing social, economic, political, and legal conditions.

Some theorists, influenced by the needs of the industrial age, have attempted in the speculative context of philosophic justification, to identify specific positive rights in advance of their legal enactment. Thus Jacques Maritain lists as the rights of the working man: rights to form trade unions, to a just wage, to work itself, to relief, to unemployment insurance, to sick benefits, to social security, and even to the ownership and joint management of an enterprise wherever an associative system can be substituted for the wage system. To set a uniform standard of achievement, a number of positive rights are proclaimed in the United Nations Universal Declaration of Human Rights of 1948.

The development in any one country of schemes of positive rights depends heavily upon three factors:

(1) *Economic Potential.* The development pattern of positive rights and welfare policies in various democracies differs from country to country. Genetically, nevertheless, there is a clear link between economic development and the organization of social dependence on a system of continued salaried income and cash wages. Because of the suffering of many under the

stresses and strains of industrial modernization, the idea has grown that protection can justifiably be claimed on behalf of those in the poorest circumstances. The result, in essence, involves governmentally set minimum standards of survival needs under conditions of industrial development.

Under the individual rights guarantees associated with the eighteenth century, security was derived from the right to property. Thus the right served an important social function in service of welfare needs. Since individual security depended greatly upon agricultural self-sufficiency or savings and accumulated reserves, it was hardly enjoyed by the propertyless. For them, the alternative welfare safety nets against disaster ranged from charity to frontier-adventurism. As the movement of workers to urban centres loosened the traditional links of family ties, the problem of poverty, old age, and unexpected destitution gene rated new social and political pressures. Consonant with minority rights and the process of political assimilation beginning in the nineteenth century, group associations played a significant role in meeting security needs. Efforts were made to minimize work-injury and health and old-age risks by transferring their financial consequences from the family to funds sponsored by the industrial community, the trade union, the farmers' cooperative, or the ethnic and religious association. But for better or for worse, the path toward national affluence has been away from the self-contained unitary economy grounded on property rights (whereby most of the necessities of life, including education, are provided in the home or extended private association). Of critical importance, the path of economically sophisticated systems has been toward nearly universal dependence by all citizens upon a continuing flow of money income for the necessities of, life. In the context of the wage system, the circumstances of educational needs, labour injuries, ill-health, and old age increasingly generate economic problem placed at government's doorstep.

(2) *Political Will.* Aside from the field of education (in which the United States led the way in supporting public schools), earliest government reform along systematic welfare lines was initiated in Germany by Bismarck. In 1883 a bill was passed insuring working men against sickness and in 1884 employers Were compelled to insure their employees against accidents. In 1887 laws. were enacted which limited the maximum number of working hours of women and children, Two years later, Germany began to insure working men against old age and disability. These policies were represented as increasing industrial efficiency, and the democratic regimes in Austria, the Scandinavian countries, the Low Countries, and finally France and Italy followed suit.

For welfare benefits to be satisfactorily conceptualized as rights, more was needed than the recognition that related policies functionally served industrial development or that moral considerations were involved. The changing jurisprudence of workmen's compensation is illustrative. The original basis for a legal claim for injury compensation in Germany and other continental countries under the influence of Roman law was the principle of "responsibility." Compensation for on-the-job injury of an industrial labourer was due only if the employer were at fault. If the victim failed to satisfy the heavy burden of showing default *on* responsibility, he could secure no compensation whatever to cover his losses. Under the common law system prevailing in Great Britain, the Commonwealth, and the United States, the victim of an accident generally had to absorb its consequences unless it was demonstrably due to the fault of a second patty-the employer in the case of work-related injury. Financial disaster was, thus, often visited on families of injured workers. On the other hand, unpredictably large damages might be assessed against employers. The winner-take-all appearance of such disputes not only provided dramatic newspaper copy, but also exacerbated industrial strife. Consequently, policy-makers were sensitive to the need for change. The result, though under quite, disparate legal systems, was to regularize (and also to lower) compensation on a principle of no-fault liability.

(3) *Administrative Capacity*. In contrast to earlier liberal assumptions about the necessity for government to leave the individual alone and to refrain from discrimination, the social and economic claims associated with newer positive rights often require that the weight of state laws and administration interfere with many things the individual would like to do. Examples include the collection of taxes, regulation of economic activities, administration of public welfare services, and enforcement of mandatory education laws. Clearly, positive rights depend on legislative definition and administrative enforcement. Their realization thus depends upon the' depth and extent of government administrative control and capacity. Will government merely license and standardize private health insurance programs, or will it take over the administration of health services? The answer concerns program legitimacy as gauged by shifting electoral majorities and patterns of

> legislative responsiveness. But the answer in administrative terms depends practically upon program effectiveness gauged by the capacity that government brings to administrative penetration into previously insulated social structures. Since positive rights are only as good as administrative enforcement services, their legal and organizational setting is important.

The penetration of government administration into every phase of society has had an important effect on legal structure. The evolution of positive rights standards has brought about a blurring of older sharp distinctions between private and public law. 16 An analogous blending of private and public organizational principles and procedures also has affected administrative enforcement services, especially during the initial stage of welfare policy development. An illustration may be drawn from French experience. In France since 1946, the existence of independent pension funds of private organizations has been illegal. The social security program of the *regime general*, nevertheless, bears the organizational marks of an earlier period when erstwhile private pension groups made and administered their own rules. Thus, at present the sickness insurance scheme for farmers, and the social security plan for the self-employed (especially shopkeepers) and others allow a certain diversity of standards and administration. Furthermore, the French supplementary retirement systems are based on freedom of choice of institutions, and the plurality of institutions is said not to impede effective government administration. The authority of the funds over the payment of benefits recalls the idea of the freedom of intermediate groups which is characteristic of the pluralism of social institutions and associational groupings authorized by earlier minority rights standards.

One of the principal difficulties involved in translating moral response to social need into modern legal change lies in society's understanding of the role of the individual. He must be seen, not only in terms of his private needs, but also in terms of his public citizenship role. The process of distinguishing between the private person and public individual (which penetrates social consciousness ideologically during the process of achieving political freedom) enters a new stage of development with the effort to define the role of the public individual in terms of legally fixed rights. To this problem the liberal response was classically framed in seventeenth and eighteenth century declarations and bills of rights. An optimistic faith in such "guarantism" was placed in documentary shields promising to the individual security from overreaching governments. The liberal idea, born of the eighteenth century, required of government chiefly those limited actions which protect freedom by forbidding interference with the individual. The resulting civil liberties which define the status of the individual are generally correlative to negative duties of the state. They are largely consistent with an optimistic view of man as a self-directing agent living in a materially sufficient environment, coupled with a pessimistic view of government seen as overreaching and potentially tyrannous. By contrast, political and civil rights largely reflect a series of more typically nineteenth century legal accommodations to the demands of various groups for guarantees of equal rights of civic participation. In the main, they are consistent with an egalitarian view of man as a politically competent participant in shaping public policy, coupled with a positive view of government as capable of using the mechanisms of law-making to mitigate the legal consequences of social inequality. The resulting civil and political rights are, by and large, correlative with positive policies of government protection and enforcement. They involve, in a phrase attributed to John Stuart Mill, "arrangements for freedom" although little more may be required of the state than that it place its power behind a set of prohibitions against interference with the exercise of equal rights on behalf of those new groups to which participation rights are extended.

During the twentieth century, new economic and social claims have come to broaden the spectrum of human rights. Because they depend for their fulfilment on affirmative government policy, they may be referred to collectively as positive rights. They are designed in legal terms to meet basic human needs not otherwise satisfied by the socioeconomic system. In the twentieth century, the combined influence of political parties and trade unions has been decisive in promoting positive-rights policies of social welfare. In the earliest phases of such policy development their spokesmen have often been effective in noting that welfare policies promote industrial efficiency, and they have been skilful in applying the symbolism and rhetoric of human rights to the field of welfare security policy. Positive rights place upon government the task of protecting the people from the misfortunes of industrial life. The aim is to remedy by welfare the needs which were privately satisfied in the earlier stages of human-rights development when negative rights were functionally linked to an ideal of individual self-sufficiency.

The classical model of developing rights and liberties which has been synthesized in this essay has both uses and limits. It is useful as a teaching device because it helps scholars to overcome the tendency to accept without question the sundry aspects (norms, concepts, and institutions) of their own legal systems. Since the study of comparative human rights seeks to explain differences and similarities, those who pursue it see their own systems in a fresh light. Explanation derived from study is also useful in generating questions for research. Inasmuch as the reasons or causes of divergencies and resemblances are often nonlegal, we must look to the socioeconomic milieu. Reliance on a model helps to supply a beginning step toward framing questions that can usefully be studied empirically.

In terms of the promotion of human rights by economic development our model is instructive. The classical path of human rights development in France, Great Britain, and the United States was favoured by gradual economic and industrial development. What brings the experience of these countries together in a coherent model is that three varieties of human rights policies can be clearly linked with three categories to which political economists refer as "public choice processes": market choice, bargaining choice and centralized choice. Thus property rights, liberty of contract, free expression, the right to travel, and related civil liberties developed side by side with processes of choice involving a largely decentralized exchange of goods, services and ideas concomitant with relatively free market-economic conditions. The political and civil rights stage of policy development which followed was associated with changing processes that emphasized collective choice: competing labour, political, associational, and social groups engaged in a variety of bargaining processes including competition, compromise, persuasion and electoral participation. The positive rights policies emphasizing health and welfare considerations have become associated in a subsequent stage of human rights development with centralized choice processes where authority is concentrated and where the hierarchical choice processes emphasize planning.

The prospect of stepping over the threshold of the post-industrial welfare state demands innovation, not simply reliance upon past lessons and experience. Inasmuch as rights and liberties conflict, and because some in any group of rights cannot be defended as a final good, the future of normative debate in the liberal tradition must focus upon the question of whether and how liberties derived from earlier stages of human rights development can be defended as conditions of the more recent welfare standards.

9

Changing Perspectives

Human rights like fundamental rights, are paramount sacrosanct, eternal and transcendental in nature and ought to be treated as inalienable and inviolable for preserving the dignity of the people. These rights, however, cannot be imagined without the security and existence of a well-regulated society. Society and the State can alone guarantee the human rights to the individual but also demand observance of social norms from the citizens. "The imperfections and frailty of human nature is the justification for the laws- of social control, They do not reject liberty but only regulate it to keep it on the trail of Social Justice Human rights are those minimal rights which every individual must have against the state or other public authority by virtue of being a "member of the human family" irrespective of any other consideration.'

There are rights which are inherent in all citizens, because of their being human. These are the rights which are inalienable because the enlightened conscience of the community would not permit the surrender of those rights by any citizen even of his own volition. These are the rights which are inviolable because they are not only vital for the development and efflorescence of human personality and for ensuring its dignity, but also because without them men would be reduced to the level of animals.

Little effort has been made to create a comprehensive map of the totality of human rights, and there has been little discussion on the detailed content of particular rights. Often even the very concept of human rights is left obscure.

The United Nations Charter refers to human rights in its preamble and six other articles. Learning about one's own rights builds respect for the right of others and points the way to more tolerant, peaceful societies. The Universal Declaration of Human Rights adopted and proclaimed by the General Assembly resolution of 10th December 1948 forms one of the main milestones in the history of Human rights. Indian Constitution contains a variety of human rights termed as fundamental rights. In India, human rights have been defined under "the protection of Human Rights 1993 (No. 10 of 1994)" as under:

> 2(l) (d) "Human rights" means the rights relating to life, liberty, equality and dignity of the individual guaranteed by the Constitution or embodied in the International Covenants and enforceable by Courts in India.

It is a matter of great national pride for all Indians that human rights concept prevailed in its hightest form in our Indian scriptures and religious books. Human rights as a concept is very ancient and some references pertaining to human rights can be found even in ancient Indian Scriptures.

> "Man is not an individual. He is a social organism. God loves him only who serves other beings: men, cattle and other creatures. His glory lies in being a member of a big family. On the one hand, man is bound by blood-kinship his parents, his wife, his children and on the

> other, he is linked with every individual of society whether near or far from his. It is given to man to link himself with those who constitute his ancestry, and also think of those who could be his posterity. Man thus lives, works and dies for society possessed of certain inalienable rights. Man is expected to develop his craft, sciences and technology and lead society from poverty to prosperity, with a happy today and a happier tomorrow".
> (from the *Atharva Veda*)

This work contains a systematic body of political ideas and embodies a comprehensive theory of kingship, Government and preservation of war. In ancient age there was a rule that after dusk upto morning don there will be no firing by the troops and there used to cease-fire with setting of the sun. The Yajinavalkya Smriti and the Narada Smriti, both are still authoritive source books of Hindu law, specifying inter alia, rules of drafting, pleading, procedure and judicial conduct. Both authoritive sources of human law specifically various rules pertaining to protection of human rights. The concept of Dharma has been eternal spring of Hindus' ethic and has been all-pervading, governing and regulating conduct of human beings. The five Yamas-ahimsa (non-violence), truth, non-theft, total abstinence and non-possession and five Niyamas-purity, contentment, penance, study of scriptures and surrender to God were enunciated by great saint Patanjali to attain self-discipline and to establish equilibrium in society. The creation of perfect man, son of eternity, was aimed at establishing an egalitarian, non-exploitive and humane social order.

India has enacted the protection of Human Rights Act 1993 (No. 10 of 1994) with a view to provide for the constitution of a National Human Rights Commission, State Human Rights Commissions in

States and Human Rights Courts for better protection of human rights and for matters connected therein or incidental thereto. The Act received the assent of the President of India on January 8, 1994 and published in the Gazette of India Extra Part 11, Section 1 dated 10 January, 1994, The Protection of Human Rights Act 1993 (Act No. 10 of 1994) contains 43 sections and is divided into the following eight chapters. Chapter 1: Preliminary-Sections 1 and 2 National Human Rights Commission. Chapter II: National Human Rights Commission Sections I and 11. Chapter III: Functions and Powers of the Commission-Sections 12 to 16. Chapter IV: Procedure Sections17 to 20. Chapter V: State Human Rights Commissions-Sections 21 to 29. Chapter VI: Human Rights Courts-Sections 30 and 31. Chapter VII: Finance, Account and Audit-Sections 32 to 35. Chapter VIII: Miscellaneous-Sections 36 to 43.

Despite the apparently fixed positions, few shifts within each perspective on human rights have been visible during past few years. Violations of human rights in India are now seen as violations of the democratic principles enshrined in the Indian Constitution as well as violation of India's international commitment of humanitarian international law and international as it defensively covenants. Another perspective on human rights has national unity, integrity and stability as the focal as it defensively justifies the use of repressive measures in the context of abnormal situations of disturbed areas like Jammu & Kashmir for maintaining national security. The shift in the Perspectives of the Amnesty International is reflected in 1992 when this well-known international body took notice of the fact that "armed Opposition groups in Jammu and Kashmir have been responsible for numerous and grave human rights abuses including hostage-taking, assassination of politicians and their families, deliberate killings of civilians including journalists and torture and rape." Condemning such abuses, the Amnesty International urged such groups to release all hostages and respect human rights and humanitarian standards. At international level, the resolution co-sponsored by India on gross violation of human rights perpetrated by terrorists groups and expressing of solidarity with the victims of terrorism was adopted by the United Nations Human Rights Commission. "The marked shift," according to Balraj Puri, "interestingly enunciated by Shri Atal Bihari Vajpayee at U.N. Conference on human rights at Geneva, asserted India's determination to maintain highest standards of human rights. He quoted at length relevant provisions of the Indian Constitution, cited the role of independent judiciary, Human Rights Commission, Free Press and NGOs in the field of Human Rights. Far from denying the fact of excesses, he quoted figures of punishments to erring officials of the security forces." Ever since early 1994, the issue of human rights was not an internal affair of a sovereign State. The appointment of the National Human Rights Commission on October 12, 1993 is another landmark in the approach towards upholding the human rights and in checking the State in its abuses of civil liberty. Allowing TADA to die a natural death is another important milestone in the history of human rights. Judicial activism and public litigation cases are also various stages in the evolution of the human right issues.

Human rights can be analysed from three perspectives: (1) Socio-economic dimensions, (2) Legal dimensions, (3) Role of international organisations and NGOs in promotion of human rights. Karel Vasak, has categorised human rights into the three generation of rights. His thesis is as following:

> The first generation rights were those rights which emerged from the American and French revolutions. They were aimed at securing the citizen's liberty from arbitrary action by the

> State. They correspond by and large to the civil and political rights in the International Bill of Rights. They are said to be negative rights in that they call for restraint from the State.
>
> The second generation rights emerged with the Russian revolution and were echoed in the welfare state concepts which developed in the West. They correspond largely to the economic, social and cultural rights and they require positive action by the State.
>
> The third generation rights, as Vasak sees them are a response to the phenomenon of global interdependence. Individual States acting alone can no longer satisfy their human rights obligations. The problems that are now being faced require international co-operation for their resolution. These problems include the maintenance of peace, the protection of the environment and the encouragement of development. The third generation rights necessarily benefit individuals and peoples.

From a sociological perspective, for proper realisation of human rights, it is essential that the society as a whole accepts the basic norms of human rights. According to Sir Hersch Lauterpacht, "the protection of human personality and of its fundamental rights is the ultimate purpose of all law, national and international." The International Bill of Human Rights is normally defined as consisting of the U.N. Declaration of Human Rights 1948, the International Covenant on Economic, Social and Cultural Rights 1966, the International covenant on civil and political rights and the optional Protocols thereto. Office of the U.N. High Commissioner for Human Rights was created in December 1993, following the recommendations of the Vienna Conference. Alston and many others have identified the following important phases of human rights activities :

1. 1945-55 was the standard setting or normative phase. The Universal Declaration on Human Rights was drafted, the bulk of the work on drafting the two Covenants was completed, Other Conventions including those on Genocide and Refugees were drafted. This lofty work, however, stood in stark contrast to the UN's inability to react to specific human rights violations.

2. 1955-65 phase was an attempt to correct this by the promotion of human rights. It was a period of attempting to influence the situation by working with governments through the procedure of periodic governmental reports and the provision of advisory services. The achievements in this phase were modest.

3. Within the next decade, 1965-75, came the phase of protection of human rights and an attempt to do something more directly about violations of human rights. New techniques were developed for appointing special rapporteurs to investigate situations. The problem of what to do with the thousands of communications received by the UN on the human rights issues was tackled, and in 1970 ECOSOC adopted the procedures under resolution 1503. The idea of a High Commissioner for Human Rights was launched.

4. After 1976 human rights have become an international concern and demand enforcement with international pressures on defaulting states. Ahmad Yamani feels that the western liberal democratic tradition is so overzealous in its defence of the individual's freedom, liberty, rights and dignity that it overlooks the acts of some individuals in exercising such rights in a way that jeopardizes the community. "Presenting another perspective, Legesse argues. If Africans were the sole authors of the universal declaration

of Human Rights, they might have ranked the rights of communities above those of the individuals.

Human rights have three basic premises which are as under:

(1) The individual necessarily remains the primary subject of international human rights law.

(2) International human rights law recognises the existence of groups.

(3) The full enjoyment of individual human rights requires certain human rights to devolve, wholly or in part, upon groups.

Human Rights have following important propositions:

(1) There is a hierarchy among the subjects of human rights law.

(2) There can be no human rights which detract from the individual's human rights.

(3) Human rights law does recognise certain rights of groups.

(4) The diversity of the cultures and civilizations, beliefs and traditions, history and aspirations reflected in polico-legal system, give rise to ever changing meaning to "human rights".

It is necessary to understand the distinction between human rights and humanitarian laws. Humanitarian law refers to those rules of International law which aim to protect persons suffering from the evils of armed international conflict, directly serving military purposes. The Status of Guerrilla in an international conflict was uncertain and people fighting wars of liberation were denied minimum humanitarian treatment by their adversaries. The Diplomatic Conference in 1977 adopted two Protocols additional to the Geneva Conventions of 1949. Article I(4) of the Protocol 1, 1977 covers the wars of national liberations while Protocol II relates to non-international armed conflict. Protocol 11, 1977 develops and supplements to Article 3 common to the Geneva Convention 1949. It covers non-internal armed conflicts in which hostilities reach a certain degree of intensity. States can easily evade their obligations to observe human rights in conflict situations by denying the armed character of the conflicts or claiming that the low level of violence does not reach the threashold required for the applicability of the Protocols.

In India, all citizens are entitled to human rights but besides women and children, there are certain groups which need greater priorities. The following groups deserve special study in the context of human rights:

(1) *Protection of minorities.* An extensive system of provisions protecting minorities was built into the network of treaties concluded at the end of the World War I. For many newly created States of Europe, a price for nationhood had to be paid in the form of a guarantee to respect the cultural, religious, and even linguistic freedom of minorities within their borders, and a promise that there would be no institutionalised discrimination.

(2) *Prescribing racial and other forms of discrimination*: Various conventions, including the International Convention on the Elimination of All Forms of Racial Discrimination, the ILO's Discrimination Convention (No. III) and UNESCO's Convention against Discrimination in education, extend their protection to members of groups defined by reference to race, colour, descent, sex, national or ethnic origin, political or other opinion, economic conditions, or birth.

(3) Protection of indigenous populations: ILO convention No. 107 concerning indegenous and tribal populations sanctions affirmative action in favour of the populations concerned. ECOSOC in its Decision 1982-84 established a Working Group to review developments relating to the promotion and protection of the human rights and fundamental freedoms of indigenous populations, with special attention to the evolution of standards concerning the rights of indigenous populations.

The founding fathers of Indian Constitution envisioned a comprehensive concept of human rights. Most of the articles of the United Nations General Assembly Resolution of 10 December 1948, Universal Declaration of Human Rights and the two International Covenants of 1966 are the building blocks of India's Constitutional Rights. The Constitution of India, in its Preamble, resolves to secure to all its citizens:

(i) Justice — social, economic and political.

(ii) Liberty — of thought, expression, belief, faith and worship.

(iii) Equality — of status and of opportunity and to promote among all.

(iv) Fraternity — assuring the dignity of the individual and the unity and integrity of the nation.

Our Constitution provides and guarantees the fundamental rights to all the citizens and these rights are the human rights.

Human rights as enumerated in the Constitution as fundamental rights are as under:-

1. *Right to Equality*
   - (i) Equality before Law (Article 14)
   - (ii) Equality of opportunity in matters of public employment: (Article 14)
   - (iii) Prohibition of discrimination on grounds of religion, race, caste, sex or place of birth (Article 15)
   - (iv) Abolition of untouchability (Article 17)
   - (v) Abolition of titles (Article 18). 2. Right to Freedom
2. *Right to Freedom*
   - (i) Freedom of speech etc. (Article 19)
   - (ii) Protection in respect of conviction for offences (Article 20)
   - (iii) Protection of life and personal liberty (Article 21)
   - (iv) Protection against detention in certain cases (Article 22).
3. *Right Against Exploitation*
   - (i) Prohibition of traffic in human beings and forced labour (Article 23)
   - (ii) Prohibition of employment of children in factories etc. (Article 24).
4. *Right to Freedom of Religion*
   - (i) Freedom of conscience and free pursuit of profession, practice and propagation of religion (Article 25)
   - (ii) Freedom to manage religious affairs (Article 16)
   - (iii) Freedom as to payment of taxes for promotion of any particular religion (Article 27)

(iv) Freedom as to attendance at religious places or religious worship in certain educational institutions (Article 28).

5. *Cultural and Educational Rights*

(i) Protection of interest of minorities (Article 29)

(ii) Right of minorities to establish and administer educational institutions (Article 30).

6. *Right to Constitutional Remedies:*

(i) Right to Constitutional remedies (Article 32).

India has ratified and acceded to the following international covenants which came into force from the dates mentioned below:

(i) International Covenant on Economic, Social and Cultural Rights of 1966 (3rd January 1976). Adopted and opened for ratification and adopted by U.N. General Assembly.

(ii) International Covenant on Civil and Political Rights (Adopted by U.N. General Assembly on 16th Dec. 1966) (Entry into Force on 23 March 1976).

All public servants including members of the State and Central Police Organisations are duty bound to uphold the Constitution of India and to adhere to the human rights enunciated to International Covenants referred above. Rights in India are only those fundamental rights and international covenants which are enforceable by courts in India and therefore a thorough analysis of all laws and acts has to be carried out to find the broad dimensions of human rights. State and Central Police Organisations are protectors of human rights and it is therefore necessary that they should understand the challenges which are before them in the field of human rights violations. Human rights can be restricted and limited by the sovereign States in the interest of the general welfare of the people of the nation-State during public emergencies which threaten the life of the nation. Limitations can be determined by law but only for the purpose of securing recognition of the rights of others and for meeting the just requirements of morality, public order and the general welfare in a democratic society. Rights cannot be exercised contrary to the purposes and principles of the United Nations.

The World Congress on Human Rights having met and deliberated in New Delhi from 10 to 15 December, 1990 has urged governments to satisfy the convention on elimination of all forms of discrimination against women and to establish commissions to monitor compliance with it. The World Congress has called upon governments and the media to disseminate freely information dealing with human rights especially those of women and to take action at every level of society with a view to changing attitudes which may result in discrimination against women and girls. The World Congress has condemned all forms of gender discrimination, including discrimination in respect of the right to be born. The World Congress has suggested legislative and other measures to ensure that no person who tends or medically examines any pregnant women shall reveal any information, either to the woman herself or to any other person, which might indicate the sex of the unborn child.

It is imperative to eliminate gender discrimination in respect of education so that education should be free and compulsory for both female and male children atleast upto the age of 16 years. The World Congress has recommended that national laws be examined and revised in order to remove discrimination in the areas by (a) marriage, (b) inheritance, (c) matrimonial property, (d) matrimonial relations, and (e) adoption and guardianship. It has recommended the establishment of family Courts based on the following principles: (a) simplified laws and procedures, (b) privacy of hearing, (c) policy of appointing family court judges in equal gender proportions and (d) providing counselling and mediation services as part of the court process. The World Congress has called upon all the governments to take immediate steps to ensure that all discriminatory laws, regulations and regulatory procedures which restrict the movement of women within a country and which restrict the rights of women to travel outside the country should be repealed.

Though the UN Convention on Elimination of All Forms of Discrimination against Women (CEDAW) was adopted by the General Assembly in 1979, India ratified it in June, 1993. In India, there has been a sharp increase in the incidence of violation of human rights of women. According to a government publication, there is one rape every 54 minutes, there is one molestation every 26 minutes, one abduction every 42 minutes and one criminal offence against women every seven minutes. Rape victims in India come mostly from the lower rings of the society. The Criminal Law Amendment Act 1983 has brought some important changes in the existing laws of rape. It amends of Section 376 of the IPC and extends the minimum period of punishment in rape cases to seven years. Section 114A states where sexual intercourse by the accused has been proved and the victim states before the court that she did not consent, the court will presume that there was absence of consent. The Act provides for trial in camera. The new Section 228(a) of the IPC also makes disclosure of the identity of the victim an offence punishable with imprisonment for two years.

By the amendment of the Child Marriage

Restraint Act 1978, the age of marriage was raised to 18 years. Section 357 of the Cr. P.C. provides for the compensation to rape victims and the offender, not the State is ordered to pay compensation to the victims. In India, in 1990 a total number of 68317 crimes were committed against women and in 1993 the figure rose to 83,954, an increase of about 23 per cent. In India everyday 32 women are raped, 16 killed for dowry and 57 are molested.

Human Rights of Children

Article 25(2) of the Universal Declaration of Human Rights (1948) provides that "Motherhood and childhood are entitled to special care and assistance. All children, whether born in or out of wedlock, shall enjoy the same social protection. Article 10 of the International Covenant on Economic, Social and Cultural Rights asserts that "Special measures of protection and assistance should be taken on behalf of all citizens and young persons without any discrimination for reasons of percentage and other conditions. Children and young persons should be protected from economic and social exploitation." The UN General Assembly adopted the convention on the rights of the children on November 20, 1989. The provisions of the convention apply for four areas of children rights, namely, survival, development, protection and participation. The Vienna Declaration of Human Rights (1993) insists that all states should, with international co-operation (a) combat "exploitation and abuse of children by addressing their root causes"; (b) device effective measures against female infanticide, harmful child labour, sale of children, child prostitution, child pornography, as well as the other forms of sexual abuse; (c) organise "means of improving the protection of children in armed conflicts and programmes of "after care and rehabilitation of children in war zones" as well as those in especially difficult circumstances." The 1989 UN Convention on the Rights of the child apply for four main areas of children's rights, namely, survival, development, protection and participation.

The Rights to Survival include provisions of adequate food, shelter, clean water and primary health care. There are the basic rights to ensure the survival of a child. The Rights to Develop include access to information, education, cultural activities, opportunities for rest, play and leisure and the right to freedom of thought, conscience and religion. The Rights to Protection include assurance of protection not only from violation of rights but also from all kinds of exploitation and cruelty, arbitrary separation from the family and abuses in the justice and penal system. Protection is vital for especially vulnerable groups among children like abandoned children, street children, displaced children, etc. The Rights to Participation include the right to express opinions and the right to play an active role in the community and society through freedom of associations, etc. Since children by virtue of the fact that they are human beings and entitled to the rights enjoyed by adults, the UN Declaration on the rights of the child affirmed by the Convention provides for States to ensure mental, physical and moral development of the children. India has ratified the Convention on Rights of child of 1989.

Human Rights to Safe Environment

The Articles 3 and 25 can form the basis of a safe and healthy environment. The rights were reiterated in the 1992 Stockhold .Declaration at the UN Conference on Environment. The recent resolution of 6 March 1990 adopted at 52nd Meeting of the Commission of Human rights of UN Economic and Social Councils. Over the last two decades, the concept of a human right to a safe and clean environment has emerged as one of the basic rights in a number of states. Article 12 of the International Covenant on Economic, Social and Cultural Rights recognize the right of everyone to the highest attainable standard of physical and mental health, and agree to take steps to activate the full realization of this right, including the improvement of all aspects of environmental and industrial hygiene."

Emergency and its Impact on Human Rights

Constitution of India, Part XVIII (Articles 352-360), provides a separate set of provisions to deal with situations such as a war or external aggression or even internal rebellion, civil war or like which render it impossible for the normal constitutional machinary to cope with the abnormal situation. During emergency, certain human rights can be derogated in the internal covenant of civil and political rights 1966. During public emergencies which threaten the organised life of the nation (communities), certain human rights can be derogated as a temporary measure till continuance of an exceptional situation of crisis or emergency crisis or threat to the nation may be either actual or imminent and such provisions exist in Article 352 (1) of the Indian Constitution which has been as under:

> "Explanation - A Proclamation of Emergency declaring that the security of India or any part of the territory thereof is threatened by war or by external aggression or by armed rebellion may be made before the actual occurrence of war or of any such aggression or rebellion, if the President is satisfied that there is an eminent danger thereof"" Article 4 of the International Covenant on civil and Political rights says: "Article 4-1. In time of public emergency which threatens the life of the

nation and the existence of which is officially proclaimed, the State parties to the present covenant may take measures derogating from their obligations under the present covenant to the extent strictly required by the exigencies of the situation, provided that such measures are not inconsistent with their own obligations under international law and do not involve discrimination solely on the ground of race, colour, sex, language, religion or social origin.

2. No derogation from Articles 6,7 and 8 (Paragraphs 1 and 2) 11, 15, 16 and 18 may be made under this provision.

Human rights are thus of two categories. One category is called non-derogable rights" and the other category is called "derogable rights" under the Indian Constitution. Articles 358359 are provisions derogating from the fundamental rights during the operation of a proclamation of Emergency by the President, under Indian Constitution "armed rebellion" implies something like the offence of waging war against the Government in power or a conspiracy or combination to overthrow lawful government by force" (Section 121 of Indian Penal Code is relevant). The 44th Constitutional Amendment Act 1978 got 352(l) by substituting "armed rebellion" for "internal disturbance". The 42nd Amendment Act 1976 empowers the President to proclaim emergency confined to a particular area only without effecting the rest of India.

Restrictions and Limitations

Under the exercise of the right of "derogation", for preserving the life and existence of the nation-State itself, the State is free from the obligations imposed by the human rights in times of "war and other public emergency. When the violation of human rights are sought to be justified under a limitation clause, the law would be saved only if the terms of the relevant clause such as reasonableness, public interest and the like as satisfied. [Chintaman Rao us State of M.P. (195) SCR 750). Article 29(s) of the Universal Declaration of Human Rights, Articles 12(3), 14(l), 18(3), 19(3), 21, 22(2) of International Covenants on civil and political rights, and Articles 8(2), 9(2), 10(2), 11(2) of European Convention on Human Rights append specific limitations to each of the human rights, apart from some generic provisions. No human-right is absolute and some limitations are needed for the protection of the society and the nation-States (Kochuni us State of Madras A 1960, SC 1960, SC 1080) (1099). Indian Supreme Court in words of Das J. has held that "putting restraint on the freedom of wrong-doing of one person is really securing the liberty of the intended victims.

Therefore restraint on liberty should be judged not only subjectively as applied to a few individuals who come within their operations but also objectively as securing the liberty of a greater number of individuals... S.C.R. 88 (292). In the Indian Constitution for human rights the limitation clauses are to be found in clauses (2)46) of Article 19, provided the conditions of reasonableness of the restrictions imposed and the grounds specified in the relevant clause are satisfied.

In Indian Constitution, Articles 31 and 31 C offer complete exceptions to the fundamental rights guaranteed by Part-III of the Constitution and if any law comes within the ambit of above referred articles (Article 31A or 31B or 31C) the law enacted with the safeguard and upheld even though' its provisions are unreasonable or arbitrary. It has been held that there cannot be anything as absolute or uncontrolled liberty for that would lead to anarchy and disorder.

Justice Bhagwati has pointed out that public interest litigation is intended to bring justice within the reach of the poor masses who constitute the low visibility area of humanity. Article 23 of the constitution is clearly designed to protect the individual not only against the State but also against other private citizens. Article 23 strikes at forced labour in whatever form it may manifest itself, because it is violative of human dignity and is contrary to basic human values. Bandhua Mukti Morcha us Union of India is a landmark judgement of the Supreme Court where the bonded labourers have been protected from exploitation. Regarding Protection of children from exploitation, Supreme Court has observed "Construction work is clearly a hazardous essential that the employment of children under the age of 14 years must be prohibited in every type of construction work. This is a constitutional prohibition which, even if not followed by appropriate legislation, must operate Proprio Viaore". In Sheela Barse us Secretary, Children and Society, the Supreme Court observed, "Every society must devote full attention to ensure that children are properly cared for and brought up in a proper atmosphere where they could receive adequate training, education, and guidance in order that they may be able to have their rightful place in the society when they grow up.

Internal Security: Challenges and Issues

In plural, secular and democratic societies violent movements arise out of socio-economic and political discontents. When available political processes are found inadequate to provide outlets for redressal of grievances, when there are credibility gaps in socio-political systems, when population of a particular area feels threatened with identify crisis, certain sections at times resort to violent political movements. When the nation States use police and security forces to put down politically violent movements, excessive use of force or aberrations in the conduct and behaviour of police officers further alienate the population and the political discontent at times gets identified. Police and PMF have a very limited role to play in combating and containing the criminality of political movements.

Terrorism, insurgency and extremism are basically violent political movements born due to the existence of political discontent and which seek redressal through violent means. Unfortunately generally at many occasion" political leaders try to put down politically violent movements with use of force through deployment of police and para-military forces. When the State uses police and para-military forces to put down such movements, excessive use of forces alienate the local population and the discontent intensifies. The first requisite therefore is to realise that political ideologies cannot be put down by force and the use of force should be limited to dealing with the criminality endemic in such situations. The problem of human rights in areas torn by intense strife and such manifestations of violence as terrorism and secessionist activities need to be looked at from a different perspective. What is the solution to the internal security challenges when the very life and integrity of the nation are at stake ? When the very existence of a secular plural and democratic society is in real peril, are human rights more important than the preservation of the nation's integrity ? Indeed who lives if the nation withers? Therefore to meet such critical situations, policing is assisted and partly replaced by the para-military forces because in the clash of arms, laws are silent. Nations make the so-called draconian laws to meet such serious situations. Political movements of disturbed areas like Kashmir and north-eastern states cannot be put down only with the use of force and deployment of security forces, because the solutions to such violent political movements lie in the political processes in the ultimate analysis.

Internal security operations are often very challenging, complex and difficult because internal security has to be maintained in accordance with the laws of the land and rule of law. During internal security operations carried out by the commandos in Punjab till 31 January 1993, there were 11 encounters, in which 222 terrorists were killed including 56 hardcore ones and 283 weapons were seized. Since 1989 in internal security operations more than 1300 police casualties took place. In Kashmir, Pakistan is waging a proxy war with the help of mercenaries. Insurgents and terrorists commit murders, kidnapping, extortions, rapes and all other types of crime which are ultimately violations of human rights. Internal security forces are performing their duties under tremendous pressure, strains and stresses.

They are highly overworked, in most hazardous working environment, without local people's support at times, thousands of miles away from their families. Often in disturbed areas ' one would find the local police highly demoralised and often infected with the dissident ideology. "Human Rights", says Claire Palley, "provide criteria for making value judgements-reflect normative judgements as to what is permissible to be done by free and responsible persons, acting either individually or collectively through the Government. Human Rights can be used to evaluate the law of States by deciding whether the standards inherent in such rights are reflected in positive law". "The path of Human Rights", says an author, "does not run smooth and straight. Every day we stumble against the irrational, reason is pushed to one side and rights are trodden underfoot." In Keshvananda Bharati's case, Justice Dwivedi observed : "The Constitution is not intended to be the arena of legal quibbling for men with long purses. It is made for the common people." Speaking in the similar tone Justice Chandrachud noted : "It is really the poor, starved and mindless millions who need the court's protection for securing to themselves the enjoyment of human rights. "Today we find that in Third World countries there are large number of groups which are being subjected to exploitation, injustice, and even violence. In this climate of conflict and injustice, judges have to play a positive role and they cannot content themselves by invoking the doctrines of self-restraint and passive interpretation. The judges in India have fortunately a most potent judicial power in their hands, namely, the power of judicial review. The judicious and sustained use of its power to further the cause of social justice has come to be regarded by many as not only beneficent but imperative in a developing country where there is large-scale poverty and ignorance. The judiciary has to play a vital and important role not only in preventing the remedying abuse and misuse of power but also in eliminating exploitation and in justice." "It would be no exaggeration to state that human rights would remain safe in a society governed by a written Constitution so long as its judges are strong and independent, do not come into pressures or influence of centres of power and are committed to the cause of human rights. The judiciary has to be ever alert to repel all attacks, gross or subtle, against human rights and they have to guard against the danger of allowing themselves to be persuaded to be attenuate or constrict human rights out of misconceived concern for the State interest or concealed political preference or sometimes ambition or weakness or blandishments or fear of executive reaction. Judicial somnambulance, indifference or timidity can be the source of greater threat to human rights enforcement than the aggression of the violators, for the greatest bulwark against State authoritarianism or arbitrariness would then be gone." "A heavy responsibility immediately falls on the shoulders of the judges in discharging the judicial function particularly in relation to enforcement of human rights. The approach of the judiciary in the interpretation of human rights should be creative and purposive and the judiciary must adopt an activist goal oriented approach and the interpretation of the fundamental rights embodied in the Bill of Rights or in a statutory legislation. The judges must boldly interpret the charter of human rights enshrined in the Constitution ... There is considerable scope for creativity for a judge if only he is dedicated to the cause of human rights and is prepared to advance human rights jurisprudence by a process of judicial interpretation. "The so-called protagonists of human rights are preoccupied only with the superstructure civil and political rights of urban and rural elite to the exclusion of other rights." "The expression 'protective custody, was a euphemism calculated to disguise what was really and in truth nothing short of a blatant violation of personal liberty guaranteed under Article 21, because there was no provisions of law under which a woman could be kept in jail by way of 'protective custody' merely because she was required for the purpose of giving evidence. Taking a bold approach he directed that all women and children who are in the jails in the State of Bihar under protective custody or who are in jail because their presence is required for giving or who are victims of offence should be released and taken forthwith to welfare homes or rescue homes and should be kept there and properly looked after. Justice Bhagwati proceeded to fill up the gap through creative interpretation of Article 21 following upon his own judgement in Maneka Ghandhi's case. He maintained that a procedure which does not make legal services available to an accused person who is too poor to afford a lawyer and who would, therefore, go through the trial without legal assistance cannot be regarded as responsible, fair and just. He held that the right to legal assistance was an essential element of any reasonable, fair and just procedure for a person accused of an offence and it must be held implicit in the guarantee of Article 21. Justice Bhagwati thus spelt out the right to legal aid in a criminal proceeding from the language of Article 21 and held that this, "is a constitutional right of every accused person who is unable to engage a lawyer and secure legal services on account of reasons such as poverty, indigence or incommunicado situation and the State is under a mandate to provide a lawyer to an accused person if the circumstances of the case and the needs of justice so require, provided of course the accused person does not object to the provision of such lawyer." The right to life protected under Article 21 of the Constitution was not confined merely to the right to physical existence but it also included within its broad matrix the right to the use of every faculty or limb through which life is enjoyed as also the right to live with basic human dignity. Using 'creative' approach and 'elaboration of rights strategy in Francis Mullan's case Justice Bhagwati elevated immunity against torture or cruel, inhuman or degrading treatment or punishment to the status of a fundamental right under Article 21, though it was not specifically enumerated as a fundamental right in the Constitution.

— Four or five police lock-ups should be selected in reasonably good localities where only female suspects should be kept and they should be guarded by female constables. Female suspects should not be kept in the same Police lock up in which male suspects are detained;

— Interrogation of women should be carried out only in the presence of women police officers/ constables;

— Whenever a person is arrested by the Police without warrant, he must be immediately informed of the grounds of his arrest and in case of every arrest, it must be immediately made known to the arrested person that he is entitled to apply for bail;

— Whenever a person is arrested and taken to the police lock-up the intimation of such arrest must immediately be given to the nearest Legal Aid Committee so that immediate steps can be taken for the purpose of providing legal assistance to the arrested person at the State cost;

— As soon as a person is arrested, the police must immediately obtain from him the name of any relative or friend whom he would like to be informed of his arrest and the police should get in touch with such relative or friend and inform him about the arrest;

— The Magistrate before whom the arrested person is produced should enquire from him whether he has any complaint of torture or maltreatment in police custody and inform him that he has a right under Section 54 of the Code of Criminal Procedure to be medically examined.

Violations of Human Rights

Shri Dharma Vira, Chairman of National Police Commission has observed, "We may modify our laws to safeguard human dignity or talk loudly about such dignity or rights but so long as the police behaviour in our country, remains as it is today, all such provisions and declarations would prove to be only on paper and not in reality". There is a general feeling of immunity that persists among police offices in India, particularly in the civil police, that they are above law and the system will provide them protection. Modern scientific methods of interrogation like the detectors, are not available at grass root levels in police and there is constant pressure from superior police officers and politicians to deliver quick results.

There are numerous causes and factors responsible for various violations of human rights by the Indian police. Inadequate police training, inadequate supervision by senior officers and corruption in police are some of the main causes of violations of human rights. Lack of adequate recognition of human rights by the police and the police subculture of violence also contribute for the violations of human rights by the police. "Clearly the rot in top echelons is responsible for the mess down below. A senior police officer commented that only extra-constitutional methods could restore law and 28 order in Punjab". When police officers violating human rights and even indicated by High Courts for violations of human rights are awarded medals, the message goes round that police could get away with such aberrations.

The apathy of the public and insensitivity of the Government have emboldened the guardians of law to go ahead with more daring forms of violations of human rights. A retired police chief says all cases of custodial deaths and police misdeanor are quietly buried after the initial furore is over. The cases are investigated and charges framed in such a manner that there are enough loopholes for the guilty to escape. The political masters are led to believe by the top police leaders that if police are taken to task, it would demoralise them and consequently they would not be able to perform their arduous tasks effectively. The police violations of human rights in India have increased over the last 5 years because of an ineffective criminal justice system.

According to Shri N.S. Saksena, the dishonest IPS Officer who cannot control his station house officers, lets this evil degenerate to a point where policemen beat any one who annoys them. Violations of human rights in terms of police excesses in torture and brutality are committed with great frequency and extensively in India where police officers are with sadistic temperament and there is lack of effective supervision by the senior officers. When there is undue delay in bringing the offenders to justice and there is reluctance on the part of the public to come forward as witnesses, police start resorting to rough and ready short-cut methods to justice. In several States of India, the police have merged into a powerful autonomous body with the senior officers having hardly any effective control over the policemen who have close links with politicians and caste lords. "Encounters" and "disappearances" are often reported by human right organisations. The Chief Minister of West Bengal Shri Jyoti Basu, admitted on the floor of the Assembly in June 4, 1992 that 78 prisoners died in police custody between April 1987 and June 1992 in West Bengal. Since independence, a large number of Commissions of Inquiry to probe into the complaints of torture and death in police custody, brutalities committed during police operations, have made various recommendations, but because of the reluctance on the part of the government to implement their recommendations, all reports are gathering dust. Justic V.V. Chandra Chud, Former Chief Justice of India in 1985, has observed, "Police officers, alone, and none else, can give evidence regarding the circumstances in which a person in their custody comes to receive injuries. Bound by the ties of a kind of brotherhood, they often prefer to remain silent to such situations and when they choose to speak, they put their own gloss upon facts and pervert the truth". It is very well established that Indian society tactly expects and approves the use of violence on suspects to get at the truth and provides social sanction to the principle of "an eye for an eye". Many unscrupulous police officers tend to play psychological factors freely in obtaining confessions and work out cases successfully.

Overwork and pressure of work also tend to cause violations of human rights in a society where professionalism is at a discount and where politicians want quick results ignoring means. Legal hurdles, like inability to keep a suspect for longer duration are also responsible partly for violations of human rights by the police. Very often policemen find themselves caught in a dilemma when they find that criminals apprehended after great difficulty and risk, are released by Courts on bail. Police brutality and violations of human rights are symptoms of a sick society where criminal justice administration has almost collapsed and political masters demand control of crime and violence. However, violations of human rights by the police are on the increase of late because the senior officers and inquiring officers are reluctant and slow to investigate cases of police excesses because of the illusion that to do so will sap public confidence in the police generally and will demoralise the policemen.

Analysis of Violations

In a significant reflection of the high incidence of human rights violations by security forces, the highest number of cases admitted by the National Human Rights Commission in its very first year are in the category of custodial deaths and other police excesses.

For the period from October 1993 to March 1994 a total of 496 cases were registered. As per record, 174 cases were admitted for further investigation and enquiry. Atleast 34 of these pertain to custodial deaths, 61 cases of police excesses and 10 cases of reported excesses by the Armed Forces. 30 Of the total cases registered the nine defaulting States and one union territory in terms of human rights violations with number of human rights violations are as under:

1.	Uttar Pradesh	102	No. of cases
2.	Tamil Nadu	61	"
3.	Orissa	51	"
4.	Gujarat	45	"
5.	Madhya Pradesh	43	"
6.	Delhi	36	"
7.	Kerala	25	"
8.	Rajasthan	24	"
9.	Andhra Pradesh	17	"
10.	West Bengal	15	"

The Human Rights Commission undertook 26 suo moto inquiries including the infamous Bijbehara massacre in Jammu and Kashmir when atleast 60 civilians died in a firing by personnel of the Border Security Force.

Punishment for Human Rights Excesses

Punishment have been meted out to 39 army personnel in the past four years for human rights excesses during operations in Jammu & Kashmir. These include 15 officers, two JCOs, and 22 other ranks. There were 245 cases of human rights violations in the past four years by the BSF in J & K. Of these 134 cases are still being investigated while punishment of varying degree has been meted in 111 cases. During the period 199094 there was one case of death of a militant in army custody for which a lieutenant-colonel was charged under Sec. 63 of the Army Act and censured with "displeasure" for not exercising effective control while a captain and second lieutenant .reprimanded" in the same case.

Of the 39 army personnel punished, 15 have been charged with rape, molestation and outraging the modesty of women. In one instance, two captains were cashiered and asked to undergo one year rigorous imprisonment for allegedly raping a Canadian woman. Twelve others, in the rank of havildars and sepoys were dismissed with punishment ranging from six months to 12 years rigorous imprisonment. They were charged with the rape of local woman and attempted molestation. In certain cases punishments varying from "reprimand" to a reduction in rank were awarded to certain personnel for failure to exercise proper control of their subordinates resulting in violation of human rights. In one case a lieutenant colonel, a major and a captain, under whose supervision an "anti-national element" sustained injuries in army custody, were censured with severe displeasure.

Functions of the Commission

The functions of the national human rights commission are given below.:

(a) inquire, suo motu or on a petition presented to it by a victim or any person on his behalf, into complaint of

(i) violation of human rights or abetment thereof or

(ii) negligence in the prevention of such violation, by a public servant;

(b) intervene in any proceeding involving any allegation of violation of human rights pending before a Court with the approval of such Court;

(c) visit, under intimation to the State Government any jail or any other institution under the control of the State Government, where persons are detained or lodged for purposes of treatment reformation or protection to study the living conditions of the inmates and make recommendations thereon;

(d) review the safeguards provided by or under the Constitution or any law for the time being in force for the protection of human rights and recommend measures for their effective implementation;

(e) review the factors, including acts of terrorism that inhibit the enjoyment of human rights and recommend appropriate remedial measures;

(f) study treaties and other international instruments on human rights and make recommendations for their effective implementation;

(g) undertake and promote research in the field of human rights;

(h) spread human rights literacy among various sections of society and promote awareness of the safeguards available for the protection of these rights through publications, the media, seminars and other available means;

(i) encourage the efforts of non-governmental organisations and institutions working in the field of human rights;

(j) such other functions as it may consider necessary for the promotion of human rights.

Inquiry into complaints: During the relatively brief period covered by this report, the commission had already registered 496 cases. Of these, 174 were admitted for further investigation/ inquiry/report while 274 were dismissed. In respect of 48 cases the Commission disposed of complaint with observations to the effect that remedies were more appropriately available in other for a, and that the complaints should seek such remedies from them. In accordance with its statute and regulations, the grounds for the dismissal of complaints were broadly that :

(i) The complaints did not fall within the purview of the Commission;

(ii) The matter was sub-judice or pending before another Commission;

(iii) The event, which was the object of the complaint had occurred more than one year before the making of the complaint;

(iv) The complaint was vague or frivolous and no specific case had been made out of a human rights violation.

On 1 November 1993, the Commission, suo motu, took cognizance of press reports about the death of about 60 persons in and around Bijbehara in Jammu & Kashmir as a result of firing by security forces operating in the area and called for reports from the Ministries of Defence and Home Affairs as also the Government of J. & K While the Ministry of Defence clarified that the army was not involved, the Ministry of Home Affairs sent a report to the Commission on the basis of the Magisterial Inquiry ordered by the State Government into the incident and the Staff Court of Inquiry ordered by BSF authorities. On examination of the report, the Commission felt that perusal of copies of evidence given by six witnesses was necessary and accordingly called for additional material, viz., the evidence given by the witnesses. That evidence having been made available to the Commission and considered by it, together with the report and material provided earlier, the Commission made the following observations recommendations:

(a) The Commission noted that disciplinary proceedings had been initiated under the Border Security Force Act against 14 members of the Force, and further that, on the basis of a Magisterial Inquiry, steps may be initiated to launch prosecutions. The commission expected that the dual proceedings would be pursued their respective logical ends and that it would be kept informed the action taken against those found guilty.

(b) Payment was recommended of interim compensation on a graded scale.

(c) It was recommended that a thorough review should be undertaken by Government of the circumstances and conditions in which Units of the Border Security Force are deployed and expected to operate in situations involving only civilian population.

These were communicated to the Central Government and the Commission has since been informed that the recommendations made by it have been accepted.

Review of Existing Laws, Implementation of Treaties and other International Instruments

Sub-sections (d) and M of Section 12 of the Act respectively empower the Commission to review the safeguards provided by or under the Constitution or any law for the time being in force, and study treaties and other international instruments on human rights with a view to making recommendations for their effective implementation. In the short period since its inception, the Commission has directed its attention to starting an in-depth study of the Terrorist and Disruptive Activities (Prevention) Act (TADA), a task in which it has enlisted the assistance of the Law Commission. A second area of study for the Commission relates to the range of issues concerning the rights of the child including the vexed and cruel question of child labour. A third area of study for the Commission relates to legislation affecting the rights of women. The National Commission for Women, which is represented in the National Human Rights Commission through its chairperson, has done considerable work in this area with the help of most eminent committee which it established for this purpose. The National Human Rights Commission intends to remain in close touch with its sister Commission on this matter, with a view to examining the issues on which it can best be of support and encouragement.

Promotion of Human Rights Literacy

The promotion of human rights literacy in a society as complex and textured as ours is a task that is, at once, both daunting and crucially important. It is also a task that calls for great perseverance, for it requires deep and lasting commitment. Indeed, there is no easy way to create a culture of human rights: all sections of society have a role to play, and an ideal to sustain, if the cause of human rights is to take root and flourish against the cruel odds of social injustice and inequality, the problems of poverty and the fanatical destructiveness of terrorism. Soon after its establishment, the Commission decided—a first series of steps-to concentrate on three key sectors of our society : first, the political parties, for ours is a nation profoundly devoted to multi-party democracy; second, the executive authority at all levels, for ours is a federal structure and third, educationists and those responsible for curricula monitoring, for human rights literacy needs its teachers-and pupils if it is to take deep root in our soil. The Commission accordingly addressed letters to the Presidents of political parties represented in the Lok Sabha, the Rajya Sabha or in the State Legislatures. The Commission observed the political parties, by their behaviour and the ideals that they propagate, can create the most powerful force for the promotion and protection of human rights of all of the citizens of our country.

In so far as the educational system is concerned, a number of steps have been taken. Meetings have been initiated with the Department of Education, Ministry of Human Resource Development and the National Council for Educational Research and Training (NCERT), for evolving appropriately graded curricula for various levels of schooling. The Department of Education and the NCERT are in the process of preparing drafts for the imminent consideration of the Commission. At the University level, the Commission has addressed communications to all Vice-Chancellors, proposing four measures:

(i) that the subject of human rights, in all of its dimensions, may find a clear place in the curriculum of the University;

(ii) that research, seminars and publications concerning human rights should be furthered;

(iii) that the Commission would encourage linkages between the academic community and non - governmental organisations so that the best academic minds can bring their talents to bear up on the practical work being done by such groups; and

(iv) that the Commission would welcome continuing contact with the universities in these areas and that it would help, within its means and possibilities.

Other training institutions have also engaged the attention of the Commission. The most notable of these is the Sardar Vallabhabhi Patel National Police Academy in Hyderabad which has included the teaching of human rights in its courses at the instance of the Commission. At the State level, too, there are increasing instances of police training institutes focussing on this key aspect of professional training, Contacts have also been instituted with the armed forces, amongst whom there is a notably heightened appreciation of the necessity and value of imparting training in respect of human rights. Indeed, at the senior-most level of the armed forces, the Commission has recently noted an increasing sensitivity towards, and recognition of, the need to develop a culture of human rights.

The Constitution expects the bureaucracy, politicians and the judiciary to play their independent roles, says the Allahabad High Court's landmark judgement in the Uttarakhand case, but .politics in India is moving away from health into a diseased power lose their perspective." Way back in 1948, the Privy Council had said: "A public servant can only be said to act or to purports to act in the discharge of his official duty, if his act is to lie within the scope of his official duty. Thus, a judge neither acts nor purports to act as a judge in receiving bribe, though the judgement which he delivers may be such an act; nor does a government medical officer act or purports to act as a public servant in picking the pocket of a patient whom he is examining though the examination itself may be such an act. The test may well be whether the public servant if challenged can reasonably claim that what he does, he does so by virtue of his office." If a minister assaults an officer within the secretariat premises, the act is not connected with his official duty and no sanction to prosecute him is needed. Cheating or abetting it is not a public duty. The Court has come down heavily on the aberrations in the administration run by UP Chief Minister Mulayam Singh Yadav and his successor Mayawati. These were the aberrations which had led to the ghastly assault on one of the women protestors, killing of men by trigger-happy police and abduction of others who were on a peaceful march to Delhi to demand a separate Uttarakhand State. One Chief Minister feigned ignorance about the bloody and beastly acts of the police and his successor, who spent a brief stint in office, defended the policemen accused of rape and killings, saying they were merely carrying out their responsibilities. Sanction to prosecute these men in uniform was denied as the accused defended their despicable acts saying these were performed in discharge of their official duties. Justice Ravi S. Dhavan and Justice A.B. Srivastava's 271 page trend setting verdict has the potential of strengthening the cause of human rights and dignity. They have questioned the accused officials' defence that they could not be prosecuted for committing penal offences like murders, rape, molestation, assault, disposing of bodies, abductions and last but not the lease tampering with records to eliminate evidence which could be conclusive. Were these not the crimes against public justice? Is firing at unarmed civil right activists or political dissenters part of the sovereign function of any State? Is burying a body with parents seeking it, part of official duty? It is a settled law that should there be an occasion to seek sanction on a prosecution, the trial court where the chargesheet is filed would decide the issue. Recently, the Supreme

Court bench headed by Justice J.S. Verma which is seized of the Hawala scam said so.

Security Forces: Combating Organised Violence

C.R.PY, B.S.F., I.T.B.P., N.S.G., C.I.S.F., Assam Rifles are some of the security forces engaged in combating organised crime today. Civil Police usually depends on security forces for all law and order duties. Security forces have to combat organised violence whether it is ethnic, communal or terrorist violence. My own experience of last thirty-three years has led me to the firm conviction that security forces, while combating organised violence, must observe human rights mainly for the following reasons:

Firstly, it is a constitutional mandate and every citizen has the fundamental rights under the constitution for a dignified human existence.

Secondly, those who violate human rights are liable to be prosecuted and made to pay compensation to the victims.

Therefore it is in the interest of the members of the security forces not to violate HR.

Thirdly, security forces no longer get any protection under sovereign immunity doctrine" because recent Supreme Court in Bilabati Behare vs State of Orissa (1993) 2-Sec-513 has held that the principle of sovereign immunity shall be inapplicable in such cases.

Fourthly, security forces can get public cooperation and support for combating organised violence only if they observe human rights and are respected by the public as their saviours against militants.

Fifthly, non-observance of human rights is counter productive and not beneficial in the long run. Violations of human rights by the security forces generally take the following shapes:

(1) Use of third degree methods during interrogation.

(2) Deaths in custody of security forces.

(3) Disappearances and fake encounters by the security forces.

(4) Illegal and unauthorised searches and raids causing inconvenience to the public.

(5) Unauthorised detentions in custody of security forces.

(6) Atrocities against women and children including cases of rapes.

(7) Discrimination against people on grounds of religion, race, caste or sex.

(8) Hand-cuffing of the people.

A number of Supreme Court judgements and human right organisations like Amnesty International and others have brought out such cases of violations of human rights by the security forces. National Human Rights Commission have also thrown light on some cases such as Bijbehara incident of Kashmir.

Sixthly, security forces must atride by the code of conduct laid out by the United Nations. They must perform their limited and well defined role. Security forces should not usurp the role of judiciary at any time and must work within the parameters of code of conduct. The code of conduct for security forces as laid down by UNO is as under:

Articel 1—Law enforcement official shall at all times fulfil the duty imposed upon them by the law, by serving the community and by protecting all persons against illegal acts, consistent with high degree of responsibility required by the profession.

Article 2—In the performance of their duty, law enforcement officials shall respect and protect human dignity and maintain and uphold the human rights of all persons.

Article 3—Law enforcement officers may use force only when strictly necessary and to the extent required for the performance of their duty.

Article 4—Matters of confidential nature in the possession of the law enforcement officers shall be kept confidential, unless the performance of duty or the need of justice strictly require otherwise.

Article 5—No law enforcement officer may inflict, instigate or tolerate any act of torture or other cruel, inhuman or degrading treatment or punishment nor may any law enforcement official invoke superior orders or exceptional circumstances, such as a state of war or a threat to war, a threat to national security, internal political instability or any other public emergency as a justification of torture or other emergency as a justification of turture or other cruel inhuman or degrading treatment or punishment.

Article 6—LEO shall ensure the full protection of the persons in their custody and in particular, shall take immediate action to security medical treatment whenever required.

Article 7—LEO shall not commit any act of corruption. They shall also rigorously oppose and combat all such acts.

Article 8—LEO shall respect the law and the present code. They shall also, to the best of their capability, prevent and rigorously oppose any violations of them.

Seventhly, security forces have to develop "a culture of human rights" where there is respect for liberty, equality and dignity of the individuals.

Eighthly, for combating organised violence, security

forces have to be equipped with

(1) uptodate and correct intelligence.
(2) sophisticate weaponry,
(3) good and modern scientific equipment and infrastructure such as lie detectors,
(4) good training for combating organised violance,
(5) dynamic leadership,
(6) high motivation, and
(7) lastly but not the least public support which cannot be earned unless human rights are protected.

Ninthly-In case security forces fail to observe human rights, it may lead to mal practices, corruption, high-handedness and arrogance in the system which will dilute its combat effectiveness to deal with organised violence. "Listening the call of the conscience" and ethical mode of righteous living is an essential requirement of security forces, State sponsored terrorism by security forces cannot be allowed in a democratic society like India.

Tenthly-"Means are as important as ends" and organised violence has to be controlled by observance of human rights by the security forces.

Today security forces are facing the greatest challenge of organised violence, insurgency, terrorism and low intensity war during the last four decades have caused lot of violations in India. Statistics reveal that more citizens have been killed in terrorist violences in Punjab and Kashmir than army men killed in the three Indo-Pak wars. In the 1947-48 war, between India and Pakistan, the Indian Army lost about 2500 soldiers including about 1000 personnel declared missing in action. Another 3261 soldiers were killed including 359 declared as missing in action in the highly intensive

1965 war while 1525 army men died in the eastern front during the 1971 war. The total number of Indian soldiers killed in these three wars stands about 7286. In contrast to this between 1981 to April 1993 as many as 21475 citizens including 8126 militants were killed in Punjab alone. In Kashmir between 1988 and 1995 these figures works out to 11656. Thus, violence in the form of terrorism and insurgency in two States alone have taken a toll of 33132, four times more than number of soldiers killed in the three Indo-Pak war. In North Eastern States of India, insurgents in Nagaland, Mizoram, Manipur, Tripura and Assam have also taken a very heavy toll. To combat organised crime, security forces need to be properly trained and equipped and provided effective leadership, motivation and will to fight organised violence. The basic question today is whether security forces which are trained in observing human rights can combat organised violences better than those who are not made aware of the human rights. From the Punjab experience, many people tend to believe that security forces cannot combat organised violence by observing human rights and they have to cut comers of law at various places. I for one do -not subscribe to this view. Police and security forces who are deployed to combat organised violences need high standard of discipline and morale, dynamic leadership and co-operation of the people. If security forces violate human rights they will not be able to get volunteer and spontaneous co-operation of the people without whose support organised violence cannot be successfully controlled and contained by the security forces.

Security forces can be divided broadly into two categories: First, category consists of those who observe human rights while combating organised violence and the second category covers those security forces who fail to observe human rights and at times deliberately violate human rights to combat organised violence. My

33 years of experience of operational areas like Mizoram, Manipur, Nagaland and Tripura in various capacities reveal and justify the contention that security forces observing human rights are always better equipped to combat organised violence. As a pragmatic practical person it is felt that police and security forces should observe human rights for their own individual interests and safe career. Political masters at times want policemen and security forces to violate human rights for some temporary gains; but long experience tells us that such temporary gains are counter-productive. The Supreme Court on January 29, 1996 has ordered CBI to prosecute 27 policemen of Punjab who were alleged to have been involved in fake encounters with terrorists in Punjab and Chief Minister Shri Brar has made it clear that his Government will not defend such officers. In such a situation, it is better that security forces combat violence by observing human rights.

Some people make a dividing line between police and security forces and in their opinion civil police is different from security forces which mainly consist of CRPF, BSF, other CPOs and the Army. Statistics prove that security forces generally observe human rights while State police at times violate human rights. During the last two years 52 allegations of excesses and violations of human rights were committed by the para-military personnel according to a statement given in the Lok Sabha by the State Human Minister and there were a total of 351 complaints against troops in Kashmir since 1991 of which 41 soldiers including 15 officers have been punished. Out of 351 complaints only 21 complaints have been found true. According to National Human Rights Commission, between 1990 to 1994, 245 cases have been registered against the BSF and 39 against the army.

National Police Commission in one of its report has

observed that police in normal situations are violating human rights by using third degree methods, fake encounters and other illegal acts and they constitute 60 per cent of the total complaints against the police. Between 1st April 1994 to 31st March 1995, there have been Ill cases of custodial deaths, 56 cases of disappearances of people from police custody and 487 cases of other police excessism have been noted. These violations of human rights by the security forces and the police are due to lack of training and awareness about human rights. Insurgency and terrorism cannot survive unless there is popular public support to their cases. Security forces by violating human rights give scope for furtherance of the cause of terrorists and insurgents. Security forces can win the hearts and minds of the people only when they observe human rights. There are numerous examples when security forces have been able to combat organised crime more effectively while observing human rights. Organised violence can be broadly categorised into the following: (i) communal violence, (ii) caste violence, (iii) industrial labour unrest, (iv) ethnic violence, (v) political terrorism, (vi) agrarian rights and violence, (vii) students violence, (viii) election violence, (ix) group violence by dacoits and other armed gangs, (ix) police violence and (xi) State violence. If security forces are not observing human rights it results in police violence and State sponsored violence. A democratic society wedded to the rule of law cannot allow State sponsored violence. Police being the agency created and maintained for combating violence and maintaining law and order cannot become law by themselves and they cannot violate human rights. Recent Supreme Court judgements have clearly indicated that police officers must observe human rights and those who violate human rights are bounded to be dealt in accordance with the law of the land and are bound to suffer in the long run. National Human Rights Commission annual report 1993-94 has given many illustrative cases. Firing by security forces in Bijbhera in Jammu & Kashmir has invited condemnation from all and disciplinary proceedings have been initiated under the Border Security Forces Act against 14 members of the force and further on the basis of a magisterial enquiry steps may be initiated to launch prosecution. In Punjab, there have been a number of cases of disappearances of people and it is suspected that these people may have been killed in fake encounters. National Police Commission has asked the concerned authorities to submit report in each case.

Analysing the anatomy of organised police David H. Beyley categorised them into three categories, (a) the violence of remonstrance, (b) the violence of confrontation, and (c) the violence of frustration. For dealing with all these types of violences, it is necessary that security forces observe human rights. It is a matter of great regret that the Indian Police is having a number of organisational deficiencies and lack of adequate infrastructure for providing proper awareness about the human rights but there is a need for genuine commitment to the human rights values in the police. There is no denial of the fact that Indian police and security forces have lack of adequate infrastructure to combat organised crime. There are hardly a few dozen light detectors with the security forces for interrogation and modern scientific methods of investigation and interrogation are not available to the security forces but this does not justify our failure to observe human rights. If we do some introspection we find that the training in police organisations is defective and does not provide enough focus on human rights. A conviction of commitment for the human rights has to be inculcated in the police and security forces if we have to implement the human rights in its true form and spirit. There is a need for sensitisation of the police and security forces in the ethos and values of human rights. Promotion of human rights literacy and awareness will go a long way in equipping security forces for better combating organised violence. Today the scene is very dismal. There have been 6835 cases of complaints registered against the police and there have been 152 cases of custodial deaths and custodial rapes between the period 1st April 1994 to 31st March 1995. These violations of human rights can be attributed to number of factors but the basic reasons are lack of faith and commitment to the human rights. Short-term successes and quick results demanded by the powers of that be at times encourage corrupt and enthusiastic police officers to violate human rights.

Human Rights Education

Section 12(h) of the Protection of Human Rights Act 1993 (No. 10 of 1994) states the functions of the Commission, which are as under: "Spread human rights literacy among various sections of society and promote awareness of the safeguards available for the protection of these rights through publication, the media, the seminars and other available means". Human rights education is most crucial for the fulfilment of the commitment made in the Indian Constitution but the task is enormously difficult. Some of the basic issues related to human rights education can be as under: (i) What kind of training is required for teachers of human rights? (ii) What sources and texts are to be drawn upon for teaching material? (iii) How human rights education to be imparted and through what training techniques? (iv) What plays, tales, stories and songs are likely to impart education of human rights with the possibility of both emotional response and further thinking? (v) What will constitute the core of its course for various levels of educational classes? (vi) Can NCERT develop model course modules for primary and secondary classes as standards to provide a basis for action by the States? (vii) Can the core book prepared by the UNESCO on human rights be adopted with necessary modification in it to suit Indian situations and conditions? (viii) Can appropriate modules be prepared and introduced in the training programmes of different levels especially in the Police and Security Forces to promote awareness of human rights? The basic question which is often asked is: Will mere human rights education stop or reduce human rights violation? There is an assumption that lack of information on human rights illiteracy is the source of violation of human rights. One of the worst form of violation of human rights in Indian society is because of intolerance.

Human Rights and TADA

The Terrorist and Disruptive Activities (Prevention) Act 1985, popularly known by its acronym TADA has stood the scrutiny of Supreme Court in many cases. The Peoples Union for Democratic Rights (PUDR) presents the statistics that of the 52998 persons arrested under TADA between May 1985 and March 1993 only 434 or 0.81 per cent of the total number of those detained, were actually convicted. With 23 of the 24 metropolitan cities declared as "notified areas", nearly 93 per cent of the country was covered under the Act. TADA has been used to fight terrorists of Kashmir and Punjab where the Government is locked in several areas of low intensity conflict against its own citizens who are armed to the teeth with ultra-sophisticated weapons. In several other States TADA has been used to fight the smugglers, drug peddlers, Naxalites (as in Andhra Pradesh) and the underworld operators in Gujarat.

Few case studies given below will indicate how TADA has been applied to Indian citizens during the last few years:

(1) In 1986-87, a student from Andhra Pradesh protesting a bus fare hike was booked under sections 3, 4 & 5 of TADA and lanquished in prison for a while year before he was released.

(2) In Andhra Pradesh Dalits asking for title to the land they cultivated were falsely charged and arrested under TADA. Though there was no material evidence against the accused, the designated Court refused to release them until civil rights advocates and PUCL President K.G. Kannabiran filed applications at the Supreme Court, High Court and Designated Court. Even then it was six months before they were released.

(3) In Baroda, a 14-year old mentally retarded boy who was out on the street during a communal riot was rounded up by the police and booked under TADA.

(4) In 1990, 45 striking workers of Universal Luggage in Aurangabad (Maharashtra) were arrested under TADA. One of them, Vishwas Bhagwan Lotange was beaten up for 16 days and died in jail. The doctor's report noted welts and cigarette burns on his body.

(5) Two hundred and forty agitating Bharatiya Kisan Sangh activists were booked under TADA during a raste roko agitation.

(6) Muslim women, youth and the aged were picked up under TADA by the Bombay Police following the bomb blasts in March 1993.

(7) In Ahmedabad, in 1991-92, a Muslim women whose husband had only a few hours ago fallen victim of police bullets, was summarily booked under TADA and held for 10 months because she had argued heatedly with the police over their unjust action.

Government of India had decided that the Terrorist and Disruptive Act will expire on 23rd May 1995. The basic issue, however, is that whether the police personnel have been able to understand the dimensions of human rights and how far that have been able to protect it. Many thinkers believe that there has been misuse of TADA over the few years that have passed because of excess politicalisation of Police Forces and neglect of training in Police Organisations.

Human Rights Record: An International Perspective

The history of mankind has been firmly associated with the continuous on-going struggle of individuals against injustice, exploitation and discrimination. Human rights remain both a statement of reality and an ever-expanding set of objectives waiting to be actualised and their realisation is possible only through a process of constant struggle. Media plays an important part in bringing out alleged violations of human rights in different countries. Violations of human rights is a global phenomenon. "Racial discrimination and religious bigotry represent a unique and frightening phenomena of human rights violations in U.S.A. In the majority of European countries racialist or Xenophobic sentiments are shared by an increasingly large percentage of population and in a number of European countries immigrants and ethnic minorities are faced with discrimination in access to housing". Charles Humana has made lot of research regarding violation of human rights by fifteen countries of the world. He has given the following human rights rating.

Global Concern for Human Rights

At international forums human rights are discussed in

great depth and UN Commission on Human Rights has been playing a very effective role. National Human Rights Commission during the last one year has visited J & K, Punjab, North-East States and many other parts of India to contact people and get first hand information about the violation of human rights. This has also given an impatus to various violations of human rights in different States.

Human Rights During Internal Conflicts

Even in situation of internal disturbances and tensions, every person can and must respect at least the following rules, without discrimination :

1. Every person shall be treated with the respect due to the inherent dignity of the human person. His or her life, moral and physical integrity, and honour shall be respected in all circumstances and regardless of the allegations against him or her. No one shall be arbitrarily deprived of his or her life.
2. Acts which are prohibited in particular are murder, torture and all other cruel, inhuman or degrading treatment or punishment, the taking of hostages, enforced or involuntary disappearance of persons, collective penalties and all acts, methods and practices of terrorism, whether committed by public officials or by any other
3. Persons exercising police powers shall, out of respect for human dignity, limit their use of force to the strictly necessary minimum.
4. No one shall be arbitrarily deprived of his or her liberty. Anyone who is arrested, detained, interned or deprived in any other way of freedom of movement shall be informed without delay of the reasons for which such measures have been

taken. The authorities responsible for the detention of a person have the duty to inform that person's family of his or her situation. The measures taken against any person shall be reviewed periodically.

5. Any person deprived of his or her liberty shall be treated humanely. He or she shall be afforded proper conditions with regard to hygiene, food, quarters and applicable work. Wounded or sick detainees shall receive the care they require. A person deprived of his or her liberty shall have the possibility of communicating periodically with his or her family.

6. Other restrictions of individual liberty, such as forcible displacement for assigned residence, may be imposed only by decision of a competent authority. Persons affected by such measures shall be treated humanely. No one may be deprived of his or her nationality nor expelled from his or her own country.

7. No one shall be held guilty on account of acts or omissions which did not constitute a criminal offence at the time when they took place.

8. No one shall be sentenced and no penalty carried out without a judgement handed down by an impartial court respecting the fundamental judicial guarantees. In particular, any person charged with an offence :

   (a) shall be presumed innocent until proved guilty according to the law;

   (b) shall be informed of the particulars of the offence alleged against him or her;

   (c) shall be afforded the necessary rights and means of defence;

   (d) shall be tried without undue delay.

A convicted person shall be advised of his or her judicial and other remedies.

9. In as much as retention of the death penalty is considered necessary, it may be pronounced only for the most serious crimes. The death penalty shall not be pronounced on persons who were under the age of eighteen years at the time of the offence, nor carried out on pregnant women or mothers of young children. A condemned person has the right to ask for clemency: he or she must be advised of this right.

   Any summary or arbitrary execution constitutes murder.

10. All wounded and sick persons shall receive care and attention, without discrimination. Medical assistance shall be facilitated. No one shall suffer harassment for the simple fact of having assisted wounded or sick persons.

11. The authorities concerned shall do everything possible to establish the whereabouts of persons reported missing, The authorities shall inform the next of kin on the progress of the investigation and notify them of any result.

12. Children, particularly if deprived of their liberty, shall be accorded the respect due to them on account of their age. They must never be compelled or encouraged to take part in acts of violence.

13. The authorities concerned shall take all necessary measures to ensure that these rules are known and respected by all. They shall include them in the training of those exercising police powers, such as members of the police forces, prison staff and, where applicable, members of the armed forces. The authorities

shall prosecute in accordance with national law anyone who violates these rules.

Above instructions and code of conduct apply in situations when police and security forces carry out operations against insurgents, terrorists and organised armed gangs.

Main Recommendations

1. With a view to removing ambiguities and impediments concerning its competence and autonomy, the National Human Rights Commission had in its report for the period ending 31st March, 1994, made certain recommendations for amendments to the protection of Human Rights Act, 1993. The Commission urges that measures be taken to bring out these amendments.
2. The Commission recommends that in states where the security forces are called upon to assist the civil authorities, local magistrates and/ or police officers, should be associated, in particular, with cordon and search operations, in order to allay misgivings regarding the conduct of personnel of the security forces and to prevent misuse of powers.
3. In insurgency affected areas, at the level of the district, the Commission recommends that district magistrates should chair regular meetings involving the security forces and be kept informed of operations by the latter. To the extent possible, leading non-officials, representatives of non-governmental organisations and others should be associated with such meetings.
4. More fundamentally, however, the Commission has considered it its responsibility to recommend

in its report on areas facing insurgencies or militancy, that while the restoration of peace may indeed by the sine qua non for the full respect of human rights, timely and sagacious political measures that are truly democratic in character are necessary, as in the long run, they have far more lasting and beneficial results than reliance essentially on security forces, however devoted and disciplined they are, or on restrictive laws, however carefully they may be applied. The Commission accordingly recommends that appropriate political measures and initiatives be taken.

5. In almost all parts of the country there is a clear and increasing need to reform the police itself, to retrain and to reorganize it and to restore to it the skills and the integrity that the country so desperately needs if the function of preserving law and order is to be improved. It is for this reason that the Commission recommends that serious action be taken on the Second Report of the Police Reforms Commission which, in 1979, made a series of proposals that remain highly pertinent today—including those suggesting the insulation of the investigative function of the police from political pressure.

6. The Commission recommends the revision of the Indian Prison Act, 1894, bearing in mind the considerable work already done by various committees and organisation and the work that is currently under way.

7. A high level committee be set up in each State to review the cases of prisoners in order to ensure that they are not detained unlawfully.

8. The Commission has raised the matter of lock-ups' and sub-jails with the State Governments

and recommends that appropriate corrective actions be taken to improve conditions in 'lock-ups' and sub-jails.

9. The Commission recommends that the Central Government accede to the 1984 Convention against Torture and other forms of Cruel, Inhuman and Degrading Treatment or Punishment.

10. The Commission recommends expeditious and effective implementation of the project prepared by the Government of Uttar Pradesh for the elimination of child labour in the glass industry in Ferozabad.

11. The Commission recommends the adoptation of appropriate legislation on compulsory primary education, matched with the necessary resources required for its purpose. The Commission supports the Government move to amend the child labour (Prohibition and Regulation) Act to make it more efficacious and recommends that early action be taken in this regard.

12. The Commission recommends vigorous implementation of the country's obligations under the Convention on Elimination of All Forms of Discrimination against Women.

13. The Commission has noted that legislation is being contemplated in regard to persons suffering disabilities. Supporting this, it strongly recommends early passage of an appropriate act on behalf of such persons whose rights must be respected and supported.

14. The Commission recommends that timely action be taken on the plans of the University Grants Commission to have support extended to five Universities by April, 1996 and various others by

1997 for the teaching of human rights at the University level.

15. The Commission recommends an improvement in the quality of training of police, military and para-military personnel and taking of special measures in order to ensure respect for the human rights of people particularly in areas of insurgency.
16. The Commission further recommends that where violations of human rights occur as a result of the conduct of armed forces personnel, prompt and effective action be taken under the law to prosecute those accused of wrong doing. This would be in the interests of all concerned-the victim, the armed forces themselves and the country at large.
17. The Commission recommends that 10th December every year be observed as Human Rights Day in all schools, colleges, universities and other educational institutions.
18. The Commission recommends that the Govt. of India takes steps for evolving suitable institutional mechanism in the Union Territories including the National Capital Territory of Delhi so that they can have their own arrangements, functionally analoguous to State Commissions, for the protection of human rights.

Mere talks, seminars, discussions and debates cannot serve a meaningful role unless there is a political will to honestly implement and observe human rights. Remedial measures need to be taken to remedy the malady of delays in the Criminal Proceedings. Experience of the working of our political system holds ample testimony to the fact that at times there is an active involvement of political figures in using the machinery of the police to gag the voice of dissent or opposition to paralyse the system. Passing laws cannot be sufficient unless effective implementation can be enforced of all laws which safeguard human rights of the individuals. Human rights and human survival are inalienably linked.

Any democratic society, while countering terrorism, becomes subject to charges of "excesses" and "violations of human rights". Implementation of human rights has come to be acknowledged nationally and internationally as a major concern of many human right organisations. It is necessary that these organisations must handle the tangled web of facts, circumstances, perceptions, compulsions and the situation more realistically and in a more holistic manner. As a watch dog body, the National Human Rights Commission has so far done a very creditable job in not only promoting human rights in the country but also raised the image of the nation in international forums.

By enacting, the Protection of Human Rights Act 1993, India has reaffirmed its strong commitment to protect and promote the human rights of its people. The voluntary organisations and the mass media can play more positive roles in promoting human rights. The time has come when the legal and judicial system has to be revamped and reconstructed so that such injustices do not occur and disfigure the fair and otherwise luminous face of our nascent democracy. 36 The talk of human rights would become meaningful only when poor, illiterate and helpless people are provided with free legal service as an unalienable right for fair and just trial. The Supreme Court has emphasised the role of people, voluntary organisations and social action groups in making legal aid meaningful, effective and purpose oriented.

Index

Absolute poor, 45
Absolute poverty, 45
Absoluteness, 79
Absolutism, 244
Activism, 187
Adjudication, 91
Administrative capacity, 261
Agrarian feudalism, 246
Agrarian rights, 311
Alternative approaches, 73
American jurisprudence, 100
Analytical techniques, 99
Anglo-Saxon jurisprudence, 177
Anti-national element, 297
Appropriate legislation, 229
Appropriate proceedings, 192
Arbitrariness, 290
Atharva veda, 269
Authoritarianism, 290

Backward classes, 45
Burgherrecht, 246
Burton bill, 75

Calorie intake, 6
Capitalism, 189
Caste violence, 311
Catholicism, 245
Child marriage restraint act, 280
Civic participation, 253
Civilian populations, 13
Communal earnages, 68
Communal violence, 311
Conciliation commission, 162
Constitutional interpretation, 98
Constitutional realism, 46
Consultative status, 10
Convention on Elimination of All Forms of Discrimination against Women (CEDAW), 280
Creative interpretation, 290
Criminologists, 187
Cultural relativism, 76

Democratic system, 2
Demonstration effect, 249
Derogable rights, 284
Diplomatic conference, 274
Disparagement, 78
Disqualification, 211
Domestic jurisdiction, 11
Domination, 243
Double standard, 87

Economic institutions, 188
Educational backwardness, 61
Effective implementation, 174

Egalitarian, 269
Egalitarianism, 255
Egregious violation, 60
Election violence, 311
Elite competition, 254
Enforcement machinery, 24
Ethnic cleansing, 37
Ethnic minorities, 138
Ethnic violence, 311
Euphemism, 290
Excessive taxation, 245
Extensive destruction, 61
Extra-judicial executions, 9
Extremism, 287

Feudalism, 244
Founding fathers, 42
Fourteenth amendment, 84
Freedom flotilla, 238
French protestantism, 245
Fundamental human rights, 19

Good governance, 75
Government administration, 262
Group violence, 311
Guarantism, 248
Guardianship, 279
Guerrilla, 274

Habeas corpus, 216
Humanism, 46
Humanitarian international law, 270
Humanitarian interventions, 13
Humanitarian task, 62

Industrial hygiene, 283
Industrial labour unrest, 311
Institutional solution, 243
Insurgency, 287
Interelection safeguards, 252
Inter-Governmental Organizations (IGO), 10
Internal disturbance, 284
Internal security, 286
International arena, 222
International community, 1
Intuitionism, 92
Invisible malnutrition, 5

Jamadras, 181
Judicial decision, 233
Judicial somnambulance, 289
Judicially enforceable rights, 230
Jurisdiction, 175

Karachi resolution, 53

Legal guarantism, 246
Legal mechanism, 79
Legal obligations, 234
Legislative-malapportionment, 252
Les politiques, 245
Limitations clauses, 34
Lok Sabha, 302

Magna Carta, 65
Mandamus, 201
Massive corruption, 68
Matrimonial property, 279
Minimum standard, 225
Minimum wage act, 181
Minority treaties, 14
Molestation, 304
Monetary obligation, 204
Moral epistemology, 98

National Council for Educational Research and Training (NCERT), 302
Neo-natural-rights, 12
Neutral approaches, 90
Nonderogability, 31
Non-Governmental Organizations (NGOs), 8

Optional protocol, 71
Organizational capacity, 252

Para-military forces, 287
Patriotism, 245
Pauperisation, 189
Peoples Union for Democratic Rights (PUDR), 314
Permissible reservations, 30
Philosophical questions, 79
Poignant paradox, 39
Police violence, 311
Political campaigns, 82
Political community, 222
Political disappearances, 2
Political freedom, 244
Political terrorism, 311
Political will, 260
Positivism, 223
Preliminary proceedings, 213
Preventive detention, 219
Price stabilisation, 71
Private insurance, 258
Private person, 244
Provisional analysis, 240
Public choice processes, 265
Public interest litigation, 176
Public order, 32
Public promises act, 204

Rajya Sabha, 302
Realism, 223
Reasonable restrictions, 43
Reformation, 244
Regime general, 262
Regional transport authority, 205
Re-nomination, 162
Reporting method, 172
Reprimand, 297
Republican constitutionalism, 254
Rhetorical affirmation, 78
Routinization, 253

Safe environment, 282
Safe-environments, 9
Sardar Vallabhabhi Patel, 303
Satisfactory paradigm, 223
Secular liberation, 42
Self-execution, 226
Sex discrimination act, 103
Shelterlessness, 7
Skeptical position, 229
Social contract, 243
Social stratification, 254
Socio-economic dimensions, 269
Socioeconomic milieu, 265
Solidarity, 73
State violence, 311
Statutory body, 205
Students violence, 311
Successive applications, 219
Sympathetic judicial forum, 185
Systematic basis, 138

Technological cooperation, 139
Territorial jurisdiction, 189
Terrorist and Disruptive Activities Act (TADA), 301

Transnational human rights, 221
Travaux preparatoires, 233
Tyrannical ruler, 244

Universal respect, 226
Utter misery, 62

Vienna declaration, 72
Western imagination, 45
Wide reflective equilibrium, 92
Writs, 201

Yugoslavia, 37

Ayan
In: 64505
Dt: 19-7-12